T0330423

Environmental Valuation, Economic Policy and Sustainability

Environmental Valuation, Economic Policy and Sustainability

Recent Advances in Environmental Economics

Edited by

Melinda Acutt
University of Lancaster, UK

Pamela Mason
University of York, UK

Edward Elgar
Cheltenham, UK • Northampton, MA, USA

Published by
Edward Elgar Publishing Limited
Glensanda House
Montpellier Parade
Cheltenham
Glos GL50 1UA
UK

Edward Elgar Publishing, Inc.
6 Market Street
Northampton
Massachusetts 01060
USA

A catalogue record for this book
is available from the British Library

Library of Congress Cataloguing in Publication Data
Environmental valuation, economic policy, and sustainability
   1. Environmental economics.   2. Valuation.   3. Sustainable
development.   4. Economic policy.   I. Acutt, Melinda, 1969–
II. Mason, Pamela, 1969–   .
HC79.E5E594   1998
333.7—dc21

                                                           98-9836
                                                           CIP

ISBN 1 85898 753 9

Printed and bound in Great Britain by
Biddles Limited, Guildford and King's Lynn

Contents

v

PART III   ENVIRONMENTAL SUSTAINABILITY

Figures

Tables

Contributors

Gayatri Acharya, Yale School of Forestry and Environmental Studies, 205 Prospect Street, New Haven CT 06511, USA. E-mail: Gayatri.Acharya@Yale.edv.

Melinda Acutt, Department of Economics, University of Lancaster, Lancaster LA1 4YX. E-mail:m.acutt@lancaster.ac.uk.

Ian J. Bateman, School of Environmental Sciences, University of East Anglia, Norwich, NR4 7JJ. E-mail:i.bateman@ uea.ac.uk.

Richard Cookson, Centre for Health Economics, University of York, Heslington, York, YO10 5DD. E-mail:rac11@york.ac.uk.

Silvana Dalmazzone, Environment Department, University of York, York, YO10 5DD. E-mail:sd103@ebor.york.ac.uk.

Vivien Foster, Oxford Economic Research Associates Ltd, Blue Boar Court, Alfred Street, Oxford, OX1 4EH. e-mail:vivien.foster@oxera.co.uk.

Purificación Granero Gómez, Deparamento de Fundamentos de Economía, Universidad de Alcalá, Plaza de la Victoria 3, Alcalá de Henares, 28802, Madrid, Spain. E-mail:ehpgg.funéco.alcala.es.

Nick Hanley, Institute of Ecology and Resource Management, University of Edinburgh, Kings Buildings, West Mains Road, Edinburgh, EH9 3JG. E-mail:n.d.hanley@ed.ac.uk.

David Harley, Royal Society for the Protection of Birds, The Lodge, Sandy, Bedfordshire, SG19 2GL. E-mail:david.harley@rspb.org.uk.

Michael Kuhn, Department of Economics, University of Rostock, 18051 Rostock, Germany. E-mail:kuhn@wiwi.uni-rostock.de.

Pamela Mason, Environment Department, University of York, Heslington, York, YO10 5DD. E-mail: pjm105@york.ac.uk.

Susana Mourato, Centre for Social and Economic Research on the Global Environment (CSERGE), Department of Economics, University College London, Gower Street, London, WC1E 6BT. E-mail:s.mourato@ucl.ac.uk.

John C.V. Pezzey, Environment Department, University of York, Heslington, York, YO10 5DD. E-mail:JCVP1@york.ac.uk.

Acknowledgements

The idea for this book arose from the inaugural meeting of the Environmental Economics Forum, held at Ambleside, Cumbria in August 1996. We would like to thank all the Forum participants for the lively and high-quality presentations and debates during an interesting and constructive weekend in the Lake District, especially: Nick Hanley; Jack Pezzey; Rosemary Clarke; and Graham Rabbitts of Associated British Ports.

A very special debt of gratitude is owed to Norman Glass of HM Treasury and Professor Richard Portes of the Royal Economic Society for the financial support provided by their organizations. Without such support, the aims of the Forum to bring together both young and more well-established researchers in this area would not have been achieved.

Thanks are also due to: Professor David Sapsford, for all his help and support; John Dodgson; Professor David Pearce; Professor Charles Perrings; Dymphna Evans at Edward Elgar; and finally, to all our colleagues at Lancaster and York.

Preface

David Pearce

Just thirty years ago I moved from my very first job as a Lecturer in Economics at Lancaster University to a lectureship at Southampton University. Within a few years, with a colleague, I established the 'UK Environmental Economics Study Group' with modest financial backing from the then Social Science Research Council. We organized all interested parties in the UK for regular discussions on environmental economics, a brand new subject which had been launched in the USA and Canada. Notable centres of excellence were the University of Wyoming, the University of British Columbia and Resources for the Future in Washington, DC. Our UK meetings rarely attracted more than six attendees, a sign of the novelty of the subject, but we benefited from luminaries such as Ed Mishan, then at the London School of Economics. More than twenty years later, environmental economics is, to put it slightly vulgarly, big business. There are associations of environmental economists in North America and Europe, boasting thousands of members. There are emerging societies in Asia and Latin America. The literature is enormous and the journals have proliferated, in general, but not always, without sacrificing the quality of work published. There are consulting companies specializing in the subject and there are repeated demands from government, international organizations and industry for professional advice.

The kinds of policy recommendations called for by environmental economists have been somewhat slower to materialize. None the less, environmental taxes – reflecting the long tradition of taxing the polluter in Pigouvian terms – have made great advances in European countries. Where political systems make it difficult for taxes to be introduced, as in the USA, tradeable quantity permits have found favour, as with sulphur trading permits. The fact that the price of a permit or quota is entirely analogous to a tax might make us think that those who have been regulated by this process are the subject of some sleight of hand. But in the political economy of things, it is important to understand why some forms of regulation are 'acceptable' and others are not. Even in the developing world, environmental charges are beginning to be introduced: charges for water rights in countries such as Chile. While I have played only a small part in all these developments, I can look back with some satisfaction at the development of environmental economics as a reasonably coherent body of thought (indeed, somewhat more coherent than the views of those who have sought to criticize it in a wholesale manner).

As the century closes environmental economics is in good shape. Like all 'paradigms', it invites detractors and supposedly competing paradigms. So-called 'ecological economics' has emerged as such a paradigm. Sadly, while it has much that is good to offer us, some of its advocates have made exaggerated claims for its distinguishing characteristics. At best it focuses more on discontinuity and non-substitutability, but one wonders why this is so different from, say, the contrast between Leontief production functions and smooth 'neoclassical' functions with which economists have lived for many years. Correcting our accounting procedures is also not a distinguishing feature of ecological economics: 'green' national and company accounting is a logical extension of the tenets of environmental economics. One might also question the skewed allocation of resources within environmental economics to green accounting exercises: do they, in the end, change anyone's behaviour? But competition, even if it is somewhat artificial, is good for any discipline and environmental economics has perhaps been sharpened by these exchanges.

Probably the most satisfying feature of the development of the subject has been the inevitable emergence of a younger group of environmental economists, 'young Turks' as my namesake Ivor Pearce used to call them. Having designed and implemented the United Kingdom's very first environmental economics graduate course at University College London, I am probably better aware than most of the extent to which these younger people have had an impact on all kinds of organizations. The editors' idea of bringing some of them together with some 'oldies' (if they will forgive me, since most of them are significantly younger than me) was therefore an excellent one. The resulting chapters are stimulating and make for a very worthwhile volume.

David Pearce
Centre for Social and Economic Research on the Global Environment
University College London and University of East Anglia

1. An introduction to environmental economics: theory and application

Melinda Acutt and Pamela Mason

INTRODUCTION

The twin aims of this book are to provide an introduction to the most important issues in the field of environmental economics, and to offer a selection of recent research in various areas of the discipline. One feature of environmental economics is the variety of both theoretical and applied areas which it encompasses. This chapter is intended partly as an overview, in demonstrating how these areas relate to each other in the general aim of improving the efficiency with which environmental resources are used. However, one should also note the wide range of attitudes towards the environment which are encompassed in various schools of thought within environmental economics. These are characterized essentially by the extent to which they consider intervention to alter the market allocation of resources to be both necessary and desirable. The perspective of mainstream economics is that any intervention must be justified by the demonstration that markets are failing to account for the full value of environmental (or other) assets. This perspective is reflected in Part I on the valuation of non-market goods. Estimated values can be used to identify the optimal allocation of resources. Green economists, on the other hand, advocate a more cautious attitude towards the environment. This can involve overriding the criterion of optimality, on the grounds that decisions which are optimal at present, such as the conversion of rain forests into agricultural land, may have unforeseen and potentially disastrous consequences in the future.

The original, and arguably still most fundamental, aim of environmental economic theory is the correction of market failures. This usually refers to the internalization of the external environmental effects of economic activity. Market failures can arise when the full cost of economic activities are not included in producers' private costs, and therefore in market prices. These costs can take the form, for example, of environmental pollution, with associated health costs, or the loss of environmental amenity. The uncorrected economic analysis by a profit-maximizing producer involves undertaking an economic activity up to the point at which the net benefit from an additional unit of the activity (the marginal net private benefit or MNPB) is zero (quantity Q_1 in Figure 1.1). In the absence of externalities, and with perfectly functioning markets, this will also be the socially optimal level of production, since marginal benefits will equal marginal costs, meaning that resources are optimally allocated. However, if external costs are generated at this level of output, then since MNPB equals zero, overall marginal costs must exceed marginal benefits so the socially optimal level of output is exceeded. The socially optimal level is where full marginal costs, the sum of private and external marginal costs (MEC), equal the marginal benefit of the activity, shown as Q^* in Figure 1.1.

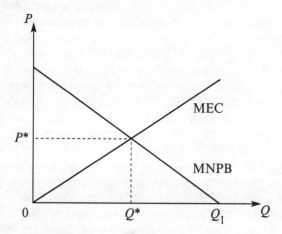

Figure 1.1 The socially optimal level of external costs

The correction of market failures, therefore entails bringing the system towards the optimal allocation of resources. It involves the incorporation of external costs into the private costs faced by the producer, so that the marginal costs which the producer sets equal to MNPB are the full social marginal costs. The private optimum will now be equal to the social optimum. Incorporation of the external costs into the producer's decision-making process requires, first, estimation of the MEC, and second, use of an economic instrument to impose the external cost on to the private producer. A study applying the most widely used method of valuation, the contingent valuation method, is described in Chapter 2, while Chapters 4 and 5 discuss alternative valuation procedures. The instruments which can be used to effect the internalization of external costs are the subject of Part II. Instruments can take the form of, for example, a tax imposed on the producer, equal to the MEC at the optimal level of production. In Figure 1.1, the tax would be equal to the distance $0P^*$, for the optimal production level Q^*. Alternatively, the optimal level of production can be imposed by the authorities, by setting a production constraint equal to Q^*. This would be a quantity-based instrument, as distinct from the price-based tax instrument.

ECONOMIC VALUATION OF THE ENVIRONMENT

As noted above, an important issue for identifying the optimal use of environmental resources is the valuation of external costs, and indeed of environmental assets in general. This area is the subject of Part I of this book. Several methods of valuation have been applied to this problem, the most popular of which has been the contingent valuation method (CVM).[1] This method is based on the use of questionnaires to create a hypothetical market in which respondents are asked for their subjective valuation of specified environmental goods or bads.

The CVM has been widely applied and has received broad acceptance in developed countries. Despite some criticisms of the validity of the estimates obtained, they have been endorsed by court decisions in the USA as constituting valid evidence in cases relating to environmental damage. In Chapter 2, Susana Mourato provides one of the first applications of the CVM to an economy in transition from central planning to a market economy, namely Hungary. This is a particularly interesting application given initial doubt as to whether the participants would be sufficiently familiar with market mechanisms to undertake a hypothetical pricing exercise. This did not prove to be problematic, and the results show that the economic benefits of improved water quality in Lake Balaton, the largest lake in Europe, are likely to be substantial. This result has immediate implications for government policy, in appraising the benefits of public expenditure on a pollution control programme.

The following two chapters, by Vivien Foster, Ian Bateman and David Harley, and by Richard Cookson, address some of the criticisms which have been levelled at the CVM technique. Foster et al. examine in Chapter 3 the charge of hypothetical bias. This is the danger that, because of the hypothetical nature of willingness-to-pay estimates, the values obtained could exceed those which would be forthcoming in a real-payment situation. They review the literature on hypothetical bias and present the results of a study comparing CVM estimates with donations made to Royal Society for the Protection of Birds (RSPB) appeals. The existing literature on hypothetical bias is based on laboratory experiments, and does not therefore involve a comparison between a hypothetical and a real-payment situation. The particular contribution of this chapter is, therefore, that it gives details of the first study to do so.

Standard CVM studies tend to adopt a conservative approach to the provision of information and discussion, in order to identify existing preferences rather than risk imposing or creating them. However, the danger of this approach is that true underlying preferences, which could manifest themselves given sufficient information and thought, could remain undeclared. Cookson addresses this problem in Chapter 4 by adopting an alternative, experimental approach to the valuation of a reduction of the risk of death associated with various activities. This approach differs from previous studies in that it makes use of increased information and allows respondents to discuss their preliminary valuations with their fellow respondents. A market for these publicly provided goods is more effectively simulated which, it is argued, provides more reliable valuation estimates.

In Chapter 5, Gayatri Acharya applies the production function approach to valuation. This is a technique which has been used widely in the analysis of optimal production decisions in standard economics but is relatively new to the valuation of environmental goods and services. She shows how the indirect use value of an environmental asset, in this case the Hadejia–Nguru wetlands in northern Nigeria, can be estimated by calculating the contribution of environmental services provided by the asset to the value of agricultural output. The results show significant positive indirect use values for the wetland areas via the groundwater recharge function which they perform. The particular value of the study is that the wetlands are currently under threat from proposed dam and irrigation projects which would divert water away from the floodplain. The values identified thus enable a more complete cost–benefit analysis of such projects.

This part encompasses a range of significant recent advances in techniques for the valuation of non-market assets. It also demonstrates the application of valuation techniques to a broad range of problems. The following part concerns the economic policies which can be used to incorporate the values identified by such procedures into actual economic decisions.

ECONOMIC POLICY TOWARDS THE ENVIRONMENT

The existence of uncorrected environmental externalities such as excess environmental pollution can result in the overuse of environmental resources and the underpricing of the environment to individuals and firms. In Figure 1.1, we saw how a tax might be imposed in order to incorporate external costs into private production and consumption decisions and so internalize any externalities. In Chapter 6, Melinda Acutt uses as a case study the UK transport sector to show how in practice environmental taxes can be implemented to correct for this underpricing. The transport sector is an important contributor to a wide range of environmental problems, in both developed and developing countries. It is also of particular policy relevance as these environmental impacts tend to rise with incomes, because increases in car ownership and travel distances are associated with income growth. Therefore, the environmental consequences of the transport sector are set to rise in terms of their relative importance. After outlining the main environmental impacts of the transport sector, Acutt examines estimates of the valuation of these problems. Valuation, as we have seen above, is vital in order to identify an optimal tax policy. The results of a number of recent valuation studies are reviewed and compared. One important difference noted is the disparity in external costs imposed by urban and rural drivers.

In practice, the imposition of a tax to raise the price of a polluting activity is more complicated than the situation outlined in relation to Figure 1.1. This is because if it is not cost-effective to base a tax instrument on all of the factors contributing to the marginal external cost of an activity, then an alternative tax base needs to be found. A range of different taxation options for the transport sector are assessed against criteria including: levels of car and public transport use; emission levels; the overall impact on government finances; administrative complexity; and equity. One of the most environmentally effective and economically efficient tax instruments is shown to be a fuel tax. However, policy relating to each environmental impact needs to be assessed separately because for some problems, the mandatory fitting of abatement technology may be more effective than a tax instrument. A further case in which regulation or local pricing policies might be preferable is when a broad instrument such as a national fuel tax cannot differentiate by location in line with differing marginal external costs, as is the case for the urban–rural divide.

This issue of location of pollution and the nonlinearity of marginal external costs is further developed by Nick Hanley in Chapter 7. This chapter focuses on an alternative policy option, that of tradable pollution permits. This is a quantity-based instrument but, as Hanley shows; utilizes a market in permits to achieve a reduction in pollution at the lowest cost. This least-cost property of tradeable pollution permits is outlined first for uniformly mixed pollutants. These are emissions such as carbon dioxide, a contributor to global climate change, whose marginal external cost (MEC) is not dependent on the location of emissions. The case of non-uniformly mixed pollutants, such as emissions of pollutants into a river at different points along its length is also outlined. The implications in this case are that the permits can no longer be traded on a one-to-one basis, as the MEC differs between sources, depending on the local concentration of the pollutant in the watercourse. The chapter goes on to provide a review of tradeable permit systems implemented to date.

Hanley then moves on to describe a simulation model of a tradeable pollution permit system for the control of water quality in a Scottish estuary. The potential cost savings for the control of water quality, if a move were to be made from the current regulatory approach, are estimated and found to be significant. A tradeable pollution permit market is simulated under both deterministic and stochastic conditions relating to the effectiveness of pollution abatement. In the second case there is uncertainty as to the effects of abatement, a particularly interesting development being the first explicit modelling of such stochastic conditions in the literature.

The next two chapters move on to consider environmental policy in the light of international considerations. In Chapter 8, Michael Kuhn discusses a much publicized worry relating to the implementation of environmental policy – that higher environmental standards may lead to a loss of competitiveness and may cause firms to relocate to regions or countries with lower environmental standards. This could lead to a loss of employment and welfare in the area introducing the environmental policy – a policy which would have been introduced with the aim of increasing welfare, by correcting for the misallocation of resources resulting from the underpricing of environmental assets in the free market. Further, if all countries reduce their environmental protection in order to attract investment then a so-called 'race to the bottom' could occur, in which countries undercut each other in terms of environmental protection, resulting in a generalized reduction in environmental quality.

In this chapter, Kuhn examines the evidence for these fears and highlights factors that might reduce this tendency to relocate. Such factors include the fact that relocation entails a certain cost, and that by remaining and complying with the environmental standards, firms have the opportunity to market products as environmentally friendly. The resulting mark-up on the price of an environmentally friendly product may or may not compensate sufficiently for the added costs of complying with the regulations. The empirical evidence to date relating to the likelihood of relocation in the face of environmental regulation is reviewed and shown to be ambiguous. The motivations and consequences of green consumerism are examined and it is this explicit analysis of green consumerism that is particularly new and interesting to the standard competitiveness and relocation arguments. A model is then presented in which the effects of environmental policies on firms' location and technology decisions are modelled, explicitly taking into account green consumer behaviour. Important findings are that the existence of green market potential acts as a counterbalance to incentives to relocate, although the existence of a relocation cost is a prerequisite for relocation not to occur. Of direct policy relevance is the finding that the presence of a green market can mean that unilateral regulation is feasible, mitigating the 'race to the bottom'.

In Chapter 9, Purificación Gómez provides an overview of the problems of environmental regulation, in an application to the problem of biodiversity conservation. She emphasizes the fact that, in the presence of full information, the various policy instruments will in theory yield equivalent results. However, under various types of uncertainty, some could be more effective than others. Moreover, different criteria of effectiveness (for example, effectiveness in reaching the conservation target as opposed to cost effectiveness) will favour different instruments. She demonstrates that it is usually impossible to predict which instrument will be most desirable, and that the decision must be taken on a case-by-case basis. The problems of regulation of biodiversity conservation involve the complicating factor of threshold effects, which are described in detail in Chapter 11. The fact that the breaching of threshold values may involve high costs, as well as the fact that their locations are often not known with certainty means that a system of regulation ought to have an innate margin of safety. The analysis in this chapter demonstrates how, for both a system of quantity controls with fines as an enforcement and a tax system, the requisite safety margins can be incorporated into the system design.

This analysis provides a demonstration of a system of regulation for the sustainable use of ecosystems. It constitutes a break with the optimality criterion, which requires only the internalization of identifiable external costs and values, and justifies limiting the use of environmental resources still further, if this is necessary to sustain what are thought to be essential environmental services.

ENVIRONMENTAL SUSTAINABILITY

The final chapter in Part II provides a link between the theory of internalization of external costs, and the problem of sustainability. It demonstrates effectively that a conflict between sustainability and optimality could arise if the former involves imposing limits on economic activity to maintain essential ecosystem services, while a criterion of optimality indicates the desirability of sacrificing the relevant ecosystems.

In Chapter 10, Pamela Mason provides an overview of the problem of sustainability arguing, contrary to a body of opinion both within and outside economics, that the concept of sustainability can be a useful one. She points out first that the lack of a generally recognized definition of sustainability stems not from vagueness of the concept itself, but from the fact that it implies different policies in different contexts. In economic analysis the desirability of a sustainable path is not taken as given, but as something that must be proved. The chapter therefore explains the economic arguments for sustainability *not* being a relevant problem. It also, however, discusses the various factors which are often omitted from economic models. The chapter argues that inclusion of these factors could alter not only the perceived optimal path, but also the likelihood that the market will be capable of identifying the said path. It is argued that the circumstances under which the market could *not* be expected to identify a desired sustainable path are sufficiently realistic as to provide a rationale for concluding that sustainability is not irrelevant.

One of the factors which is discussed as being omitted from the economic process is the essential life-support services provided by global ecosystems. The issues pertaining to the sustainable use of ecosystems are discussed by Silvana Dalmazzone in Chapter 11. This chapter covers the theory on the stability and resilience of ecosystems, the interaction between economic and ecological factors and so the sustainability of ecosystem-dependent economic activities. Two types of resilience are defined: Pimm-resilience, referring to the speed with which a disturbed ecosystem returns to its initial equilibrium, and Holling-resilience, referring to the extent to which an ecosystem can be disturbed and still retain the capacity to return to the original equilibrium. Analysis of this concept proves to be particularly useful in the management of systems in which economic growth changes the parameters of the ecological systems, which in turn have implications for the optimal and sustainable allocation of resources. The most important feature of the sustainable use of ecosystems is the possibility that there may be a discontinuity in the damage function, or a threshold value beyond which the system could be destroyed, or switch suddenly to a degraded state.

These concepts are analysed with respect to the impacts of both harvesting and pollution on ecosystem dynamics, both of which reduce ecosystem resilience. The most important contribution of this approach is in improving the use of ecological information for the management of renewable resources, by accounting for the effects of stress on the resilience of ecosystems and the danger of feedback effects and threshold values.

One of the most important roles for environmental policy is the identification of critical lower bounds, above which ecosystems must be maintained. The approach emphasizes the fact that in identifying these bounds, economic factors must be accounted for, since the stability domain will be directly affected by the optimum harvesting decisions. The identification of such bounds is essential to the design of regulatory systems for the conservation of ecosystems, of the type analysed in Chapter 9.

A further point brought out in Chapter 10 is that the context in which an economy implements a policy of sustainability determines the policy requirements, in terms of which assets and which sectors must actually be sustained in order to sustain well-being. For example, when the context is that of a small economy, then most external parameters, such as the rate of interest, can be taken as given, and optimal consumption and investment decisions taken on such a basis. This point is analysed by John Pezzey in Chapter 12. He examines the case of a resource-owning economy that is open to trade with the rest of the world, and is sufficiently small that its actions do not affect prices or interest rates in the rest of the world. Assuming that resources have no value other than as inputs to production, the model proves that if the economy moves from a strategy of maximizing the present discounted value of utility to one of sustainability of consumption, then the strategy of resource management is unchanged. Sustainability of well-being does not depend in any way on sustainability of the resource sector. The constant exogenous interest rate means that, in effect, whatever the objective function in terms of the distribution of welfare over time, it is maximized by maximizing the value of the resource endowment, and therefore of wealth. The ability to invest in the international capital market means that this wealth can be distributed over time so as to maximize any objective function, be it maximization of the present value of utility, or maximization of sustainable consumption.

This conclusion implies that if the market value of natural resources is maximized by rapid depletion, then this is the optimal strategy for a small economy whether or not it wishes to sustain consumption. However, the chapter does stress the strength of the assumptions necessary for this conclusion to hold. First, it is necessary that no value be placed on the resource stock other than as a source of inputs to production, while in fact many renewable resource stocks, such as forests, are valued for their own sake. Second, it is necessary that the rest of the global economy does not follow a similar depletion path, but maintains the structure of production so that the return to invested capital is itself maintained. The possibility that this assumption is not satisfied is examined by considering the case of a closed economy, which represents the equivalent of many small economies following the same path. In this case the rate of interest cannot be assumed to be constant, but is determined by internal investment decisions. A switch from a present value-maximizing objective to one of sustainability necessitates, in this case, a change in resource management. These results demonstrate clearly the point that the practical strategies required for sustainability vary according to the context in which the policy is implemented.

CONCLUSIONS

This chapter has outlined the role played by each branch of environmental economics in improving the efficiency with which environmental resources are used in the economic system, and the contributions to this aim of the following chapters. Part I provides a broad range of topics in environmental valuation. The application of valuation techniques is described for environmental assets in a developed country, an economy in transition, and a less-developed country. The last of these illustrates a technique which has been little used in environmental valuation. Also analysed is a new method for estimating the true underlying values which people attach to non-market assets.

The valuation techniques analysed in Part I allow the identification of the optimal scale of production. Part II illustrates both the theory and application of the policy instruments necessary to internalize the identified values into the economic process, and so achieve the optimal allocation of resources. In particular, many of the non-market values required to identify the optimal allocation are the kinds of factors, such as the value of health risks, for which people tend not to have well-developed preferences. The type of information and psychological analysis described by Cookson in Chapter 4 may therefore result in a more accurate valuation.

A further step is to consider the possibility of a conflict between the optimality of the scale of production, and its sustainability. It is possible, for instance, that activities which are optimal from the point of view of the present have costs which are felt mainly in the future. The regulatory instruments necessary to implement these further restrictions on the use of environmental resources in production are described in Chapter 9. The economic theory behind this possible conflict is outlined in Chapter 10, in its analysis of the circumstances under which the optimal scale of production exceeds the maximum scale at which global ecosystems are able to support economic activity. Chapter 11 describes the theory on the sustainable exploitation of ecosystems in the presence of threshold and feedback effects, and demonstrates the restrictions which would be required, effectively providing the ecological–economic analysis required for the regulation of ecosystem use. Chapter 12 shows that it is possible under certain, rather restrictive assumptions, for the optimal and sustainable strategy for a resource-owning economy to be the stripping of the resources and investment of the proceeds abroad. However, the very restrictive nature of the assumptions necessary for the anticipated optimality to be realized, means that the analysis is more of a warning than a recommendation.

The use of valuation techniques to improve the efficiency of resource allocation is, in theory at least, relatively uncontentious. However, the constraining of currently optimal activities in order to ensure that global ecosystems and therefore human well-being are not seriously damaged at some point in the future would require a degree of political will which cannot simply be assumed. For sustainability to have policy relevance, it must be shown that the current generation is prepared to make the necessary sacrifices. The analysis described in the latter part of this book provides a theoretical basis on which this important discussion can be based.

NOTE

1. For an overview of alternative methods of valuation, such as the travel cost method and hedonic pricing, see Chapter 10 of Perman et al. (1996).

REFERENCE

Perman, R., Y. Ma and K. McGilvray (1996), *Natural Resource and Environmental Economics*, London: Longman.

PART I

Economic Valuation of the Environment

2. Economic valuation in transition economies: an application of contingent valuation to Lake Balaton in Hungary

Susana Mourato*

INTRODUCTION

In recent years, the estimation of economic values of environmental resources has become an important part of the discipline of environmental economics. The purpose of economic valuation is to reveal and translate into monetary terms the true costs and benefits of alternative decisions regarding public goods such as environmental resources. The need for valuation arises from the fact that most environmental goods and services are not traded in the market and hence do not have a price. Examples are air and water quality or forest preservation. This does not imply that these goods and services do not have a value, only that markets fail to capture it directly ('market failure').

If decisions regarding the environment are to be fully informed and efficient then it is necessary to take into consideration all benefits and costs of a particular decision or project. For example, the disposal of sewage into a river may cause damage to the aquatic fauna and flora and the surrounding environment which, if taken into consideration, may make alternative solutions – such as improving the sewage treatment facilities – more appealing. In any case, the value of these 'external' environmental losses should be reflected in the private costs of sewage disposal (either through appropriate taxation, environmental standards or permit systems).

* The research underlying this chapter was funded by the European Union PECO 1994 Programme. The author gratefully acknowledges a grant provided by the Portuguese Junta Nacional de Investigação Científica e Tecnológica (JNICT) through the PRAXIS XXI Programme. Sandor Kerekes, Maria Csutora, Zsusza Szerenyi and Ezter Kovacs made valuable contributions to the survey design and implementation. The author is also indebted to Giles Atkinson for insightful comments.

Translating all benefits and costs into monetary terms is thus a necessary first step to enable external factors to be taken into consideration by decision makers. This does not imply that decisions regarding the environment should be made solely on the basis of efficiency criteria, simply that valuation exercises provide important information to guide the allocation of scarce public resources.

Economists have developed special techniques for placing monetary values on goods and services that are not traded in the market place. In recent years, one such technique, the contingent valuation method (CVM), although surrounded by ongoing controversy, has managed to gain widespread acceptance among both academics and policy makers, being considered by many as the most complete method of environmental appraisal. Chapters 3 and 4 address in more detail some of the criticisms that have been levelled at the CVM.

Contingent valuation techniques (Mitchell and Carson 1989) are survey based and involve the creation of a hypothetical market (described in the questionnaire) in which the environmental good or service in question can be traded. Respondents are then asked their willingness to pay (WTP) for a positive environmental change or their willingness to accept (WTA) compensation for a deterioration.

Contingent valuation is well rooted in the theory of welfare economics, namely on the neoclassical concept of economic value based on individual utility maximization. It assumes that stated WTP amounts are related to respondents' underlying preferences. The values obtained correspond to the correct monetary welfare measures, namely Hicksian compensating and equivalent variations (ibid.; Freeman, 1994).

In recent years, CVM has been extensively applied in developed countries to the valuation of a wide range of environmental goods and services (Carson et al., 1996). Much of the impetus for this acceptance came from the conclusions of the special panel appointed by the US National Oceanic and Atmospheric Administration (NOAA). The NOAA panel concluded that CVM studies could produce estimates reliable enough to be used in a judicial process of natural resource damage assessment (Arrow et al., 1993).

The challenge remains to apply such techniques successfully to the more complex situations existing in the developing world or in transitional economies. In the former case, where income, educational constraints and imperfect markets could be seen as precluding valuation attempts, some studies have been successfully implemented in recent years. Georgiou et al. (1997) summarizes the existing literature. This chapter focuses on the latter case, where existing research efforts are much more scarce,[1] and describes the design, implementation and results of what is one of the first applications of contingent valuation to a transitional economy: the economic valuation of water quality improvements in the largest lake in Europe, Lake Balaton in Hungary.

RATIONALE FOR THE STUDY

The first broad motivation for the Lake Balaton study was to determine whether contingent markets could be used accurately in the distinguishing characteristics of transitional economies where common economic instruments like taxes are relatively undeveloped. That is, whether consumers would be able to adjust quickly from a centrally planned economy to the opposite end of the spectrum, namely hypothetical markets.

Second, given the country's typical combination of high levels of pollution and low levels of environmental awareness, an investigation into the degree of environmental sensitivity of Hungarian citizens and the effects of information was also conducted.

Under the former communist regime, Hungary (with, arguably, a comparative advantage in agriculture) underwent rapid industrialization. The implementation of this policy was at the root of the massive environmental degradation that resulted: the growth of production pursued at any cost; economic inefficiency; a low priority for conservation; 'dirty' technologies; and heavy industry. Today, about 11 per cent of the country has been declared to be dangerously polluted and approximately 40 per cent of the population lives in these polluted regions. According to Peter (1993), it is estimated that pollution damage amounts each year to nearly 4 per cent of national income.

In parallel, Bochniarz and Kerekes (1994) have argued that communist ideology engendered a loss of civil responsibility which in turn was reflected in the absence of an ethic of respect for nature, as people did not seem to see beyond the value of consumptive uses. With the beginning of the transition to a market-orientated economy in 1989, also came some awareness of the scale of environmental damage. Nevertheless, some years down the line of transition, environmental awareness is still considered to be generally low. Moreover, Bochniarz and Kerekes (ibid.) point out that public outcries related to environmental issues are motivated more by a poorly understood fear of danger than by a conscious reaction based on knowledge of the problem.

Lastly, within this general framework, the more specific goal of this study was to estimate the benefits Hungarian citizens derive from water quality improvements at Lake Balaton and to explore the scope for generating additional funds for remedial and preventive conservation actions.

For that purpose, three different funding possibilities were explored: an increase in general tax levels (ascertained by surveying a representative sample of the Hungarian population, interviewed in various locations throughout the country); an increase in local taxes, mainly affecting residents and people who own homes in the vicinity of Balaton (examined through a survey of usual residents and second-home owners); and an increase in local tourist daily taxes (investigated by on-site interviews of tourists). In addition, the notion that sufficient tax revenues are currently targeted at Balaton is examined through a budget reallocation exercise.

LAKE BALATON CASE STUDY

Lake Balaton is the largest lake in Europe and is situated in the centre of Hungary. It stretches for almost 80 km with a shoreline of 197 km, a surface of 596 km^2 and a 2552 km^2 catchment area. Its waters are shallow, reaching an average depth of 2–3 metres so that the lake maintains a pleasant temperature from May to October. There are approximately 130 000 permanent residents in close proximity to Lake Balaton, plus 420 000 residents in its catchment area.[2]

Although its uses have varied over time, today Lake Balaton is used mainly for recreational purposes: swimming, sunbathing, sailing and fishing. There are approximately 123 beaches occupying some 206 hectares and massive waterfront development occupies most of the shoreline. The lake generates more than a third of Hungary's income from tourism. The average weekend occupation of the lake during the peak season (summer period) in 1991 was 570 000 people with a maximum of 930 000. This exceeds the optimal load of the Balaton by 1.6 times. Once seen as the Hungarian sea it is still considered to be the nation's playground although rising prices are pushing out domestic in favour of foreign tourists. Presently, four-fifths of the tourists are foreigners, mainly from former socialist countries and from Germany and Austria.

Water quality at Lake Balaton has become a problem since the 1970s and reached critical levels around 1982. The primary source of deterioration that has occurred is eutrophication, a type of biological pollution that can be described as an increase in the nutrient concentration of the water (phosphorus and nitrogen). The main source of water pollution is the direct sewage flow from neighbouring villages. The existing treatment facilities are scarce and overloaded during the peak season (only 34 per cent of waste water was treated in 1991). This explains the seasonal characteristics of pollution at the lake where water quality reaches its lowest levels in the summer.

Over the years, there have been a number of programmes designed to clean up the water and beaches of Balaton. These attempts have been unsuccessful because of lack of money and political commitment. Current clean-up projects are based exclusively on cost considerations. No attempt has been made to determine the economic benefits of water quality improvements at the lake. By determining the total benefits of a cleaner Balaton, new sources of funding may be identified and feasible financing schemes for measures to reduce water pollution may be devised and implemented.

ASSESSING SURFACE WATER QUALITY IMPROVEMENTS

Water quality improvements in surface waters generate a wide variety of market and non-market benefits.[3] For the particular case study of Lake Balaton, benefits include direct on-site uses comprising mainly recreation – swimming, boating, beach sports, sun-bathing, sightseeing, hiking/walking, angling, amenity values from the surrounding environment – and indirect use values such as increased employment from tourism or pleasure from reading or seeing pictures of the lake.

Water quality improvements may also produce a different type of benefit known collectively as 'non-use values' that correspond to a wide range of motivations for which individuals might value environmental improvements in Lake Balaton, irrespective of their use of it: benefits from protecting the quality of the lake for future generations (bequest values), from knowing that others are currently enjoying the lake (altruistic values) or simply from the knowledge that the lake is being preserved for its own sake, providing a natural habitat for fish, plants and wildlife (existence values). This knowledge may be experience based or education based. Non-use values arise from the landscape, the biodiversity, the ecosystems and even the national symbolism related to the lake and may well extend beyond the frontiers of Hungary. Between use and non-use values are the so-called 'option values' that refer to benefits derived from guaranteeing the opportunity for future recreational use of the lake.

The economic evaluation of rivers and lakes has traditionally focused on the demand for on-site recreational use (Sanders et al. 1990). However, non-use values may play as important a role in justifying expenditures on water protection as the more conventional use benefits. This is especially true in the case of unique and irreplaceable sites such as the Balaton not only the largest lake in Europe but, together with Budapest, the most famous Hungarian landmark.

In this study, we estimate the *total* benefits of improving water quality levels in Lake Balaton, from the point of view of Hungarian citizens. It is currently considered impossible to isolate the several components of total value accurately (Cummings and Harrison 1995). Estimating total values, incorporating the range of existing attributes, is thus the correct way of obtaining valid and reliable results. In this framework, the adoption of the contingent valuation method was warranted by the fact that it is the only technique theoretically capable of estimating the whole range of benefits produced by water quality improvements, including non-use values.

In addition, the method has been applied successfully to a variety of water-related issues including sanitation, water supply, recreation, flow enhancement and health risks.[4] It has also been used in very different contextual frameworks: lakes and rivers, groundwater, bathing water (both salt and freshwater), fishing sites, urban water parks, wetlands and marine and coastal areas.[5]

SURVEY DESIGN AND IMPLEMENTATION

This section provides an overview of the lengthy process of design and implementation of the Balaton contingent valuation surveys, from the sampling and piloting stages through to final questionnaire design.

Sampling Issues

The benefits of water quality improvements and the mechanisms through which they may be captured vary geographically and according to population characteristics.

Residents and home owners in the Balaton area benefit directly from water quality improvements in the lake. They pay local taxes ('contribution to settlement development') that help finance local sewage and waste treatment facilities. For many, the Balaton home is a second home, used mainly for weekend breaks, holidays or rented out for the summer. Hungarian tourists who actively use the area, although they do not possess a house there, also derive direct benefits from improvements at the lake. Daily tourist taxes are charged to those staying in paid accommodation. In addition, the whole population of Hungary, whether users of the area or not, may derive option and non-use benefits from the preservation of the lake, which reflect individual preferences for the existence of a clean environment, especially when related to an asset that is simultaneously a national symbol in historical, scenic, environmental and economic terms. These latter values may be captured through national taxes.

To try to estimate separately the benefits derived by the different population groups described above, linking them to the relevant payment mechanism in each case, a split sample design was used:

- an on-site *random local sample* of 1094 individuals. The sample includes residents (217), second-home owners (219), Hungarian tourists (336) and foreign tourists (322) all of whom actively derive use benefits from the Balaton;
- a *random national sample* of 737 Hungarians, representative of the (adult) Hungarian population.

A comparison of survey and census data from 1995 shows that the national sample seems to be representative of the Hungarian population with regard to sex, age, education and income. In contrast, the age distribution of Hungarian tourists interviewed on-site is skewed towards younger generations while the reverse is true for the, on average, much older owners of a weekend home. Furthermore, the average net monthly income in the national sample is between 20 000 and 25 000 HUF (1995 US$140–175), which accords to the estimated mean income per capita in Hungary in 1995 of 23 000 HUF (1995 US$161). This is slightly more than the mean income of onsite Hungarian tourists and considerably less than the declared monthly earnings of second-home owners that falls in the 30 000–35 000 HUF interval (1995 US$210–245). Also, education levels are much higher for the on-site sample than at a national level. For example, nearly half of all second-home owners have university degrees. Thus, owning a second home at Balaton, unsurprisingly perhaps, seems to be an indicator of higher-income levels.

Pre-testing Stages

A comprehensive background study was conducted prior to the design of the questionnaires. The surveys were administered by a market research organization with experience in conducting surveys in Hungary, including environmental surveys. Special training sessions were provided to the group of chosen enumerators.

Both survey instruments were extensively pre-tested – a fact which assumes a particular importance in the novel circumstances of transitional economies. A series of consultations with local experts and informal groups preceded the design of the questionnaires. First drafts were tested and refined in several in-depth group interviews. Nearly 100 pre-test interviews were conducted on-site at the Balaton area and in Budapest. Apart from testing several aspects of the survey instrument, the pilots also provided a training opportunity for the enumerators.

The final versions of the on-site questionnaire were administered on location at Balaton during July and August 1995. Four different variations were adopted: a version for local residents, a version for second-home owners, another for Hungarian tourists/recreational visitors and a final one for foreign tourists (in German). The off-site national survey took place in December 1995 at several sampling points around Hungary.

Overall it appears that the survey was highly successful in capturing the interest of the population. The vast majority of the interviewees found the questionnaire interesting and very few people thought it was difficult although some 13–22 per cent found it too long (the duration of the interview varied from 20 minutes to more than one hour, with an average of 30–35 minutes).

The Survey Instrument

The Balaton questionnaires comprised sections on attitudes and perceptions, uses of the area, travel costs, scenario information, value elicitation, debriefing and socioeconomic characteristics.

Regarding the scenario, extensive information was provided about the lake. Maps, photographs and a water quality ladder were used to show the length and location of Balaton and to illustrate the pollution problems and proposed changes. The water quality improvement would be brought about by a hypothetical Balaton Clean-Up Programme (BCUP) consisting of a set of measures to regulate the discharge of pollutants into the lake expected to ensure bathing water quality by the year 2010. If the clean-up operation was not implemented, respondents were informed that the water quality would be expected to deteriorate over the following 15 years.

The financing mechanism for the clean-up would be based on taxation: (i) in the on-site survey, all users who directly contribute to the pollution process would have to pay a local compulsory contribution (paid on an annual basis by residents and second-home owners, and on a daily basis by tourists);[6] (ii) in the off-site national survey, all Hungarian households would pay a share of the costs through increased taxes.

A number of follow-up questions were included in the Balaton national survey to determine the degree of credibility and acceptance of the proposed BCUP. On average, the programme seemed to generate very positive responses. In all, 56 per cent of Hungarians felt that there would be widespread community support for the programme, 75 per cent thought it would be approved by the parliament, 56 per cent trusted that it could be enforced adequately by the Hungarian authorities and, most importantly, a large majority of 88 per cent were confident it would achieve the proposed objectives. As expected, the only aspect of the BCUP that respondents reacted negatively to was the payment vehicle: 60 per cent considered taxes to be an unfair mechanism (very unfair for 22 per cent). This position explains some of the stated zero WTP answers analysed below.

The contingent market was posed as a dichotomous choice referendum (a vote 'for' or 'against' the proposed BCUP) and requested the individual monetary valuation. In its single-bounded version (Bishop and Heberlein 1979; Hanemann 1984; Cameron 1988) respondents were faced with a single valuation question asking whether they would be willing to pay a certain amount of money for some environmental improvement (the bid level was varied across different subsamples). In the study, a double-bounded elicitation procedure was adopted (Hanemann et al. 1991) whereby the initial elicitation was followed by a second payment question that depended on the response to the first bid level: if the respondent accepted the initial bid he or she was asked to pay a higher bid; if the answer to the first bid level was 'no' he or she was presented with a lower one. Open-ended valuation questions, consisting of simply asking respondents directly for their maximum WTP, were also elicited.

ENVIRONMENTAL ATTITUDES

Eastern European countries have undergone drastic political, economic, cultural and social changes during the last decade. These changes impact on the public's perception of the importance and urgency of environmental problems. However, studies of environmental attitudes in transition economies are scarce and, in this respect, Hungary is no exception. The Balaton on-site and off-site questionnaires included specific sections on attitudes towards the environment in general with a special emphasis on water-related problems.

Attitudes towards the Environment in General

Table 2.1 ranks respondents' perceptions of the most serious problems in Hungary. Among the national sample, unemployment, inflation and public health services were voted the worst problems. The on-site survey results were, however, very different: on the whole, health, environment and education received the highest ranks. These figures probably reflect the fact that, in the on-site version of the questionnaire, the section containing general questions about the environment was positioned *after* the information about Lake Balaton and the initial valuation question.[7]

Respondents were, at that stage, very focused on pollution problems and this may have resulted in an upward bias in favour of the relative importance of the environment category. This illustrates the fact that minor changes in questionnaire design may engender a large disparity in answers.

Table 2.1 Ranking of the most serious problems in Hungary

Most serious problems in Hungary	National sample	On-site sample
Education	7	3
Environment	6	2
Inflation/economy	2	4
Health	3	1
Poverty	4	6
Security	5	7
Unemployment	1	5

However, the ranking of the most important problems within the environment sphere was not affected by the particular placement of the question. This is due to the fact that water pollution (in its various forms including drinking water pollution) was considered the most serious environmental problem by the national Hungarian sample (Table 2.2). The fact that the users of the lake had previously been informed about water deterioration at Balaton did not change the direction of these preferences. Air pollution and waste management came second and third in the ranking. Furthermore, it is interesting to note that, within the on-site sample, the local residents' subsample ranked air pollution third. Air pollution is linked more to large cities and industrial areas. Hence, the fact that it is not a local priority in the Balaton area probably impacts on the respondents' assessment of national priorities.

Table 2.2 Ranking of the most serious environmental problems in Hungary

Most serious environmental problems in Hungary	National sample	On-site sample
Air pollution	2	2
Forest nature	4	—
Soil pollution	5	4
Waste management	3	3
Water pollution	1	1

Contrary to common perceptions, the majority of respondents were found to be interested or very interested in environmental issues (67 per cent and 80 per cent in the national and local samples, respectively) with only 5–7 per cent declaring a lack of interest in the topic. However, only 3–4 per cent were members of an environmental organization. Once more, second-home owners generally performed 'better' in terms of environmental concern, possibly a reflection of the higher level of income and education in this subsample relative to the population as a whole.

For 40 per cent of national respondents, old technologies and the low level of economic development were the principal causes of environmental degradation in Hungary and only 2 per cent attributed it to the previous state ownership of property. The majority of respondents thought the general public, local and state authorities and the scientific community should all be involved in environmental decisions and 64 per cent also considered their knowledge of environmental problems to be sufficient to allow them to play an active part in finding solutions.

Uses of and Attitudes towards Balaton

Most Hungarians have visited Lake Balaton: 98 per cent of the representative national Hungarian sample had visited the lake and 93 per cent visited more than once, regularly or occasionally. So almost every respondent can be classified as a 'user', with the distinction being whether the interview took place on- or off-site.

Of the on-site users, the average tourist visits the lake on an annual basis while second-home owners visit regularly throughout the year. Tourists tend to stay for one or two weeks while nearly a third of second-home owners stay for longer periods. The majority of residents and home owners have owned a house or lived in the area for more than ten years. The main motivation for acquiring a house in the area is linked to the local amenities and only 8 per cent consider it as an income source (which is compatible with the fact that most of those interviewed do not rent out their homes/rooms on a regular basis). Most of these subsamples spent at least part of their holidays in the lake area. The main activity at the lake is relaxing and enjoying the scenery for both residents and second-home owners. Tourists appear to prefer resting on the beach and swimming while fishing and water sports do not seem to be very popular with any group of users.

Only 6–10 per cent of the sample thought the Balaton waters were not polluted, with 51–56 per cent of respondents considering the lake to be polluted or very polluted (the lower percentage being for the on-site users – since they are actively using the lake, they are not likely to find it very polluted, perhaps reflecting some form of cognitive dissonance). However, the differences between the two samples are small and some consensus does seem to exist. It is important to recall in this respect that almost every respondent, on- or off-site, could be classified as a 'user'.

Interestingly, a majority of 54 per cent of national respondents consider industrial discharges and agriculture run-off to be the main causes of water pollution in the Balaton. The actual main source of pollution, sewage flow from local users (whether residents or tourists), is only cited by 43 per cent of the population. Respondents consider industry and agriculture to be the sectors most responsible for environmental degradation and these general feelings seem to have been extrapolated to the particular case of Balaton.

Adverse effects from pollution on wildlife (plants and animals) supported by the lake seem to be the main concern for respondents which is indicative of the existence of non-use values (given that angling is not common in the Balaton). Respondents were also not surprised by the assertion that some 2 000 people get sick every year because of pollution at the lake.

WILLINGNESS-TO-PAY ESTIMATES

To recap, the Lake Balaton study explored three different funding mechanisms: general taxes, local resident taxes and local tourist taxes. Three different samples were surveyed to address each of these different possibilities: a representative sample of the Hungarian population, interviewed in various locations throughout the country, a sample of habitual residents and second-home owners in the Balaton proximity and a sample of Hungarian tourists interviewed on-site. A number of econometric models were used to analyse the survey data arising from single- and double-bounded dichotomous choice and open-ended questions.[8] Table 2.3 depicts mean estimated benefits across the different subsamples, using the three different statistical specifications referred to above.[9]

Table 2.3 Mean annual WTP estimates across models and subsamples

Subsample	Single bounded	Double bounded	Open ended
National	4340.7	3901.8	3756.8
Second home	2965.2	2998.2	3144.3
Residents	2939.9	2925.2	2768.4
Hungarian Tourists	979.0	903.6	791

Notes:
(i) $N = 1509$.
(ii) All data in Hungarian forints (HUF).

Inspection of the values included in Table 2.3 shows a significant disparity in WTP estimates across subsamples which indicates that the choice, and specifically the temporal dimension, of the payment vehicle crucially affects the results. Estimates vary from 791 to 4341 HUF (1995 USS6–30). Hence, with the exception of local residents and second-home owners, it cannot be inferred from these results that on-site local tourists value water quality improvements less than citizens interviewed off-site, given the differences in the payment vehicles used in the questionnaires. The relatively lower values obtained by local taxes may be due to the fact that: (i) Hungarians object to paying locally for something that is of avowed national interest; (ii) on-site elicitation exacerbates particular use values while a less-contextual scenario may highlight broader non-use concerns; (iii) daily taxes tend to invoke more consumptive-use values (that is, something you may easily pay for on a daily basis) than non-use benefits (that may be perceived to be on a more long-term basis and thus be better captured by annual payments); (iv) or, less plausibly, that local authorities may be perceived as less capable of implementing and managing the BCUP.[10]

The lower estimated benefits for each subsample can be used for policy purposes, given the desirability of quoting conservative estimates for values elicited in contingent markets, and they correspond approximately to a reasonable 1 per cent of respondents annual net income. The results also suggest that an annual tax levied at the national level maximizes the revenue that can potentially be obtained from Hungarian citizens.[11]

Confidence intervals for the mean calculated from referendum data, estimated using the Krinsky and Robb procedure, show that the differences between the alternative econometric models are not statistically different from zero.[12] It seems to have become the received wisdom in CV studies that the mean WTP resulting from dichotomous choice data is consistently larger than that obtained from open-ended elicitations. In this study such differences were, however, not statistically significant and were in the opposite direction to that expected for second-home owners. Basic valuation functions were estimated and are given in the appendix.

Follow-up questions included after the valuation section revealed that, on average, respondents were split almost equally between choosing non-use motivations or use-related benefits as the main reason for supporting the BCUP. The most-cited non-use benefit is a bequest motive followed by nature and wildlife preservation.

One of the motivations for including a maximum WTP question as a follow-up to the referendum elicitation process is the identification of zero bidders. The proportion of zero WTP values was 16 per cent in the national sample, 24 per cent in both the residents' and Hungarian tourists' subgroups and 22 per cent for the owners of a weekend home.

These values are within the same magnitude, if smaller, of those usually found in CV studies. Further debriefing revealed that about 40 per cent of those stating a zero WTP could not afford to pay more taxes or considered that there were more important goals than the BCUP. A little more than 50 per cent of respondents protested against some aspect of the proposed programme. Reasons included: unwillingness to pay more taxes; disbelief in the effectiveness of the programme; or a perceived lack of responsibility for pollution of the lake. For these people, the survey instrument did not elicit the true benefit of cleaner water at Balaton. They were, however, included in the overall estimate of an average WTP because: (i) of the dangers inherent in arbitrarily removing observations from the sample; (ii) a conservative approach was favoured throughout the study and the inclusion of potential protest answers in the final calculations can only bias the results downwards.

BUDGET REALLOCATION

The possibility that 'high enough' taxes were already being targeted at the Balaton was also explored in the national questionnaire. This was achieved through a novel budget reallocation exercise. It constitutes a test of the tax mechanism and *not* an estimation of benefits from water quality improvements (which can be elicited only through the hypothetical market described in this chapter). The standard proportion of zero WTP answers found seem to indicate, however, that externalities exist that are not already being captured by existing tax mechanisms.

After the valuation section, respondents were introduced to the hypothetical public expenditure breakdown (based on real data) depicted in Figure 2.1. Additionally, they were informed that implementing the BCUP in the following year (1996) would have an estimated cost of 3.5 billion HUF.

A new alternative hypothetical scenario was introduced. Instead of increasing taxes to finance the Balaton clean-up, the government was now considering financing the BCUP by reducing by 3.5 billion HUF the budget previously allocated to (A) other areas of public expenditures, (B) other environmental expenditures or (C) other expenditures in the water sector, and reallocating the amount to the Balaton programme. Respondents were then asked to vote for or against this reallocation mechanism operating on all three levels A, B and C.

A. SHARE OF MAIN PUBLIC EXPENDITURES IN STATE BUDGET

Health	Education	Pension/social security	Defence	Roads and transport	Environment	Security
16%	12%	25%	5%	5%	1%	4%

B. ENVIRONMENTAL EXPENDITURES

Air quality	Cultural heritage	Waste management	Nature protection	Water quality	Soil conservation
33%	6%	8%	4%	45%	4%

C. WATER EXPENDITURES

Drinking water	Sanitation/sewage treatment	Other rivers and lakes	Lake Balaton	Groundwater
33%	56%	7%	3%	1%

Figure 2.1 *Hypothetical public expenditure distribution, 1996 (1707 billion HUF)*

At level A, a majority of 58 per cent of respondents voted in favour of the budgetary switch. Defence and social security were the sectors indicated most often as possible candidates for the budget cut. On level B, only a minority of 29 per cent was in favour of a money switch, probably reflecting public feelings that not enough is being spent on each of the areas of the environmental budget. Air quality and cultural heritage were the preferred areas for any reduction in funds. Finally, on level C, only 28 per cent agreed with budgetary changes from sanitation and other rivers and lakes. Again, this low percentage may be indicative of a feeling that funding is generally scarce for water management needs (it should be recalled that water pollution was unanimously considered the most serious environmental problem in Hungary).

The next step consisted of inquiring whether respondents preferred any of the budget reallocation options just described, or the tax increase option described in the valuation section of the questionnaire, as a means to finance the Balaton clean-up operation. Results indicated that 41 per cent would actually prefer the reallocation approach, 16 per cent voted for the tax increase and 36 per cent chose a combination of the two.

To make these results resemble a WTP answer,[13] the last question introduced a possibility of a tax cut due to a reduction of 3.5 billion HUF in administrative costs. Respondents were asked to choose one of four alternatives: (i) reduce the total tax burden; (ii) allocate the surplus money to the BCUP; (iii) allocate the surplus to other areas of public expenditure; or (iv) a combination of all these options. A vote for any category apart from the tax cut constitutes an indirect payment for the chosen purpose (although obviously not a maximum WTP). After some adjustments, it can be seen that approximately 52 per cent of respondents preferred the money to be allocated to Balaton, which in essence constitutes a tax cut refusal; 20 per cent chose the tax cut and a further 22 per cent would like to see the money allocated to other areas.

How should these results be interpreted? In the national survey, the valuation exercise shows that only 16 per cent of respondents refused to pay any positive amount for water quality improvements at Balaton, with the remaining 84 per cent stating a positive WTP. On the whole, the surveyed population was willing to pay up to one per cent of their annual income for the proposed clean-up operation. This means not only that a clearly positive benefit exists from the proposed programme, but also that the large majority of respondents, although naturally disliking paying taxes, do not reject wholly the proposition that they might pay more for environmental purposes.

The budget reallocation exercise shows that 74 per cent of the population is willing to forgo some monetary gain to contribute to allow extra spending in some area (52 per cent mention the BCUP as the preferred area although that result is almost certainly biased upwards by the asymmetric amount of information provided about the lake versus other possible options). Considering the margins of error in both approaches this is indicative of the fact that the estimate of an 84 per cent acceptance rate of a tax increase specifically for Balaton may be biased upwards only slightly.

It is important to reiterate that this outcome implies nothing about the existence of significant positive benefits from water quality improvements at Lake Balaton but suggests instead a possible need to carefully consider adequate mechanisms to capture those benefits. Budget reallocation exercises of this kind can provide a benchmark against which to compare the number of protest answers and indicate the relative importance of the proportion of the population that may object to paying more taxes as a way to finance particular causes. The use of a portfolio of different economic instruments should reduce protests against any particular payment mechanism.

CONCLUSIONS

The main purpose of this study has been to illustrate the potential of contingent valuation to estimate the total benefits that Hungarian citizens derive from water quality improvements at Lake Balaton and to explore the scope for generating additional funds for remedial and preventive conservation actions. For that purpose, three different funding possibilities were explored. These were an increase in general tax levels affecting all Hungarian taxpayers, an increase in local taxes, applicable mainly to residents and second-home owners in the Balaton neighbourhood and an increase in local tourist daily taxes.

Our results show that water pollution is perceived as the most serious environmental problem in Hungary and that the economic benefits from water quality improvements at Lake Balaton are likely to be substantial. The related externalities would be better captured by an increase in the national tax level affecting all taxpayers. Hungarians are willing to pay an average of 3900 HUF (1995 US$27) every year for clean-up operations, which corresponds approximately to one per cent of *net* annual earnings. Implementation of such a mechanism would substantially increase the effectiveness of efforts to protect Balaton.

The study also shows that contingent markets can be used accurately in the case of transition economies. Furthermore, by carrying out a budget reallocation exercise, the survey showed that a large majority of Hungarians are willing to forego a tax cut in order to finance a number of areas of public expenditure. The implications are that taxes seem, on the whole, to be an acceptable mechanism to finance and redistribute resources, and that Hungarian consumers were able to adjust quickly from a centrally planned economy to the opposite end of the spectrum, namely hypothetical markets.

NOTES

1. See Mourato and Danchev (1997) and Zylicz et al. (1995) for other examples.
2. A comprehensive review of Lake Balaton's characteristics, uses, water quality and related legislation can be found in Andrasi et al. (1997).
3. For general texts about total economic value and its components, see Pearce and Turner (1990) and Mitchell and Carson (1989); for specific references to total and partial values in the water context, see Smith and Desvousges (1986) and Sanders et al. (1990).
4. CVM is the valuation technique recommended by US federal guidelines (US Water Resources Council 1983) as suitable for the valuation of water-based recreation and environmental resources.
5. Listings and overviews of related CV studies of water-based recreational benefits can be found in Mitchell and Carson (1989), Georgiou (1993), Carson et al. (1996), Georgiou et al. (1997) and Mourato et al. (1997).
6. The pre-test showed that respondents protested against the use of taxes as a payment vehicle, whereas the, for our purposes, similar 'compulsory contribution' concept seemed to resolve the problem! What happened is that compulsory contributions have existed in Hungary for years while taxes are a relatively new concept for the population. This small example shows the importance of pre-testing the wording of questionnaires

to be applied in a novel setting and illustrates how small, apparently innocuous, word changes can elicit very different behaviours.

7. After the attitudinal section, respondents were given the opportunity to revise the valuation question, which the large majority did not.

8. Care should be taken when interpreting the open-ended maximum WTP results. Since these were not determined independently of the dichotomous choice elicitation process (that is, in a split-sample context) but resulted from follow-up questions in the same questionnaire, the resulting estimates will be influenced by the bid amounts presented beforehand.

9. The results are obtained from the original data set, without any arbitrary truncation or elimination of observations.

10. In this respect, it is worth mentioning that the direction of the above results does not reveal any signs of temporal embedding as noted in other studies: that is, the present value of a series of (daily) payments does not seem to exceed the corresponding one-time (annual) payment.

11. Aggregating over all taxpayers would provide an estimate of total benefits that could then be compared with the implementation costs for Balaton's clean-up measures.

12 Detailed econometric results from all the different models applied to the data and referred to in this chapter can be found in Mourato et al. (1997).

13. Note that the initial budget reallocation questions are not comparable to the CV WTP question: they do not imply a monetary cost to the individual directly but simply a reallocation of existing funds between possible areas of expenditure. What then is being evaluated is the optimality of the initial resource allocation between competing uses which is a different matter altogether. But if a surplus can be created in such a way that none of the existing areas of interest are impoverished (by reducing bureaucracy, for example) and respondents can choose between a tax cut or an application in some public area of interest, that constitutes in a sense an indirect payment and is thus comparable with a willingness to contribute any positive amount.

REFERENCES

Andrasi, M., M. Csutora, A. Gorbe, S. Kerekes, E. Kovacs, S. Mourato and Z. Szerenyo (1997), 'Water quality at Lake Balaton, Hungary', Report to DGXII, European Commission, Brussels.

Arrow, K., R. Solow. P. Portney, E. Leamer, R. Radner and H. Schuman (1993). 'Report of the NOAA Panel on contingent valuation', *Federal Register*, **58** (10), 4602–14.

Bishop, R. and T. Heberlein (1979), 'Measuring values of extra-market goods: are indirect measures biased', *American Journal of Agricultural Economics*, **61**, 926–30.

Bochniarz, Z. and S. Kerekes (1994), 'Deficiencies in the existing system of environmental protection in Hungary', in Z. Bochniarz, R. Bolan. S. Kerekes and J. Kindler (eds), *Designing Institutions for Sustainable Development in Hungary: Agenda for the Future*, Minneapolis, Minn.; Budapest: Regional Environmental Centre for Central and Eastern Europe, pp. 9–21.

Cameron, T. (1988), 'A new paradigm for valuing non-market goods using referendum data: maximum likelihood estimation by censored logistic regression'. *Journal of Environmental Economics and Management*, **15**, 355–79.

Carson, R., N. Carson, A. Alberini and N. Wright (1996), *A Bibliography of Contingent Valuation Studies and Papers*, La Jolla, CA: Natural Resource Damage Assessment, Inc.

Cummings, R. and G. Harrison (1995), 'The measurement and Decomposition of nonuse values: a critical review', *Environmental and Resource Economics*, **5**, 225–47.

Freeman III, A.M. (1994). *The Measurement of Environmental and Resource Values: Theory and Methods*, Washington, DC: Resources for the Future.

Georgiou, S. (1993) 'Economic valuation of eutrophication damage in the Baltic Sea region: a review of relevant valuation studies', Report for the Contingent Valuation Method Network.

Georgiou, S., D. Whittington, D.W. Pearce and D. Moran (1997), *Economic Values and the Environment in the Developing World*, United Nations Environment Programme. Cheltenham: Edward Elgar.

Greene, W.H. (1997), *Econometric Analysis*, 3rd edn, New York: Macmillan.

Hanemann, W.M. (1984), 'Welfare evaluations in contingent valuation experiments with discrete responses', *American Journal of Agricultural Economics*, **66**, 332–41.

Hanemann, W.M., J. Loomis and B. Kanninen (1991), 'Estimation efficiency of double-bounded dichotomous choice contingent valuation', *American Journal of Agricultural Economics*, **73**,1255–63.

Mitchell, R. and R. Carson (1989), *Using Surveys to Value Public Goods: The Contingent Valuation Method*, Baltimore, MD: Johns Hopkins Press.

Mourato, S., M. Csutora, S. Kerekes E. Kovacs and Z. Szerenyo (1997), 'Estimating the value of water quality improvements in Lake Balaton: a contingent valuation study', Report to DGXII, European Commission, Brussels.

Mourato, S. and A. Danchev (1997), 'Preserving cultural heritage in transition economies: a contingent valuation study of Bulgarian monasteries', Report to DGXII, European Commission, Brussels.

Pearce, D.W. and R.K. Turner (1990), *Economics of Natural Resources and the Environment*, Hemel Hempstead, Herts: Harvester Wheatsheaf.

Peter, S. (1993), 'New directions in environmental management in Hungary', B. Jancar-Webster (ed), *Environmental Action in Eastern Europe. Responses to Crises*, New York: M.E. Sharpe.

Sanders, L., R. Walsh and J. Loomis (1990) 'Toward empirical estimation of the total value of protecting rivers', *Water Resources Research*, **26** (7), 1345–57.

Smith, V.K. and W. Desvousges (1986), *Measuring Water Quality Benefits*, Boston, MA: Klumer-Nijhoff.

US Water Resources Council (1983), *Economic and Environmental Principles and Guidelines for Water and Related Land Resources Implementation Studies*, Washington, DC: US Government Printing Office.

Zylicz, T., I. Bateman, S. Georgiou, A. Markowska, D. Dziegielewska, R.K. Turner, A. Graham and I. Langford (1995), 'Contingent valuation of eutrophication damage in the Baltic Sea region', Centre for Social and Economic Research on the Global Environment Working Paper, GEC 95–03, CSERGE, University College London and University of East Anglia, UK.

APPENDIX 2A VALUATION FUNCTIONS

Table 2A.1 illustrates basic valuation functions with the bid level as an explanatory variable. The single- and double-bounded models (SB and DB, respectively) were estimated using a logit and probit link function, respectively (Greene 1997). All estimated functions depend negatively on the bid level as expected: the higher the amount the lower the probability of accepting to pay. Extended valuation functions including socioeconomic and attitudinal regressors were also found to perform well, with the coefficient signs according to prior expectations (see Mourato et al. 1997).

Table 2A.1 Bid functions

Sample type	National sample		2nd home owners		Residents		Hungarian tourists	
Model	SB	DB	SB	DB	SB	DB	SB	DB
Cte	0.9602	1.1568	1.0731	0.8153	1.2221	0.9092	1.0156	0.8509
	(6.876)	(10.93)	(3.232)	(6.732)	(3.410)	(6.578)	(4.592)	(8.572)
Bid level	−0.0002	−0.0003	−0.0004	−0.0003	−0.0004	−0.0003	−0.0081	−0.007
	(−10.6)	(−18.1)	(−4.53)	(−12.2)	(−4.77)	(−11.9)	(−6.07)	(−19.5)
Log L	−424.66	−974.55	−137.11	−276.1	−132.44	−265.77	−210.5	−455.1

Notes: T-ratios in parenthesis

3. Real and hypothetical willingness to pay for environmental preservation: a non-experimental comparison

Vivien Foster, Ian J. Bateman and David Harley

INTRODUCTION

Environmental policy makers in the United Kingdom (UK) are turning their attention increasingly to contingent valuation (CV) estimates of public willingness to pay for changes in environmental quality. In this context, the method has been applied to issues as diverse as landscape preservation, bathing water quality, recreational forests, beach nourishment and low flow rivers. Furthermore, the Foundation for Water Research (1996) has published a manual for assessing the benefits of surface water quality improvements based on the transfer of willingness-to-pay estimates from a variety of existing CV studies. Mourato, in Chapter 2, provides an application of the technique to the valuation of water pollution reduction in Hungary.

While considerable improvements in survey practice during the last ten years have enhanced the reliability of CV estimates significantly, the methodology continues to have its critics (Diamond and Hausman 1994). Arguably the most substantive charge that has been levelled against the approach is that known as 'hypothetical bias'. This refers to the fact that respondents to CV surveys are asked to express their willingness to pay, without ultimately being required to make the stated financial contribution. Under these circumstances, it would appear to be all too easy for respondents to overstate their true desire to contribute, whether deliberately or unwittingly, given that they do not face any personal cost in doing so. The concerns raised by hypothetical bias are perhaps best summarized by the expression 'talk is cheap'.

The reason why the charge of hypothetical bias is potentially so pernicious to the CV method is that it is not something which can readily be resolved by more scrupulous attention to survey design. The hypothetical nature of the payment context is, almost by definition, intrinsic to the whole approach.

The research community has therefore responded with a substantial body of experimental studies expressly designed to compare real and hypothetical willingness to pay under carefully controlled laboratory conditions. The aim has been to provide a rigorous empirical test of the hypothesis that the willingness to pay estimates derived from CV studies could be substantially larger than real contributions requested under similar circumstances.

This chapter reviews the existing literature on this issue. It also provides a new contribution based on comparisons between donations to six large-scale fund-raising appeals by the Royal Society for the Protection of Birds (RSPB) and a number of recent UK CV studies which focus on similar environmental amenities and payment contexts. This exercise differs significantly from the existing literature in that it takes the testing of hypothetical bias out of the rather artificial laboratory environment. However, while this renders the study more realistic it also makes the resulting comparisons less rigorous, in the sense that the real and hypothetical payments are not conducted under strictly identical conditions. A more technical presentation of the methodology and results can be found in Foster et al. (1997).

LITERATURE REVIEW

The empirical literature on hypothetical bias has two related objectives. The first is to establish whether or not such bias is a phenomenon which impacts significantly on the results obtainable from CV studies. As mentioned above, this is done by setting up experiments which control for all other differences except for the real or hypothetical nature of the payment elicited. The second objective is to consider – where hypothetical bias is found to exist – whether it follows any regular pattern which might permit a standardized adjustment to be made. Clearly, hypothetical bias only represents a problem for CV to the extent that it takes an erratic and unpredictable form. Were the effect found to be systematic in nature, it could always readily be removed by a simple process of rescaling hypothetical payments.

This possibility has given rise to discussion of 'calibration factors' (Loomis et al. 1995). These are standardized adjustments based on ratios of hypothetical to real payments in experimental studies, which show the factor by which hypothetical payments could be expected to exceed real payments. For example, if it proved possible to establish definitively that willingness to pay from a CV survey was always twice as large as a real payment made under exactly comparable circumstances, then it would be a straightforward matter to correct for hypothetical bias by dividing the CV estimates through by a factor of two. However, a solid weight of systematic evidence would be required before such corrections can be undertaken with any degree of confidence.

The literature suggests that two different types of problems may be encountered as a result of hypothetical bias. First, respondents may disregard the limitations of their income when stating their willingness to pay. This could be expected to lead to a higher *level* of hypothetical willingness to pay relative to that which would arise in a real payment context. Second, because of the absence of any financial cost associated with making a mistake, respondents may not expend very much mental effort in formulating their response to the survey. This effect potentially introduces inaccuracies of ambiguous sign, and could therefore be expected to show up in a higher *variance* of hypothetical willingness to pay relative to real payments.

An overview of the empirical literature on hypothetical bias is given in Table 3.1. The columns of the table summarize a number of important methodological features of each study: whether it was performed in the field or under laboratory conditions; whether it focused on a private (or consumer) good versus a public (or environmental) amenity; whether the real and hypothetical payments were administered to different experimental groups (enabling a 'between group' comparison) or sequentially to the same group of people (entailing a 'within group' comparison); and whether the comparison variable used was the mean level of payments or the percentage of respondents acquiescing to a fixed offer price.

The central concern of this literature has been to establish whether there are statistically significant differences in the level of valuations between real and hypothetical contexts. Thus, the final columns of the table indicate whether or not a statistically significant divergence between real and hypothetical payments was established in each study, providing the corresponding calibration factors (or ratios of hypothetical to real payments). The larger the calibration factors the greater the suggestion of hypothetical bias. Although the differences in *variance* between real and hypothetical valuations have not been a central research issue, evidence from those studies which publish the relevant summary statistics suggests that the variance in valuations is indeed greater in hypothetical contexts, Loomis et al. (1995), Neill et al. (1994).

Many of the studies cited took the form of laboratory experiments. While there are obvious advantages associated with the strictly controlled environment of such experiments, arguably the very laboratory context may engender a bias of its own. This is so in the sense that subjects are placed in a purchase situation which they would not necessarily have chosen for themselves, and have their interest artificially focused on the subject of the experiment. As a result, the real willingness to pay in the simulated market may exceed that which the subjects would exhibit outside of the laboratory.

Table 3.1 Summary of studies comparing real and hypothetical payments

Study	Type of experiment	Type of good(s)	Type of comparison	Comparison variable	Significant divergence	Calibration factor
Bishop and Heberlein (1979)	Field	Private	Between groups	Response	✓	0.3–1.6
Bishop and Heberlein (1986)	Field	Private	Between groups	Payment and response	✓/✗	1.3–2.3 and 0.8
Bohm (1972)	Laboratory	Private	Within groups	Payment	✗	0.9–1.0
Brown et al. (1996)	Field	Public	Between groups	Payment and response	✓/✗	4.1 and 6.5
Cummings et al. (1995)	Laboratory	Private	Between and within groups	Response	✓	2.6–5.3 and 2.6–10.5
Dickie et al. (1987)	Field	Private	Between groups	Response	✓/✗	n/a
Kealy et al. (1988)	Laboratory	Private	Between and within groups	Response	✓	1.4 and 1.4
Kealy et al. (1990)	Laboratory	Private and public	Between and within groups	Response	✓	1.3 and 1.0–2.0
Loomis et al. (1995)	Laboratory	Private	Between and within groups	Payment	✓	1.8–2.9 and 2.0–3.6
Navrud (1992)	Field	Private and public	Within groups	Response	✓	3.2 or 1.6–2.1
Neill et al. (1994)	Laboratory	Private	Between groups	Payment	✓	3.1–25.1 or 6.0–12.0
Samples et al. (1986)	Non-experimental	Public	Between groups	Payment	✓	1.6+ or 32–300
Seip and Strand (1992)	Field	Private and public	Within groups	Response	✓	10.3
Sinden (1988)	Laboratory	Public	Within groups	Payment	✗	0.8–1.5

These deficiencies may to some extent be overcome by means of field experiments, which are typically based on mail surveys. Although beset by drawbacks of their own, such field experiments do have the advantage of freeing the subject from the intensity of the laboratory environment. However, even here, it could be argued that the subjects' behaviour is influenced by the experimental context. For example, Seip and Strand (1992) asked people via a CV survey whether they would be willing to join an environmental group at the current subscription fee. Those who said that they would were subsequently sent a real application form through the mail, however only 10 per cent of these actually became paid-up members of the society. While this appears to be very low in comparison with the number of people who said they would join, it is actually very high compared with the background unsolicited join-up rate. The authors comment that if the purely voluntary propensity to join environmental groups was as high as that evidenced in their own field experiment, the Norwegian society for the preservation of nature would have six times as many members as it currently has.

In view of this problem, there is therefore a place for studies which undertake a comparison of contributions to environmental causes outside of the experimental context, as an alternative benchmark for the evaluation of hypothetical willingness to pay. Although such studies do not permit formal conclusions about the precise magnitude of hypothetical bias, in the way that controlled experiments do, they do at least avoid some of the problems which may be associated with an experimental methodology

A rare example of such an informal study is the one undertaken by Samples et al. (1986). It performs a comparison between the hypothetical willingness to pay obtained in a number of US CV studies relating to the preservation of unique environmental resources, and the aggregate value of environmental donations made by the US public during the course of a year. The comparison is complicated by the low degree of correspondence between the environmental resources which form the subject of the two payment contexts. None the less, it is interesting to note the authors' conclusion that 'on the average, individuals are hypothetically willing to pay nearly as much to preserve one animal or amenity resource as they in fact actually paid in 1984 for all civic and public causes' p.6. The category of 'civic and public causes' comprises some of the major US environmental groups – such as the Sierra Club, the National Audubon Society and the National Wetlands Conservation Project. It also includes a whole range of other causes such as equal rights protection, legal defence funds, crime prevention and neighbourhood rehabilitation.

A striking feature of the literature is that the vast majority of experiments have been undertaken with private (or consumer) goods, ranging from hunting permits and strawberries, to posters and solar calculators, as opposed to the public environmental amenities which typically form the subject of CV surveys. This has been justified on the grounds that subjects are more familiar with market transactions for consumer goods, which makes it possible to abstract away from many of the other problems and biases potentially besetting the CV of unfamiliar environmental goods for which there is no market-trading experience. The argument is then that, where private goods are used, any divergence between real and hypothetical payments can more confidently be attributed to hypothetical bias.

In spite of these obvious advantages, the use of private goods in investigations of hypothetical bias carries certain drawbacks. In particular, there is the difficulty of getting respondents to indicate their own true valuation of the commodity, as opposed to simply recalling the current market price of the good (Cummings et al. 1995). The recalled market value of the good may act as a common anchor or reference point which itself serves to reduce the divergence between real and hypothetical payments.

Interestingly, however, the empirical evidence does not support the preconception that hypothetical bias may be less of an issue in the case of private goods. The Sinden (1988) laboratory experiment which focuses on the public good of soil preservation is one of the most favourable to CV in its finding of no statistically significant difference between real and hypothetical responses. Moreover, the Kealy et al. (1990) experiment which examines both a private good (a chocolate bar) and a public good (donations towards an acid rain prevention fund), finds very little difference between the extent of hypothetical bias arising in the two cases.

As far as the weight of evidence on hypothetical bias is concerned, most experiments find some positive statistically significant difference between hypothetical and real payments. Comparisons between the calibration factors resulting from different studies should be undertaken with caution, given the widely differing methodological approaches they adopt; some making use of auctioning mechanisms, with others simply requesting a 'yes or no' answer to a specific offer price.

Laying these concerns to one side, Table 3.1 suggests that most calibration factors fall in the range 1.3–12.0. It is interesting to note that these results are comparable with those obtained from the market research literature, where it has been found that the demand predicted by studies of new consumer goods is typically between 1.5 and 10.0 times higher than the level which results when these are eventually released on to the market (Diamond and Hausman 1994). For this reason it has become common practice in the market research community to adjust the survey predictions for this pattern of systematic overstatement.

Seen in the context of the existing literature, the present study should be understood as an informal non-experimental comparison between real and hypothetical willingness to pay for the public good of environmental preservation. As such, it is most closely in line with the work of Samples et al. (1986). However, unlike that study, the present one is based on a far richer set of disaggregated data regarding actual financial responses to environmental appeals. These provide a much closer match with the results of the CV studies which are used as hypothetical comparators, than did the aggregated donations data used by Samples et al.

Like the studies by Seip and Strand (1992) and Navrud (1992), the present analysis is based on real donations to environmental groups. However, unlike the earlier Norwegian work, it considers mean payment levels (as opposed to responses to a take-it-or-leave it membership subscription), and looks at behaviour in the real world as opposed to a field experiment situation. Another important difference relative to these earlier studies, is that the focus is clearly on the public good of environmental preservation, as opposed to environmental group membership, which combines both private and public good characteristics.

STUDY METHOD

The analysis in this chapter is based on a set of summary statistics describing responses to RSPB fund-raising appeals. The RSPB is Europe's largest voluntary nature conservation organization with more than 890 000 members. Funds raised through mail appeals accounted for 9 per cent of the Society's £33.9 million budget in 1994/95, that is about £3.1 million.

The appeals data, summarized in Table 3.2, relate to a variety of environmental resources and cover six out of a total of eight appeals which took place over the period November 1992 to January 1994. The projects covered fall into one of three general categories: land purchase, species preservation and habitat conservation, all of which have a distinctive bird focus. Half of the appeals relate to the funding of projects on specific sites, whereas the other half are focused on some more general environmental issue.

Table 3.2 provides data on each of the following aspects of the appeals: the number of members mailed (S); the number of those mailed responding with a donation (R^+); and the aggregate value of the donations made (V). Using this information, it is possible to calculate three

Table 3.2 *Summary of RSPB appeals data (current prices)*

Appeal	Site-specific	Appeal issue	S	R⁺	V(£)	R⁺/S(%)	V/R⁺(£)	V/S(£)
Ramsey Island (1992)	✓	Land purchase of maritime heath habitat	372772	28399	644460	7.6	22.69	1.73
Cantley Marshes (1993)	✓	Land purchase of low-lying wet grassland	300000	20783	418493	6.9	20.14	1.40
Shorebirds (1993)	✗	Campaign to protect coastal habitats for shorebirds	249994	18885	343185	7.6	18.17	1.37
Bittern (1993)	✗	Campaign to protect reedbed habitat for bittern	300417	15392	268430	5.1	17.44	0.89
Caledonian Pine (1993)	✓	Preservation of ancient coniferous woodland habitat	299783	18323	308215	6.1	16.82	1.03
Heathland (1994)	✗	Preservation of lowland heath habitat	241172	14128	260614	5.9	18.45	1.08
Overall	—		1764138	115910	2243397	6.6	19.35	1.27

Notes: S = No. of mailings; *R⁴* = No. of people responding with a donation; *V* = Total value of donations.

Table 3.3 *Summary of comparable UK contingent valuation surveys (current prices)*

Study	Resource	S	R	R⁺	R⁺/S (%)	V/R⁺ (£)	V/S (£)
Hanley and Craig (1991)	Flow Country	400	100	78	19.5	21.53	4.19
Hanley and Munro (1994)	Heathlands	226	211	207	91.6	26.06	23.87
Hanley and Spash (1993)	Birkham Wood	500	161	112	22.4	18.53	4.15
Spash and Hanley (1995)	Caledonian Pine general public	198	152	133	67.2	11.92	8.01
	students	121	104	95	78.5	19.64	15.42

Notes: S = Sample size; *R* = No. of respondents; *R⁺* = No. of respondents with a positive willingness to pay; *V* = Aggregate willingness to pay over whole sample.

ratios of particular interest: the positive response rate (R^+/S); the mean donation per respondent (V/R^+); and the mean donation per mailing (V/S). Unfortunately, data on medians and standard deviations were not available for these appeals.

A set of UK CV studies were identified as suitable for comparison with the RSPB mail appeals (CSERGE and DoE 1994). The selection aimed to be comprehensive in the sense of encompassing all the UK CV studies which have covered the relevant types of resources: heathland, wetland and ancient woodland. The degree of comparability of these studies with the RSPB appeals data was assessed along two dimensions: resource comparability and methodological comparability.

Resource comparability was evaluated by examining the degree of similarity between the amenities forming the subjects of the RSPB mail appeals and the CV studies. If the studies were concerned with precisely the same environmental goods a 'high' degree of resource comparability was awarded. Any CV studies concerned with the preservation of the kinds of habitat featuring prominently in the RSPB appeal, and specifically referring to birdlife, were accorded a 'medium' degree of comparability. The remaining studies were accorded only a 'low' degree of resource comparability.

To facilitate methodological comparability, the CV studies and RSPB appeals should use the same provision and payment rules, hence providing the same incentive structure. In CV terms, RSPB appeals were characterized as 'mail surveys', conducted 'off site', using 'open-ended elicitation' involving a 'once-off donation' to a 'charitable trust fund'. The CV studies were then compared with this characterization to see how many of the purely methodological characteristics were common to each.

Only those studies exhibiting a high degree of both resource and methodological comparability could be used for the purposes of the study. The application of these criteria reduced the number of CV comparators available from an initial eleven to as few as four. Clearly, reliance on such a small number of observations will render estimates of the mean effect of the difference between real and hypothetical payments less precise.

Table 3.3 provides a summary of the response rates and donation ratios for the selected CV studies. Some transformation of the results was required in order to express them in a form that is strictly comparable with the RSPB data. Thus, the first ratio (V/R^+) can be understood as the mean willingness to pay among those expressing a positive willingness to pay, while the second ratio (V/S) can be interpreted as the mean willingness to pay across the entire survey sample. It is important to note that the ratio V/S is not exactly equivalent to the mean willingness to pay usually reported in CV studies, in as much as the latter is typically calculated by excluding respondents whose refusals to contribute are judged to represent 'protest votes' rather than zero values, whereas the former measure includes these.

The discussion thus far has laid much of the methodological foundation for the comparison of hypothetical CV studies with real RSPB appeals. However, there remain two further features of the data which weaken the analogy between an RSPB appeal and a CV study, and consequently serve to complicate any comparison between the two. The first relates to the differing natures of the target populations used in the two contexts (this is termed the 'population effect'). The second relates to the different information sets presented to these two target populations (this is termed the 'information' effect).

Regarding the 'population effect', the RSPB appeals are targeted towards a very specific subsample of the population who have a proven interest in environmental issues, as evidenced both by their membership of the RSPB and their tendency to contribute regularly to previous appeals. This is not the case with CV surveys which are, in general, administered to a representative random sample of the general public. Consequently, one would anticipate a stronger response from the target population for an RSPB appeal than could be expected from sending the same literature to a sample of the general public. Such effects are well known in CV surveys, where membership of an environmental group is often found to be associated with a significantly larger willingness to pay than the rest of the population. For example, Bateman et al. (1995) find that environmental group members are willing to pay on average 30 per cent more than non-members towards the preservation of the Norfolk Broads. Hanley and Craig (1991) find a difference of 20 per cent in their study of the Flow Country.

Regarding the 'information effect', CV studies aim to be relatively dry and objective in their presentation of information about the survey good, whereas the RSPB appeals literature is obviously designed to be persuasive in its treatment of the issues. Once again, the likely consequence of this is to put upward bias on the response to the RSPB appeals, relative to what it would have been had a more dispassionate style been adopted. As before, there is some empirical evidence from the CV literature regarding the order of magnitude of such 'information effects'. Hanley and Spash (1993) found that supplying additional information as to the relative scarcity of heathlands in the south of England as well as photographic material covering the associated flora and fauna, was enough to increase mean willingness to pay towards a hypothetical trust fund by as much as 80 per cent. The effects of both increased information, and discussions of issues of preferences are analysed by Cookson in Chapter 4 of this book.

In combination, the 'population and information effects' are likely to inflate the value of the RSPB donations relative to those which could be expected from a real donation context which was designed to be strictly comparable to a CV survey. Although it is not possible to gauge the size of these effects with any degree of precision, the evidence from recent CV surveys cited above suggests a potential combined inflationary effect of between 160 per cent and 240 per cent depending on which of the results are used. That is to say that if the RSPB appeals had been conducted in such a way as to be strictly comparable to the CV surveys, the resulting donations could be expected to have been 45 per cent to 65 per cent lower than those actually received. The implication is that the calibration factors between CV studies and RSPB appeals will be biased downwards.

RESULTS

Bearing in mind the methodological issues discussed above, a series of calibration factors for specific matched pairs of studies were calculated and are reported in Table 3.4. Before calculating the calibration factors, the results of all the relevant CV studies and RSPB appeals were converted into 1995 prices. These calibration factors form the basis of the comparison between real and hypothetical payments, and are the ratios of the values of each of the three summary variables defined above (R^+/S, V/R^+ and V/S) between CV studies and RSPB appeals (that is, they are ratios of ratios).

Cursory inspection of Table 3.4 reveals a striking result. The mean value of contributions to hypothetical charitable appeals (V/S) is 3.64–25.32 times higher than the mean value of contributions to real charitable appeals. However, this overall result conceals an interesting underlying pattern, namely that the calibration factors for the mean positive valuation (V/R^+) are much lower than those calculated for the positive response rate (R^+/S). Thus, the calibration factors for the mean positive valuation (V/R^+) are always close to one (in the range 0.69–1.62), indicating that there is very little difference between real and hypothetical charitable appeals as regards the size of the mean donation made *by those who actually contribute*. However, the calibration factors for the positive response rate (R^+/S) are generally greater than three (in the range 2.83–15.52), implying that the proportion of people who claim that they would make a donation to a hypothetical charitable appeal is several times larger than the proportion of people who actually do make donations to real charitable appeals.

Table 3.4   Summary of calibration factors from CV studies and RSPB appeals (1995 prices)

CV survey / RSPB appeal	$V/R^+{}_{CV}$ / $V/R^+{}_{RSPB}$	Mail survey?	R^+S_{CV} / R^+/S_{RSPB}	V/S_{CV} / V/S_{RSPB}
$\left(\dfrac{\text{Caledonian Pine (general public)}}{\text{Caledonian Pine}}\right)$	$\left(\dfrac{12.28}{17.83}\right)= 0.69$	✗	$\left(\dfrac{0.672}{0.061}\right)= 11.02$	$\left(\dfrac{8.25}{1.09}\right)= 7.56$
$\left(\dfrac{\text{Caledonian Pine (students)}}{\text{Caledonian Pine}}\right)$	$\left(\dfrac{20.23}{17.83}\right)= 1.13$	✗	$\left(\dfrac{0.785}{0.061}\right)= 12.87$	$\left(\dfrac{15.88}{1.09}\right)= 14.55$
$\left(\dfrac{\text{Southern England Heathlands}}{\text{Southern England Heathlands}}\right)$	$\left(\dfrac{30.75}{19.00}\right)= 1.62$	✗	$\left(\dfrac{0.916}{0.059}\right)= 15.52$	$\left(\dfrac{28.17}{1.11}\right)= 25.32$
$\left(\dfrac{\text{Birkham Wood}}{\text{Caledonian Pine}}\right)$	$\left(\dfrac{20.75}{17.83}\right)= 1.16$	✓	$\left(\dfrac{0.224}{0.061}\right)= 3.67$	$\left(\dfrac{4.65}{1.09}\right)= 4.26$
$\left(\dfrac{\text{Flow Country}}{\text{Cantley Marshes}}\right)$	$\left(\dfrac{27.77}{21.35}\right)= 1.30$	✓	$\left(\dfrac{0.195}{0.069}\right)= 2.83$	$\left(\dfrac{5.41}{1.48}\right)= 3.64$

What this means is that in a hypothetical context fewer people are likely to opt out of making a donation; however, those donations that are made are generally no larger than might be expected from a real payment context. The pattern of results suggests that the differences between real and hypothetical payments are not so much attributable to donors exaggerating the amount that they would pay in a hypothetical appeal, but rather to the greater tendency for people to 'free ride' on the generosity of others when it comes to a real charitable appeal.

This tentative conclusion is reinforced by considering the variation in the calibration factors for the positive response rate (R^+/S) according to whether the CV study is based on a mail survey or a face-to-face interview. Specifically, when mail surveys are used the calibration factors are always below five (ranging from 2.83 to 3.67), whereas when interview-based surveys are used, the calibration factors are invariably in excess of ten (ranging from 11.02 to 15.52). This reflects the substantially higher positive response rates which are obtained from face-to-face interviews (typically in excess of 50 per cent) versus mail surveys (usually less than 25 per cent). It seems plausible to suggest that the presence of an interviewer would make respondents more embarrassed about 'free riding' on the generosity of others, and that this accounts for the observed differences in the calibration factors.

As regards comparisons with the conclusions of the earlier literature (see Table 3.1), the study which provides the closest parallel to the present

one is that by Brown et al. (1996), because it relates to an open-ended elicitation process for the public good of environmental preservation using a
charitable fund payment vehicle based on a mail survey. The study by
Brown et al. (ibid.) obtains a calibration factor of 3.98, when the results of
that study are expressed in terms of the variable V/S used in the present
study. This figure lies within and towards the upper end of the range for
the V/S calibration factor of 3.64–4.26 found in the present study.

To summarize, for the narrowly defined case of open-ended mail surveys based on charitable donation payment vehicles, this chapter has
provided evidence that the ratio V/S is likely to be at least four times
larger in hypothetical data than in real data. The implications of this
result for the interpretation and use of CV estimates, depend on one's
view as to whether real or hypothetical payments lie closer to true
underlying values.

From a theoretical point of view, it is to be expected that neither real
nor hypothetical payments would equate with true underlying economic
values, particularly when these represent voluntary charitable donations.
Rather, the expectation would be that the underlying values would lie
somewhere in the range defined by the two. The reason for this is that real
donations are likely to be deflated owing to the tendency of people to 'free
ride' on the generosity of others, while hypothetical donations are likely to
be inflated because of the fact that respondents are not required to make
the donations they claim to be willing to pay. Since theory suggests that
underlying economic values cannot be measured directly either from real
or hypothetical donations, these should merely be used to put upper and
lower bounds on the likely magnitude of the true benefits. The calibration
factors found in this study could be used to generate lower-bound estimates from CV values for resources where no appeals evidence exists, or
upper-bound estimates from donations data for resources which have been
the subject of an appeal, but for which no CV study has been carried out.

An alternative stance would be to argue on the basis of the pattern of
results uncovered in the empirical analysis, that underlying economic
values probably lie closer to the level of hypothetical payments than
they do to the level of real payments. This is based on the finding that
the divergence between real and hypothetical payments was largely
attributable to the greater number of people 'opting out' of making a
contribution in the real setting, and had very little to do with donors
exaggerating the positive amount they would be willing to contribute in a
hypothetical context. According to this view, there is no need to undertake any calibrating adjustment to the results of CV surveys.

Finally, in certain circumstances one might wish to reject the goal of
measuring true underlying values altogether, and argue that what really

matters is whether or not a particular sum of money could actually be raised. In this case it is the real payments which form the relevant benchmark. Where evidence on real donations does not exist, the calibration factor could be used to estimate their likely level from CV evidence, in the same manner that the results of consumer surveys tend to be calibrated in the market research literature.

CONCLUSIONS

This chapter has undertaken a non-experimental comparison between hypothetical willingness to pay for environmental preservation – from a selection of recent UK CV surveys, and real payments made in response to a series of recent RSPB fund-raising appeals. A number of features of the study are of particular interest and distinguish it from most of the existing literature. First, the actual payments are made in a 'real-world' context as opposed to a more artificial experimental environment. Second, the study focuses on the public good of environmental preservation, whereas most of the earlier studies have used private consumer goods. Finally, a framework for comparing real and hypothetical behaviour has been set up which makes it possible to distinguish between the decision to opt in or out of the market and any alteration in the stated positive valuation.

None the less, it is important to recognize that the study also suffers from a number of significant limitations. The most fundamental of these is that the real and hypothetical data used in the analysis were not designed to be strictly comparable in the way that is possible in an experimental context. Furthermore, the differing respondent populations and information conditions underpinning the two data sources were such as to create a clear upward bias in the real donations data and thus a downward bias in the calibration factors. Based on recent empirical evidence, it was estimated that the reported calibration factors could fall short of the true ones by as much as one-half. In addition, there were very few CV studies which met even moderately stringent criteria for comparability, so that the results are subject to small numbers limitations. Finally, the study was only concerned with one particular subset of CV studies, namely, those relying on open-ended elicitation in the context of a charitable donation payment vehicle. Together these limitations must necessarily lend some caution to any application of the results obtained.

The evidence suggests that V/S may be at least four times as high in an open-ended CV mail survey as in a comparable real donations context; although neither could be expected to correspond to true underlying values, which can only be bounded within this range. It should be noted that this result applies specifically to the variable V/S which is not exactly the same as the mean willingness-to-pay variable reported in most CV studies.

A second important finding was that the difference between real and hypothetical payments could be attributed largely to much higher positive response rates in the hypothetical data. A much higher proportion of people claimed that they would make a donation to a hypothetical charitable appeal than actually did so in response to a real charitable appeal. However, the amount that donors said they would contribute to a hypothetical appeal was, on average, very similar to that which donors tended to contribute to real appeals. While it is not possible to reach rigorous conclusions given the deficiencies of the data, the implication is tentatively that the difference between the two has more to do with the tendency to 'free ride' in real charitable appeals, than with the tendency to exaggerate the level of contributions that would be made to a hypothetical appeal.

The practical application of these results should await the accumulation of more substantive evidence. However, their implication is that calibration factors of the kind estimated in this study could be used to convert data on either real or hypothetical donations into a confidence range within which the true economic values are likely to be found. The findings of this study suggest that the underlying values may lie towards the upper end of the range defined by real and hypothetical payments.

REFERENCES

Bateman, I.J., I.H. Langford, and A. Graham (1995), 'Survey of non-users' willingness to pay to prevent saline flooding in the Norfolk Broads', Global Environmental Change Working Paper 95–11, Centre for Social and Economic Research on the Global Environment, University of East Anglia and University College London.

Bishop, R.C. and T.A. Heberlein (1979), 'Measuring values of extramarket goods: are indirect measures biased?', *American Journal of Agricultural Economics*, **61**, 926–30.

Bishop, R.C. and T.A. Heberlein (1986), 'Assessing the validity of contingent valuations: three field experiments', *Science of the Total Environment*, **56**, 434–79.

Bohm, P. (1972), 'Estimating demand for public goods: an experiment', *European Economic Review*, **3**, 111–30.

Brown, T.C., P.A. Champ, R.C. Bishop and D.W. McCollum (1996), 'Which response format reveals the truth about donations to a public good?', *Land Economics*, **72**, 152–66.

Centre for Social and Economic Research on the Global Environment (CSERGE) and Department of the Environment (DoE) (1994), *UK Studies of the Economic Valuation of Environmental Impacts: Central Directory*, University College London and University of East Anglia.

Cummings, R.G., G.W. Harrison and E.E. Rutstrom (1995), Homegrown values and hypothetical surveys: is the dichotomous choice approach incentive compatible?', *American Economic Review*, **85**, 260–66.

Diamond, P.A. and J.A. Hausman (1994), 'Contingent valuation: is some number better than no number?', *Journal of Economic Perspectives*, **8**, 45–64.

Dickie, M., A. Fisher and S. Gerking (1987), 'Market transactions and hypothetical demand data: a comparative survey', *Journal of the American Statistical Association*, **82**, 69–75.

Foster, V., I.J. Bateman and D. Harley (1997), 'Real and hypothetical willingness to pay for environmental preservation: a non-experimental comparison', *Journal of Agricultural Economics*, **48**, 123–38.

Foundation for Water Research (1996), *Assessing the Benefits of Surface Water Quality Improvements*, Marlowe: Foundation for Water Research.

Hanley, N. and S. Craig (1991), 'Wilderness development decisions and the Krutilla–Fisher model: the case of Scotland's "Flow Country"', *Ecological Economics*, **4**, 145–65.

Hanley, N. and A. Munro (1994), 'The effects of information in contingent markets for environmental goods', Discussion Paper in Ecological Economics 94/5, Department of Economics, University of Stirling.

Hanley, N. and C. Spash (1993), *Cost Benefit Analysis and the Environment*, Aldershot: Edward Elgar.

Kealy, M.-J., J.F. Dovidio and M.L. Rockel (1988), 'Accuracy in valuation is a matter of degree', *Land Economics*, **64**, 158–71.

Kealy, M.-J., M. Montgomery and J. Dovidio (1990), 'Reliability and predictive validity of contingent values: does the nature of the good matter?', *Journal of Environmental Economics and Management*, **19**, 244–63.

Loomis, J., T. Brown, B. Lucero and G. Peterson (1995), 'Improving validity experiments of contingent valuation methods: results of efforts to reduce the disparity of hypothetical and actual willingness to pay', Paper presented at the W–133 Regional Research Meeting, Monterey, California.

Navrud, S. (1992), 'Willingness to pay for preservation of species: an experiment with actual payments', in S. Navrud (ed.), *Pricing the European Environment*, Oslo: Scandinavian University Press, pp.231–46.

Neill, H., R.G. Cummings, P.T. Ganderton, G.W. Harrison and T. McGuckin (1994), 'Hypothetical surveys and real economic commitments', *Land Economics*, **70**, 145–54.

Samples, K.C., M.M. Gowen and J.A. Dixon (1986), 'The validity of the contingent valuation method for estimating non-use components of preservation value for unique natural resources', Paper presented to the annual meeting of the American Agricultural Economics Association, Reno, Nevada.

Seip, K. and J. Strand (1992), 'Willingness to pay for environmental goods in Norway: a contingent valuation study with real payments', *Environmental and Resource Economics*, **2**, 91–106.

Sinden, J.A. (1988), 'Empirical tests of hypothetical bias in consumers' surplus surveys', *Australian Journal of Agricultural Economics*, **32**, 98–112.

Spash, C. and N. Hanley (1995), 'Preferences, information and biodiversity preservation', *Ecological Economics*, **12**, 191–208.

4. An alternative approach to valuing non-market goods

Richard Cookson[*]

INTRODUCTION

Non-market goods (and bads) can range from the preservation of Amazonian forests through to the protection of consumers from food poisoning. What they all have in common is that they impose costs upon society, often through higher taxes or higher prices in the shops, but their precise value is unknown. Environmental economists have developed a standard way of valuing them, called 'contingent valuation'. The basic idea, as described in Chapter 2 of this book, is to find a suitable sample of people and then to ask each of them individually how much they would be willing to pay for the environmental nonmarket good in question.

However, as noted in Chapter 3, this approach has been seriously criticized from within the economics profession (Diamond and Hausman 1994). Perhaps the most serious criticism is that willingness-to-pay responses tend to be insufficiently sensitive to the quantity of the good being valued – or that contingent valuation suffers from 'part–whole bias' (Baron and Greene 1996; Dubourg et al. 1998; Bateman et al. 1997). This chapter describes a small-scale study that developed an alternative approach which avoids this and other problems. The study was about the value of safety, but this alternative approach could equally well be applied to any other area of environmental valuation.

* This chapter is a brief and non-technical summary of research supported by the Economic and Social Research Council (ESRC), under postgraduate studentship R00429424071 and research award R000234987, 'Theoretical and Empirical Issues in the Valuation of Safety'. The details are reported in Cookson (1996). I am particularly grateful to Graham Loomes for his help in designing this study, to John Hey for his help in analysing the results, and to the editors of this book for helping me turn my scholastic prose into something resembling plain English. I am also grateful to Gabriella Berloffa. Judith Covey, Paul Dolan, Mike Jones-Lee and Anne Spencer for many helpful discussions and comments.

THE ALTERNATIVE APPROACH

The alternative approach consults a smaller number of people than contingent valuation but in greater depth. It departs from contingent valuation in four main respects:

- *Relative valuation* People are asked to value a whole range of comparable non-market goods, rather than just a single one. Comparing like with like is often easier, and more meaningful, than directly stating an 'absolute' monetary figure.
- *Multiple question formats* Asking the same valuation question in different ways encourages people to adopt different perspectives and checks that their answers are not influenced by the way in which the question is framed.
- *Small group discussions* This allows people to discuss the issues and evidence, to hear a wide variety of opinions, and to consider and reconsider their answers in the light of reflection and discussion.
- *Qualitative research methods* Careful investigation of the qualitative *reasons* that people give for their quantitative answers allows researchers and policy makers to determine what those answers really mean.

The basic justification for this alternative approach is that non-market goods are unfamiliar and hard to understand. Imagine you had to state how much an Amazonian forest is worth to you. You could no doubt think of a number, if pushed. It would probably depend to a large extent on how the question was framed and what mood you were in – and to a lesser extent on how many acres of forest, or millions of acres of forest, we were actually talking about.

Now imagine you wanted to think seriously about the question, and to give a meaningful response. To start with, you would need to think about the different ways in which Amazonian forests might be valuable to you. One way, presumably, is that they help to prevent global warming by absorbing carbon dioxide. So you would need to get to grips with the available scientific evidence on global warming. Then you would have to relate this evidence to your own life. How is global warming likely to affect you in the future? How do these effects compare with other uncertainties in the future? What about your feelings towards other people affected by global warming? How does all of this compare with the changes you would make in your current lifestyle in order to save money? And then there are all of the other ways in which Amazonian forests might be valuable to you.

All in all, this is not an easy task. Most people lack the time, the resources and the motivation to undertake it thoroughly. So, to the extent that preferences can be stated about Amazonian forests, they are extremely 'raw' and may contain any number of errors and misunderstandings. The alternative approach assumes that people make mistakes when dealing with difficult and unfamiliar issues. It concentrates on one specific aspect of the valuation and gives people as much help as possible in thinking about it. Unlike contingent valuation, it does not aim to measure the 'raw' preferences which drive people's behaviour. Rather, it aims to measure 'true' economic preferences which represent people's interests or well-being. To summarize, whereas the contingent valuation approach simply aims to measure existing public opinion, the alternative approach aims to measure informed public opinion.

THE VALUE OF SAVING LIFE

Typically, health and safety considerations are incorporated into economic valuations by multiplying the expected number of lives saved (or lost) by a suitable monetary value for life saving. Of course, the very idea of placing a monetary value on human life is highly controversial. Economists argue that, because the resources available for life saving are strictly limited, an explicit analysis of costs and benefits can help policy makers to make sensible and fair decisions. Opponents of the idea argue that it is callous and cynical for ethical questions of life and death to be explicitly driven by financial considerations.

In assessing this controversy, it is important to note that an economic 'value of life' does not represent the value of any particular person's life. Rather, it represents the value of what is known as a 'statistical' life, made up of many tiny changes in the probability of dying among a large population of individuals. Hence, paradoxical as it may seem, one can accept the need for the economic valuation of life without denying the widely held ethical conviction that life is invaluable. Life is invaluable; statistical life is not.

There are further ethical difficulties, of course, about how values of life should be determined. According to standard economic theory, the value of life is the sum total of the small amounts that each of the individuals in a given population is willing to pay to save a single 'statistical' life among that population. Now, what an individual is willing to pay for a small reduction in his or her probability of dying will depend, among other things, on his or her wealth and life expectancy. So standard theory has the controversial implication that values for saving the lives of the rich should be higher than values for saving the lives of the poor. It also has the controversial implication that values for saving the lives of the young and the healthy should be higher than values for saving the lives of the elderly and the infirm.

Leaving aside these controversies let us turn to the specific issue dealt with by this study. Contingent valuation studies have found up to 700-fold differentials in estimated values of life between different areas of safety (Beattie et al. 1997).[1] These differentials might be due to one of four things: first, differences in the wealth and life expectancy of the sample populations; second, aspects of the situation that are not incorporated in standard economic theory but which nevertheless enter into 'true' economic preferences; third, errors and misunderstandings in people's 'raw' preferences: and fourth, survey design biases in measuring people's 'raw' preferences.

A handful of studies have controlled for this first possibility by asking several 'willingness-to-pay' (WTP) questions across different areas of safety to the same sample of people (Mendeloff and Kaplan, 1989; McDaniels et al. 1992; Savage 1993; and Gregory and Lichtenstein 1994). These questions were followed by 'psychometric' rating questions of the kind that psychologists use to explain people's perceptions of risk.[2] The three principle psychometric factors are 'dread' (the extent to which contemplation of the hazard evokes feelings of anxiety), 'unknown' (the extent to which the hazard seems to be unknown or ill-defined), and 'number' (the perceived number of deaths and injuries from the hazard). These studies found up to sixfold variations in values of life across different areas of safety which were strongly correlated with these psychometric factors.

However, these studies aimed to measure the raw preferences that motivate behaviour, not true economic preferences. So, even if we set aside the possibility of survey design bias these studies cannot distinguish between the second and third possibilities. We are thus left with an important question. To what extent do public perceptions of risk enter into true economic preferences? Given that risk and uncertainty is fundamental to almost all environmental issues, this question has tremendous significance for almost all areas of environmental policy. The study summarized below is a first attempt at answering this question.

DESIGN OF THE STUDY

This small-scale methodological study used a sample of 52 parents from a local school, who were paid £15 each with a further £5 donated to the school fund. This sample was adequate for the methodological purpose of the study – although obviously a larger and more representative sample would be needed for the purpose of policy guidance. The study consisted of ten 'workshops', with four to six participants, each lasting about two hours. The design of these workshops was extensively pre-tested and refined using two pilot studies, also with paid members of the public.

Six areas of public safety were valued: air pollution (A), birth control pills (B), car accidents (C), food poisoning (F), medical radiation (M) and rail accidents (R). Public policy scenarios were used, rather than consumer purchase scenarios, to encourage subjects to come to an appropriate understanding of the policy situation in which their answers might ultimately be used. To enable relative valuations to be made, subjects were asked to assume that possible safety improvements were available in each area of safety that would prevent 100 deaths in the UK over the next ten years. Each public safety improvement was described briefly to subjects on separate 'information cards', one of which is reproduced in Figure 4.1.[3]

IMPROVEMENT A
100 fewer deaths over the next ten years from

AIR POLLUTION
- This risk of dying stems from both lung diseases and heart diseases
- Those most at risk of dying from air pollution are people with existing lung or heart conditions, especially the elderly
- Most air pollution in the UK is caused by road traffic
- Masks may have little protective effect

Figure 4.1 Example scenario description

Subjects answered four different types of relative valuation question. The question formats were:

- *Priorities* This was an ordinal ranking question that asked respondents to place each public safety improvement in rank order of priority, allowing ties.
- *Matching* This was a cardinal scaling question that first asked respondents to choose between two public safety improvements, allowing ties. Those who stated a strict preference were then asked to mark on a numerical scale how many deaths prevented in their preferred context they would regard 'equally as good as' 100 deaths prevented in the other context.

- *Willingness to pay* This was an open-ended question that asked respondents how much their household would be prepared to pay each year in extra taxes over the next ten years for a particular public safety improvement. To obtain relative valuations, subjects were asked to answer each WTP question in isolation from the other WTP questions – that is, on the assumption that the other payments and safety improvements would not take place.
- *Monetary values* This was an open-ended question that asked respondents to place monetary values on each public safety improvement relative to a value of £100 million for public safety improvement C.

The 'priorities' question and the 'willingness-to-pay' question are well known; the 'matching' question was adapted from Jones-Lee and Loomes (1995). The 'monetary values' question was developed for the purposes of this study. During pre-testing it was found that subjects felt more comfortable with this question than with various other questions that have been used before. In particular, comparisons in units of 'social loss' (Slovic et al. 1979) provoked many clarificatory questions and complaints that it was 'too abstract', and division of a budget to yield 'relative WTP' (Savage 1993) caused difficulties of mental arithmetic when there were more than two or three items to compare.

The workshops began with a structured group discussion, moderated by myself, lasting about 20 minutes. Subjects then had about 35 minutes to give initial answers to the first three types of valuation question – on an individual, rather than group basis. Two pairs then discussed the monetary values question together, and any remaining subjects took part in a 'feedback interview' with myself. These pair discussions and interviews lasted about 20 minutes. Subjects were then brought back to the main table and asked to give final answers to all four types of valuation question on a fresh questionnaire.

THE QUANTITATIVE RESULTS

Subjects valued food safety and rail safety about the same as car safety, safety from air pollution about 50 per cent higher, and safety from birth control pills and medical radiation about 50 per cent lower. However, nearly a quarter of the subjects gave equal valuations to each safety improvement in each question. The aggregate rankings of the six safety improvements were strictly consistent across all four valuation questions. The aggregate ratios, however – the relative values of life – were only broadly consistent, as can be seen in Table 4.1. These relative values were all estimated relative to area C, car accidents, which automatically gets a valuation of 1.[4]

Table 4.1 Relative values of life (C = 1)[a]

	Food poisoning (F) $N = 52$[b]	Birth control pills (B) $N = 27$[c]	Medical radiation (M) $N = 27$[c]	Air pollution (A) $N = 52$	Rail accidents (R) $N = 52$
Willingness to pay[d]	1.0	0.4	0.6	1.3	0.8
Monetary values	0.9	0.6	0.7	1.8	0.8
Matching[e]	1.2	n/a[f]	n/a[f]	n/a[f]	1.2

Notes:
a. Since the individual ratios were approximately lognormally distributed, the relative values presented in Table 4.1 were estimated using geometric means.
b. N is the number of respondents to each question.
c. Half of the subjects were asked to value only car accidents, food poisoning, air pollution and rail accidents.
d. One subject returned missing values for his or her four final WTP answers.
e. The matching results are inflated by three subjects giving rather extreme responses.
f. Subjects did not value birth control pills, medical radiation and air pollution using

In a large-scale study, relative values of life of this kind could be converted into 'absolute' monetary values by using one or more monetary 'pegs' – for instance, the UK Department of Transport's national figure for road accident fatalities. This conversion is not meaningful for a small-scale methodological study of this kind. This study is intended to be illustrative, showing how the alternative approach might be used. A larger sample size would be necessary for a study to be suitable for national policy guidance.

The WTP results in Table 4.2 provide further evidence that responses to WTP questions tend to be insufficiently sensitive to the quantity of the good being valued. The 'absolute' value of life estimates implied by these responses lie between £30–110 million for arithmetic means and £12–25 million for medians.[5] Now, these values are about 50 times higher than value of life estimates from contingent valuation studies. Why? The most likely explanation is that the magnitude of risk reduction in this study was a great deal smaller than that used in most standard contingent valuation studies. If WTP responses are insufficiently sensitive to the magnitude of risk reduction, then we would expect that smaller magnitudes would multiply up to yield larger value of life estimates.

Table 4.2 Household willingness to pay (£ per year for ten years)

	Car accidents (C) $N = 51$	Food poisoning (F) $N = 51$	Birth control pills (B) $N = 27$	Medical radiation (M) $N = 27$	Air pollution (A) $N = 51$	Rail accidents (R) $N = 51$
Arithmetic mean	24.90	31.80	13.10	14.10	43.70	23.30
Median	10.00	10.00	5.00	10.00	10.00	10.00

QUALITATIVE RESULTS

The main reason that subjects gave for valuing safety differently across the six areas was the degree of 'choice' and 'control' they felt themselves to have. 'Choice' generally meant the ability to choose to be exposed to the hazard (for instance, by owning a car); and 'control' generally meant the ability to control one's own level of risk from exposure to the hazard (for instance, by driving carefully). Almost all of the subjects mentioned one or both of these factors as primary considerations, and agreed that the degree of choice and control was lowest in area A (air pollution) and highest in areas B and M (birth control pills and medical radiation).

Both of these 'contextual factors' are closely related to the first of the three primary psychometric factors from risk perception research, namely the 'dread' factor. They also both appear to be reasonable justifications for people's answers. Although they have not traditionally been incorporated into economic models they are intelligible reasons why true economic preferences might vary from one area of safety to another. Greater perceived freedom to choose and to control the risks that you face may improve your well-being – even if it actually ends up reducing your life expectancy (as estimated by yourself or by the safety experts). So you may be prepared to trade off the value of living longer against the value of living in freedom from bureaucratic controls.

Interestingly, only a handful of subjects gave the kinds of reasons one might expect from standard economic theory. A few said that they had what they called a 'selfish' reason for placing a lower value on rail safety than car safety, since they were infrequent rail users. Only one of the subjects spontaneously raised the issue of age or life expectancy in discussions. This was surprising, because life expectancy plays an important role in the standard economic theory of the value of life, and subjects were presented with information about the age groups most at risk.

Several subjects mentioned various apparently confounding factors. In connection with air pollution, some mentioned ongoing benefits beyond the stated time of ten years and associated non-fatal lung diseases as well as the stated number of deaths. A handful were more concerned with the costs of the safety improvements than with the benefits. One or two did not believe that 100 deaths could be prevented over the next ten years from either rail accidents or medical radiation.

Some also mentioned factors which are incompatible with the purpose of the study in a rather less straightforward sense. For instance, several were concerned about the baseline probability of dying in a particular area of safety as opposed to the stated change in the probability of dying. This is a natural thing for people to pick up on, as the third standard risk perception factor is the perceived 'number' of deaths and injuries from the hazard. Now, one can see why a different total baseline probability of dying might affect the benefit you obtained from a given change in that probability, but it is hard to see how the composition of that total baseline probability, in terms of baseline probabilities from different causes, could make any difference. This is more likely to be a misplaced concern related to a common confusion between levels and changes.

Finally, some subjects mentioned benefits other than safety – in particular, those of environmental protection in general and of a better public transport system. It is easy to see how these considerations might relate to individual self-interest or well-being. However, it is hard to imagine that they would be taken into account as part of the safety component of an economic valuation. Rather, they would enter as separate costs and benefits. So, once again, these concerns appear to be misplaced once one fully appreciates the purpose of the study and the practical uses to which its results will be put.

THE EFFECTS OF FURTHER REFLECTION AND DISCUSSION

The qualitative evidence suggests that, during the pair discussions, subjects were not simply negotiating a joint answer on the basis of fixed individual opinions. Rather, they seemed to be genuinely persuading each other to see things in a different light. Of the 38 respondents who took part in pair discussions, 17 gave individual responses to the monetary values question which were identical to their jointly agreed pair response. In all but one of these cases, both partners had proceeded to give these same responses. This suggests that the two partners were not simply compromising in order to reach agreement, but that at least one of them had changed his or her mind about the relative valuations. In particular, the pair discussions tended to lead subjects to place a higher value on rail safety relative to car safety. The qualitative evidence suggests that this was because discussions made subjects more aware of the issues of choice and control.

The discussions also helped to make people's answers more consistent. The proportion of subjects whose individual rankings were precisely consistent (including ties, and across all four valuation questions) rose from 17 per cent to 37 per cent after the discussions. One possible way to reduce inconsistencies still further would be to engage in a more formal procedure of decision analysis with participants, over a period of days or weeks rather than a period of hours (Gregory et al. 1993). However, research into group psychology suggests that highly intensive group discussions may produce final answers that are more consistent and more confidently expressed than initial answers – and yet no closer to the truth (Irwin and Davis 1995). Worse, it increases the danger that the researcher will allow the discussions to continue until subjects return desired answers.

CONCLUSIONS

The new approach attempts to find the true economic value of goods and services by attempting to bridge the gap between public opinion and expert opinion. A small-scale study estimated values for life saving which varied by plus or minus 50 per cent across six different areas of safety due to considerations of 'choice' and 'control'. Unlike the 700-fold value of life differentials estimated by contingent valuation, these results were (i) justified by clearly articulated reasons for preference, (ii) free from clearly identifiable 'part–whole' bias, and (iii) consistent across four different question formats in terms of aggregate rankings.

Of course, for many environmental applications, it will not be possible to establish a standard unit of value such as the 'value of life'. This would be particularly difficult in cases involving a high degree of irreversibility or uniqueness. Nevertheless, it will always be possible to identify a range of substitute goods. For example, there may be substitute areas of remote wilderness, substitute sites of historical interest, or substitute humanitarian causes. So, in principle, the new approach can be applied to any area of environmental policy in which policy makers wish to engage in explicit priority setting.

NOTES

1. It should be noted that contingent valuation studies of health and safety typically depart in significant ways from the standard survey guidelines for environmental damages assessment (Arrow et al. 1993).

2. Psychometric research into risk perception is reviewed in Slovic (1992). Subjects answer a series of questions in which they rate different risks according to overall risk and then according to various psychometric dimensions of risk. Typically, the major patterns of correlation between overall risk and the psychometric dimensions can be captured by three principal factors ('dread', 'unknown' and 'number').

3. These valuation scenarios were all carefully researched and pre-tested for clarity and credibility. Since there were six scenarios, rather than one, they were briefer than is standardly recommended for contingent valuation surveys. In fact, this brevity may be an advantage, given the psychological fact that people tend in any case to simplify their cognitive tasks and to use various mental short-cuts or 'heuristics' (Slovic 1995). Hence, the inclusion of too much detail may distract attention away from the essential value-bearing characteristics of the non-market good and towards theoretically irrelevant 'cues'.

4. The priorities question obtains ordinal rankings, so no cardinal relative value is implied. For the other three question formats, relative values were calculated as follows. Denote the ith individual's relative valuation of public safety in area X by $l_i(X) = V_i(X), V_i(C)$. The $V_i(.)$ represent 'absolute' valuations of life by the individual. The WTP estimate of $l_i(X)$ is his or her WTP in area X divided by his or her WTP in area C. The monetary values estimate is his or her monetary value in area X divided by £100 million. The matching estimate is his or her stated ratio, $\Delta C / \Delta X$, where ΔC represents the expected number of deaths prevented in area C, and ΔX the number prevented in area X.

5. These are 'rough-and-ready' estimates which assume (purely for the sake of argument) that this sample of households was representative of the UK population. There are roughly 25 million households in the UK. Since each safety improvement saves an average of ten lives a year, the corresponding values for saving a single life among the UK population were estimated from Table 4.2 by multiplying each figure by 2.5 million.

REFERENCES

Arrow, K.J., R. Solow, P.R. Portney, E.E. Leamer, R. Radner and H. Schuman, (1993), 'Report of the NOAA Panel on contingent valuation', *Federal Register*, **58**(10), 4602–614.

Baron, J. and J. Greene (1996), 'Determinants of insensitivity to quantity in valuation of public goods: contribution, warm glow, budget constraints, availability and prominence', *Journal of Experimental Psychology: Applied*, **2**, 106–25.

Bateman, I., A. Munroe, B. Rhodes, C. Starmer and R. Sugden, (1997), 'Does part–whole bias exist? An Experimental Investigation', *Economic Journal*, **107**, 322–33.

Beattie, J., S. Chilton, R. Cookson, J. Covey, L. Hopkins, M. Jones-Lee, G. Loomes, N. Pidgeon, A. Robinson and A. Spencer (1997), 'Valuing health and safety controls: a literature review', Contract Research Report 171/1988 Health and Safety Executive.

Cookson, R. (1996), 'Contextual factors in the valuation of safety: an exploratory study', York Economics Discussion Paper Series No. 96/41.

Diamond, P.A. and J.A. Hausman (1994), 'Contingent valuation: is some number better than no number?', *Journal of Economic Perspectives* **8**(4), 45–64.

Dubourg, W.R., M.W. Jones-Lee and G.Loomes (1998), 'Imprecise preferences and survey design in contingent valuation', *Economica*, **64**(256), 681–702.

Gregory, R. and S. Lichtenstein (1994), 'A hint of risk – tradeoffs between quantitative and qualitative risk factors', *Risk Analysis*, **14** (2). 199–206.

Gregory, R., S. Lichtenstein and P. Slovic (1993), 'Valuing environmental resources: a constructive approach', *Journal of Risk and Uncertainty*, **7**, 177–97.

Irwin, J.R. and J.H. Davis (1995), 'Choice/matching preference reversals in groups: consensus processes and justification-based reasoning', *Journal of Organizational Behavior and Human Decision Processes*, **64** (3), 325–39.

Jones-Lee. M.W. and G. Loomes (1995), 'Scale and context effects in the valuation of Transport Safety', *Journal of Risk and Uncertainty*, **11**, 183–203.

McDaniels, T.L., M.S. Kamlet and G.W. Fischer (1992), 'Risk perception and the value of safety', *Risk Analysis*, **12** (4), 495–503.

Mendeloff, J. and R.M. Kaplan (1989), 'Are large differences in "lifesaving" costs justified?' A psychometric study of the relative value placed on preventing deaths', *Risk Analysis*, **9** (3), 349–63.

Savage, I. (1993), 'An empirical investigation into the effect on psychological perceptions on the willingness-to-pay to reduce risk', *Journal of Risk and Uncertainty*, **6**, 75–90.

Slovic, P. (1992), 'Perception of risk: Reflections on the psychometric paradigm', in S. Krimsky and D. Golding (eds), *Social Theories of Risk*, New York: Praeger, pp. 117–52.

Slovic, P. (1995), 'The construction of preferences', *American Psychologist*, **50** (5), 364–70.

Slovic, P., S. Lichtenstein and B. Fischhoff (1979), 'Images of disaster: perception and acceptance of risks from nuclear power', in G. Goodman and W. Rowe (eds), *Energy Risk Management*, London: Academic Press, pp. 223–45.

5. Valuing the environment as an input: the production function approach

Gayatri Acharya

INTRODUCTION

The assignment of monetary values to economic goods and services is a normal and necessary result of economic activity. Assigning monetary values to environmental resources, particularly those for which there are no market values, is however, a somewhat more difficult concept for many people to accept. Yet, without attempting to value environmental goods and services, we essentially allow the opportunity for them to be mismanaged. Krutilla (1967) noted the difference between use and non-use values of environmental resources. While there may be a moral argument for not measuring non-use values in monetary terms, goods and services obtained through extraction from or by interaction with the ecosystem have a use value which may be measurable in monetary terms. Use value may derive from the direct use of goods and services, such as food resources, or from the indirect use of the ecosystem services, such as flood control. In general, the direct use of marketed products of ecosystems is easier to measure since a market value exists and may be adjusted for distortions. In contrast, ecological functions, such as groundwater recharge or discharge, may have indirect use values which are reflected in the economic activities these functions support. The indirect use value of an environmental function is therefore related to the change in the value of production or consumption of an activity or property that it is protecting or supporting (Barbier 1994).

The valuation of direct use values (that is, benefits derived from the direct use of a wetland's resources) and indirect use values (deriving from environmental functions) require different approaches. Direct use values are generally measured by observing commercial uses of resources or services derived from wetlands and by applying market prices or shadow prices. The valuation of indirect use values deriving from environmental functions requires that the linkages between these functions and dependent economic production activities are known or are at least estimable.

This chapter presents the theoretical arguments made in the current valuation literature for using the production function approach to valuing environmental functions (Barbier 1994; Freeman 1993; Mäler 1992). It then presents a recent application of this approach in valuing the groundwater recharge function of the Hadejia–Nguru wetlands in northern Nigeria, briefly discussing the methodological requirements of this approach to measure the value of environmental functions.

THE PRODUCTION FUNCTION APPROACH

Ellis and Fisher (1987) note that when the services of an environmental resource are inputs in the production of some marketed or marketable good, the appropriate basis for determining the value of the environmental service is to view it as a *factor input* into the production process. The impact on the product supply of a change in an ecosystem function depends therefore on the demand for the product and the shift in the supply curve of the factor input. For example, a service such as the capacity of wetlands to improve the quality of drinking water (ibid.), enters into the utility function indirectly through the consumption of the final good, that is, drinking water. Since wetlands can be said to reduce the cost of water treatment by removing or settling pollutants, this reduction in cost can be represented as a shift in the marginal cost or supply curve for fresh water along a given demand curve. An environmental improvement, such as an increase in wetlands, as suggested by Ellis and Fisher (ibid.) would involve a supply shift downward and to the right. The theoretically preferred measure of welfare change is the area of the change in combined consumer and producer surplus (Figure 5.1). It is important to note that this area is bounded by the market demand curve and the old and new supply curves. The identification of demand for an environmental good is therefore necessary in order not to overestimate the benefits of an environmental improvement. However, as noted by Freeman (1991), the impacts of market conditions and regulatory policies are also important.

Mäler (1992) develops the use of the production function for measuring the value of an environmental resource when the output of the production function is measurable. If the output is measurable and the production function can be defined as for example:

$$Y = f(x_1, ..., x_k, q)$$

where Y is the measurable output, $x_1, ..., x_k$ are inputs of goods and services and q is the output of the unpriced environmental resource, then the

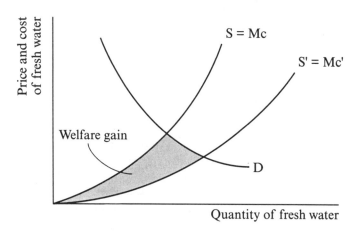

Source: Ellis and Fisher (1987).

Figure 5.1   Change in combined consumer and producer surplus from a shift in product cost curves

economic value of a small change in the resource supply (holding all other prices constant) is the value of the production change that will accompany the change in the resource availability.[1] The welfare change, as noted above, is the sum of the consumer and producer surplus measures. However, if the production units are small relative to the market for the final output, and they are essentially price takers, it can be assumed that product and variable input prices will remain fixed after a change in the environmental resource, q. In this case the benefits of a change in q will accrue to the producers (Freeman 1993).

The production function approach provides a useful way in which to value environmental functions. However, the pervasive lack of adequate data on how an environmental function is linked to the production of other goods often means that the welfare analysis may require a number of assumptions. None the less, there may be sufficient information on related variables which could help strengthen the validity of these assumptions. Narain and Fisher (1994), for example, use a production function approach to model the value of the Anolis lizard. They estimate crop production functions for various crops and assume that the contribution of the lizard to pest control is reflected in the production function as a shift in the intercept term. For example, they estimate that the production function for sugar is expected to shift by 1000 per cent for a one per cent decrease in the lizard population. Although this approach develops the appropriate production functions for the crops being produced, it is unable to actually predict the change in output due to changes in lizard population because of a lack of information about the lizard populations and its contribution as a pest control for agricultural crops.

APPLYING THE PRODUCTION FUNCTION APPROACH: A CASE STUDY OF THE HADEJIA–NGURU WETLANDS, NORTHERN NIGERIA

This section briefly describes the Hadejia–Nguru wetlands in northern Nigeria and highlights the role of these wetlands in recharging the shallow aquifers within the region. It then applies the previously described methodology of valuing environmental functions as inputs in the production of a marketable good and calculates a value for this ecosystem function by hypothesizing changes in recharge rates due to changes in flooding extent.

The Hadejia–Nguru Floodplain and Wetlands

The basin of the Komadugu–Yobe river covers an area of 84 138 km² in northeastern Nigeria and flows into Lake Chad. The rivers Hadejia and Kano, arising in Kano state, and the Jama'are river arising in Plateau and Bauchi states, drain into the Yobe. The portion of the floodplain where the Hadejia and Jama'are rivers meet is known as the Hadejia–Jama'are wetlands. The area of floodplain lying between the towns of Hadejia and Gashua and south of Nguru, are widely referred to as the Hadejia–Nguru wetlands[2] (see Figure 5.2).

Historically, the floodplain of the Hadejia and Jama'are rivers spanned an area of about 3200 km² at peak flood (Drijver and van Wetten 1992). Inundation begins in June and peak flood extents are attained in August–September (Thompson and Hollis 1995). The climate of the region is dominated by the annual migration of the Inter Tropical Convergence Zone (ITCZ) which reaches its most northerly position above Nigeria during July–August. The influence of the ITCZ produces the distinct wet and dry seasons characteristic of Sub-Saharan Aflica. The peak rainfall months in northeastern Nigeria are June–August and the mean annual rainfall for Nguru for the period 1942 to 1990 was 487 mm (ibid.). The rivers have periods of no flow in the dry season (October–April) and a marked concentration of run-off in the wet season with almost 80 per cent of the total annual run-off occurring in August and September.

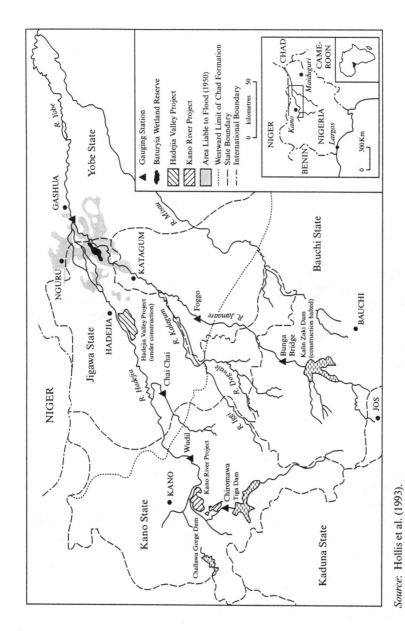

Source: Hollis et al. (1993).

Figure 5.2 The Hadejia–Nguru wetlands and study area

The floodplain wetlands of the Hadejia–Jama'are Basin are located at the downstream end of the Hadejia–Jama'are River Basin, around and just upstream of the confluence of the two rivers. At the town of Gashua the area drained by the Hadejia and Jama'are is 61 120 km^2 (Adams and Hollis 1988). In the dusty, dry environment of northeastern Nigeria, the floodplain is a source of food and the most essential resource of all – water. The floodwaters rejuvenate the floodplain, providing new soil and moisture. Floodplain activities have adapted to suit this cycle, making use of the floods in an ingenious way and taking advantage of a combination of the wetland's resources.

The floodwaters of the Hadejia and Jama'are rivers accumulate in low-lying areas known as *fadamas* in Hausa,[3] which then provide valuable opportunities for grazing, agriculture and other economic uses. *Fadamas* are defined as 'land which is seasonally waterlogged or flooded' (Turner 1977). This complex of pools created by the flooding and accumulation of water forms the Hadejia–Jama'are wetlands. These areas are waterlogged or flooded during the wet season and gradually dry out until they are flooded again during the next wet season. *Fadamas* are used extensively for fishing, farming and grazing, with the uses varying in accordance with the seasonal changes in flood extent.

The wetlands are threatened by upstream developments in the form of dams and irrigation projects which divert water away from the floodplain. As populations of cities like Kano grow and the water demands of the urban areas increase, more water will be diverted further upstream, resulting in a reduction of the flow in the rivers within the floodplain (Barbier and Thompson 1997).

Studies of the hydrological and economic environment of the Hadejia–Nguru wetlands have noted that these wetlands support a wide range of economic activities, including wet and dry season agriculture, fishing, fuelwood collection, livestock rearing and forestry (Hollis et al. 1993; Adams and Hollis 1988; Adams, 1993; Thomas et al. 1993). The wetlands are, in addition, a valuable site for wildlife conservation and, in particular, for waterfowl.[4] Table 5.1 summarizes the available key flood-plain resources and the main methods of utilization within the wetlands.

Grazing within the wetlands is crucial for the cattle and livestock kept by the nomadic Fulani populations and by some farmers. During the dry season the Fulani from both north and south of the wetlands move their camps and their herds to graze on the seasonally exposed grasslands. The wetlands are therefore an essential part of the seasonal cycle of migration undertaken by the nomadic Fulani. Traditionally the Fulani and the farmers have had a tense but cordial relationship. Certain traditions, such as allowing the Fulani herds to graze on the last of the harvest crops in return for some compensation, are still practised, although this is becoming increasingly rare and wrought with conflict.

Table 5.1 Resource utilization

Resource	Utilization
Water	Domestic use, irrigation, livestock watering, navigation
Vegetation	Food, grazing, thatching material, ropes, fuel
Land (*fadamas* and upland), soil	Flooded agriculture, irrigated agriculture, dryland farming, building material
Fish	Fishing, important source of protein
Birds, reptiles, amphibians	Food, hunting, tourism, minor trade

Fisheries, fuel, fibre and food resources are important products of the wetlands. Thomas et al. (1993) note that the wetlands are an important centre of fish production in the region. Fishing is undertaken mainly during the flooded season although some villages and individuals fish throughout the year. Thomas et al. estimated that the annual fish production from the wetlands may vary between 1620 and 8100 metric tonnes, and may well be an underestimate. The floodplain is also a producer of large quantities of doum palm, reeds and sedges (Kalawachi 1995). Polet and Shaibu (in preparation) estimate that the annual value of doum palm produced from the area may be about 35 million Naira.[5] A recent study by Eaton and Sarch (1997) provides additional information on the wild food resources found within the wetlands and the extensive use of these resources by the wetland populations.

Water is used directly from *fadamas*, from river and from the groundwater resources maintained by the regular flooding of the wetlands. It is estimated that more than one million people living within the wetlands depend on groundwater (Kimmage and Adams 1992). Hydrological studies conducted on the wetlands have concluded that the wetlands are particularly important for the recharge of the shallow and deeper aquifers of the Lake Chad Formation which is facilitated by the wet season flooding of the wetlands.[6] The majority of the floodplain villages draw their drinking water from hand dug village wells (ibid.). A few villages near rivers may rely more heavily on river water.

The use of groundwater by rural households and urban dwellers over a vast area across the states of northeast Nigeria and parts of Niger, is dependent upon the recharge of the Lake Chad aquifer. With reference to the important function performed by these wetlands, Hollis et al. (1993, p. 67), state;

> There is no doubt that groundwater recharge comes mainly from the inundation of the fadamas and floodplain and not from the river channels themselves. Much literature refers wrongly [to] 'losses' with the implication that reductions in river flow represents water going to waste. In fact, the reduc-

tion in flow in rivers crossing the Chad formation is an essential natural process which supports a range of productive ecological and human activities including potable water supplies to villages over a wide area.

The present study aims to value the groundwater recharge function performed by these wetlands by studying the use of groundwater in irrigated agriculture, in areas where there is hydrological evidence for groundwater recharge by *fadamas*. By isolating the economic value of groundwater attributable to *fadama* inundation (that is, separate from the recharge of groundwater by river channels), this study aims to shed greater insight into the specific role played by flooding in the wetlands.

Agricultural Water Use within the Wetlands

The flood cycle is very important in the order and intensity of activities undertaken. In agriculture, the seasonal rise and fall of floodwaters results in the establishment of four cropping systems, namely, rainfed upland cropping, *fadama* or flood cultivation, recession farming and irrigated cropping. Total cultivated area in the floodplain is estimated as 230 000 hectares of which approximately 77 500 hectares is dry season farming and 152 500 hectares is wet season farming (Barbier et al. 1993). Upland or dryland farming is rain fed, and millet, sorghum and cowmelon are cultivated. *Fadama* farming is mainly rice cultivation and planting is done with the onset of the rain. By the time the land is flooded, the rice is expected to be high enough to withstand the inundation. Recession farming follows the *fadama* cultivation. As the floods recede the exposed land is planted with recession crops such as beans, cotton or cassava. These crops utilize the residual moisture in the soil. Dry-season irrigated farming has been traditionally practised in the area with simple irrigation technologies, often associated with channels cut from the rivers (Adams 1993). These *lambu* or irrigated lands are now increasingly (since the 1980s) being irrigated with the use of small petrol-powered pumps, which can lift water relatively short distances from river channels or from shallow groundwater within the wetlands.

Pumps may be used to lift water from flooded areas, rivers or groundwater resources. This study focuses on pump irrigation using water from shallow aquifers. Irrigation farming begins in October, after the floods have receded, and continues up until March/April. The crops grown using this irrigation technology include tomatoes, sweet and chilli peppers, onions, spring onions, wheat, and to a lesser extent, sweet potatoes, irrigated rice, lettuce and garlic. The floodplain has experienced a dramatic rise in small-scale irrigation following the introduction of small petrol-powered pumps for surface water irrigation and tubewells to tap the shallow aquifers under the floodplain (Kaigama and Omeje 1994; Kimmage and Adams 1992).

Although the extent of small-scale tubewell irrigation within the Hadejia–Jama'are wetlands is not well documented, it appears to be changing rapidly because of changes in hydrological conditions, economic conditions, government initiatives, and in particular because of the policies of the World Bank-supported Agricultural Development Programs (ADPs) which have promoted the use of small irrigation pumps through subsidies and/or loans for tubewell drilling and pump purchase.

The expansion of dry season cultivation in the area has resulted from the increased availability of small-scale irrigation technology and higher producer prices for some dry-season crops such as peppers, onions and wheat. The availability of pumps has also resulted in irrigation of certain dry-season crops such as sweet potato, to increase yields, and farmers in the area are experimenting with new commercial crops such as lettuce and garlic. Availability of, and access to, groundwater resources ensures the farmers a more secure and year-round water supply for these crops.

The growth of tubewells in this area is expected to continue to increase and although there is at present apparently little concern for the over-exploitation of this resource, this optimism is based on relatively little data on aquifer recharge and the effect of increased or reduced flooding of *fadama* areas. Cropping patterns in the area have changed because of these credit and technological facilities as well as because of changing hydrological conditions. Increasing dependence on small-scale irrigation for dry-season crops may result in increased sensitivity of small farmers to changes in prices and market demand. However, farming in this area is generally subsistence, and to hedge against uncertainty farmers practice multicropping and intercropping.

Welfare Measures and Technological Considerations[7]

We begin by assuming that farmers produce $i =$, 1, ..., n crops, irrigated by groundwater. Let y_i be the aggregate output of the i'th crop produced by the farmers. The production of y_i requires a water input W_i, abstracted through shallow tubewells, and $j = 1$, ..., J of other variable inputs (for example, fertilizers, seed, labour), which we denote as x_i, ..., x_J or in vector form as $\mathbf{X}_J$. Because of the relationship between recharge and the level of water in the aquifer, we also assume that the amount of water available to the farmer for abstraction is dependent on the groundwater level, R. The aggregate production function for crop i can be expressed as:

$$y_i = y_i[x_{i1}, ..., x_{iJ}, W_i(R)] \quad \text{for all } i \quad (5.1)$$

and the associated costs of producing y_i are:

$$C_i = \mathbf{C}_x \mathbf{X}_J + c_w(R)W_i \quad \text{for all } i \quad (5.2)$$

where C_i is the minimum costs associated with producing y_i during a single growing season, c_w is the cost of pumping water and $\mathbf{C}_x$ is a vector of $c_{xi}, ..., c_{xJ}$, strictly positive, input prices associated with the variable inputs $x_{i1}, ..., x_{iJ}$. Note that we assume c_w is an increasing function of the groundwater level, R, to allow for the possibility of increased pumping costs from greater depths.

We further assume that the demand curve can be expressed as a price–quantity relationship (that is, an inverse demand curve) for the aggregate crop output,

$$P_i = P_i(y_i) \qquad \text{for all } i \tag{5.3}$$

where P_i is the market price for y_i, and all other marketed input prices are assumed constant.

Denoting S_i as the social welfare arising from producing y_i, S_i is measured as the area under the demand curve (5.3), less the cost of the inputs used in production (5.2):[8]

$$S_i = S_i[x_{i1}, ..., x_{iJ}, W_i(R); c_w(R)] = \int P_i(y) \, dy - \mathbf{C}_x\mathbf{X}_J - c_w(R)W_i \quad \text{for all } i,j \tag{5.4}$$

From the above relationships, we are interested in solving explicitly for the effects on social welfare of a change in groundwater levels, R, due to a fall in recharge rates. This effect is observed in the production function through an impact on water input, w_i. We assume that all other inputs are held constant and at their optimal levels, and that all input and output prices, with the exception of c_w, are unchanged. For a non-marginal change in groundwater levels from R_0 (old level) to R_1 (new level), the welfare change measure associated with a change in naturally recharged groundwater is the resulting change in the value of production less the change in pumping costs. *The net welfare change is therefore the effect of a change in groundwater levels on the value of the marginal product of water in production, less the per unit cost of a change in water input.* A marginal change in pumping costs also affects the total costs of water pumped. The effect of a change in water input due to a change in groundwater levels occurs both directly and indirectly through the marginal effect of a change in pumping costs on water input. As long as per unit pumping costs are not prohibitively high, one would expect an increase in groundwater levels to lead to a welfare benefit, or at least to maintain the initial welfare levels, whereas a decrease in groundwater levels would result in a welfare loss, either due to increased pumping costs and/or to a change in productivity.[9] If we further assume that farmers face the same production and cost relationships for each crop *i* and are price takers (that is, they cannot affect the market price of their produce) then it is possible to aggregate the welfare effects of a change in groundwater levels for the individual farmer, for all farmers.

A second issue we consider before estimating production functions and welfare changes is the technological relationship between groundwater levels and tubewells. A typical tubewell consists of a length of pipe pump casing sunk into the ground below the maximum depth to the water table. This maximum depth should be such that during pumping, the aquifer's water level does not fall below the pipe's reach. If the rate of withdrawal from the aquifer exceeds the recharge, and groundwater levels do not recover to the original base level, the use of the shallow tubewell may need to be abandoned.[10] For the purpose of this study, we consider two possible effects of a fall in groundwater levels:

1. as groundwater falls below a certain level, the costs of pumping water are likely to rise, and
2. if groundwater levels fall below the maximum depth of the sunk tube-wells, then the farmer will have to cease pumping for the rest of the dry season and thus agricultural production will fall and may even cease.

For case (1) to occur, we expect that the speed of the pump will be affected by a drop in groundwater levels but water will still be available to the farmer using the given technology. The pumps being used in the floodplain are surface mounted pumps, and it is likely that at depths approaching seven metres these pumps will slow down because of the increase in lift. To maintain water input levels, the farmer would have to increase pumping hours, thereby incurring higher costs of production.

The tubewells in the study area are sunk to depths of approximately nine metres and the groundwater table would have to fall to a level below nine metres before pumping capabilities fall to zero (that is, for case (2) to occur). If water levels stay below nine metres, the farmer will not be able to irrigate at all and the associated drop in yield can be calculated from the production function by setting water input to zero. This is expected to occur in the wetlands only if there is a long period of very low flooding and no technological adaptation. Hence we only concern ourselves with case (1) for the purpose of this study. Since there is little evidence that groundwater levels could fall much below seven metres we restrict our present analysis to this level for both wheat and vegetable production.

Estimating Production Functions for Wheat and Vegetables

We estimate production functions for wheat and vegetable production using survey data from the Madachi *fadama* located within the Hadejia–Nguru wetlands. In estimating these production functions, we assume that the output depends on a combination of purchased goods and water inputs. The farmers in the Madachi area grow mainly wheat, irrigated rice and vegetables. The crops are divided into these three groups because of the different nature of irrigation, fertilizer application and other farming decisions. Wheat and rice are generally grown earlier in the season and vegetables are grown well into the dry season. We estimate production relationships for wheat and vegetables only since irrigated rice is grown by very few farmers in the sample.[11]

We consider linear, log-linear and quadratic functional forms for wheat and vegetable production. The linear form assumes constant marginal products and excludes any interaction between the inputs. Although the lack of interaction terms is restrictive, we observe in the literature that linear relationships are likely, particularly for wheat production and with low levels of inputs. The quadratic form is also estimated, allowing for interactions between variables. This form also allows us to observe the effect of increasing quantities of inputs on output levels. The log-linear form assumes constant input elasticity and variable marginal products. The production function for wheat is described for example in general form as:

$$Y = f(L, B, S, F, W)$$

where Y = total output of crop (kg)
                L = land (ha)
                B = labour (workers)
                S = seeds (kg)
                F = fertilizer (kg)
                W = water application = irrigation (litres).

The production function for vegetables was estimated as a single function since all the vegetables are grown at the same time (after the wheat has been harvested) or in quick succession, and receive similar quantities of inputs. Data on seeds/seedlings was unreliable and this variable was dropped from the production function. The econometric results indicate that the log-linear model is the most satisfactory version of the wheat and vegetable production functions.[12]

Valuing the Recharge Function

Hydrological evidence for the relationship between flood extent and recharge to village wells show that there is some fluctuation with flood extent and mean water depth of the shallow aquifer The effect of planned upstream water projects will have an impact on producer welfare within the wetlands through changes in flood extent and therefore groundwater recharge. By hypothesizing a drop in groundwater levels from six metres to seven metres in depth (due to reduced recharge), we calculate the expected change in welfare associated with this reduction in recharge. This exogenous change affects the farmers' decision-making process *during* the farming season, that is, after decisions on other inputs have already been taken. This is because the effect of the reduced recharge will not be felt until after the dry-season agriculture has started.

The welfare change measures described above are used together with the results of the production function estimates to calculate welfare changes for individual farmers. We assume also that farmers in the Madachi area are price takers and hence face a 'horizontal' demand function. We hypothesize a drop in groundwater levels to approximately seven metres and consider the effect of changing pumping costs on water input and use the production function estimated earlier for the purpose of estimating welfare changes.

The production functions are used to calculate the associated change in productivity due to a metre fall in recharge levels. From the measure of welfare change discussed earlier, we find that average welfare change per hectare for wheat production is approximately 54459 Naira (US$618) and 3566 Naira (US$40) for vegetable production, over the growing season. The welfare change associated with the effects of groundwater loss on wheat production is very high, possibly because wheat production requires high water inputs and productivity is severely affected by changes in water input.

CONCLUSIONS

From our survey data, we estimate that there are 175 wheat and vegetable farmers and 134 vegetable farmers in the Madachi *fadama* influence area of about 6600 hectares.[13] Using the estimated production functions, the change in welfare associated with a decrease in recharge to the aquifer is calculated as 2863 Naira (US$32.5) for each vegetable farmer and as 29110 Naira (US$331) for farmers growing wheat and vegetables. The total loss associated with the one metre change in naturally recharged groundwater levels (resulting in a decline of groundwater levels to approximately seven metres) is estimated as 5 477 938 Naira (US$62 249) for the influence area of the Madachi *fadama*. It is estimated that shallow aquifers could irrigate 19 000 hectares within the wetlands through the use of small tubewells (DIYAM 1987). Using this figure together with the average welfare change for the Madachi *fadama* (5478 Naira/hectare or US$62/hectare), we estimate a welfare loss of 1.04×10^8 Naira or US$1 182 737 for the wetlands, due to a decrease in groundwater levels to approximately seven metres in depth, within a single year.[14] As previous studies have asserted, and as this study confirms, groundwater recharge is of considerable importance to wetland agriculture and reduced recharge resulting in lower groundwater levels will result in a loss of welfare for the floodplain populations.

This study uses the production function approach together with appropriate welfare measures to capture the value of the recharge function in terms of agricultural production during the dry season. The chapter reviews the theoretical basis for using this approach, where the environmental function is valued as an input in the production of a marketed good. The application shows the relative difficulty of identifying the physical relationship between the environmental good or function and the economic activity it supports. At the same time, this study shows the possibility of using crop production and input data to estimate these relationships empirically and measure correctly the welfare changes related with changes in the environmental function. There are few applications of this approach in the valuation of non-marketed environmental resources. With increased understanding of data requirements, the production function approach, where the environment enters as an input in the production process, may prove to be as useful a methodology in environmental valuation as it is in conventional production analysis.

NOTES

1. If the output Y cannot be measured directly, then either a marketed substitute may be used, if it exists, or possible complementarity or substitutability between the resource and other inputs must be explicitly defined (see Mäler 1992 for a complete discussion).
2. The Hadejia–Jama'are wetlands refer to the entire Basin, including the area beyond the town of Gashua in the northeast, whereas Hadejia–Nguru is the term used to describe the wetlands between Gashua and Hadejia.
3. A major northern Nigerian language and ethnic group.
4. Note that this study carries out a *partial valuation* of the wetlands by valuing one ecological function performed by the wetlands. Other use and non-use values listed here are not addressed by the valuation exercise presented in this chapter.
5. 88 Naira = US$1.
6. Schultz (1976) and DIYAM (1987), cited in Thompson and Hollis (1995).

7. Full derivations of these welfare measures can be found in Acharya and Barbier (1997).
8. We assume here that the demand function in (5.3) is compensated, so that consumer welfare can be measured by the appropriate areas; or that the consumer surplus estimate of the ordinary demand function is a reasonable estimate of consumer welfare. See Freeman (1993) for a discussion.
9. We expect dS/dR to be positive as long as the water table is not so high as to cause waterlogging and subsequently cause direct damage to crops and/or changes in soil conditions.
10. However, increased costs of pumping from a greater depth may cause pumping to be curtailed until a new groundwater level is established. Because the farmer is forced to stop pumping, water levels may recover, allowing some sporadic pumping throughout the season. This introduces uncertainty into the problem and makes it a dynamic problem. This is beyond the scope of the present chapter.
11. Since crop-level data is often not available, many studies analyse farm level aggregated input demands. Although fixed factors, such as land, may cause jointness in the production process, we argue that crop-level production functions can be estimated in this case for wheat and for vegetables since (i) crop-level data was collected through the survey and is available and (ii) vegetables are clearly grown only after the winter wheat production implying that input decisions may be considered as separate in terms of the production processes.
12. See Acharya and Barbier (1997) for full econometric results.
13. Size of Madachi influence area is derived from Thompson and Goes (1997).
14. Note that this figure is based on 32 per cent of installed tubewells actually working and could be much higher for a higher percentage of operational tubewells within the wetlands.

REFERENCES

Acharya, G. and E.B. Barbier (1997), *Valuing the Hadejia–Jama'are Wetlands of Northern Nigeria*, Report prepared for IUCN – the World Conservation Union, Gland, Switzerland.

Adams, W.M. (1993), 'Agriculture, grazing and forestry', in Hollis et al. (1993), pp. 89–96.

Adams, W.M. and G.E. Hollis (1988), *Hydrology and Sustainable Resource Development of a Sahelian Floodplain Wetland*, Report for the Hadejia–Nguru Wetlands Conservation Project.

Barbier, E.B. (1994), 'Valuing environmental functions: tropical wetlands', *Land Economics*, **70** (2), 155–73.

Barbier, E.B., W. Adams and K. Kimmage (1993), 'Economic valuation of wetland benefits', in Hollis et al. (1993), pp. 191–209.

Barbier, E.B. and J.R. Thompson (1997), 'The value of water: floodplain versus large-scale irrigation benefits in northern Nigeria', forthcoming in *Ambio*.

DIYAM (1987), *Shallow Aquifer Study*, 3 Vols, Kano: Kano State Agricultural and Rural Development Authority.

Drijver, C.A. and C.J. van Wetten (1992), *Sahel Wetlands 2020: Changing Development Policies or Losing the Sahel's Best Resources*, Leiden: Centre for Environmental Studies, University of Leiden.

Ellis, G. and A. Fisher (1987), Valuing the environment as an input', *Journal of Environmental Management*, **25**, 149–56.

Freeman, A.M. (1991), 'Valuing environmental resources under alternative management regimes', *Ecological Economics*, **3**, 247–56.

Freeman, A.M. (1993), *The Measurement of Environmental and Resource Values: Theory and Methods*, Washington, DC: Resources for the Future.

Hadejia–Nguru Wetlands Conservation Project (HNWCP) (1996), Internal report prepared on the survey of the Madachi *fadama* influence area, Hadejia–Nguru Wetlands Conservation Project, Nguru.

Hollis, G.E., W.M. Adams and M. Aminu-Kano (eds) (1993), *The Hadejia–Nguru Wetlands: Environment, Economy and Sustainable Development of a Sahelian Floodplain Wetland*, Switzerland and Cambridge, UK: IUCN – the World Conservation Union, Gland.

Hollis, G.E. and J.R. Thompson (1993), 'Water resource developments and their hydrological impacts', in Hollis et al. (1993), pp. 69–79.

Kaigama, B.K. and M.U. Omeje (1994), 'Soil fertility and water conservation management practices in *fadamas*, in A. Kolawole, I. Scoones, M.O. Awogbade and J.P. Voh (eds), *Strategies for the Sustainable Use of Fadama Lands in Northern Nigeria*, Zaria: CSER/ABU, and London: International Institute for Environment and Development (IIED), pp. 133–7.

Kalawachi, M. (1995), 'The dilemma of sustainable water resources management of Komadugu-Yobe Basin: the Yobe view', in M. Aminu-Kano (ed.), *The Critical Water Resources of the Komadugu-Yobe Basin*, Proceedings of a National Institute for Policy and Strategic Studies and the Hadejia–Nguru Wetlands Conservation Project Workshop, Kuru: NIPSS/HNWCP.

Kimmage, K. and W.M. Adams (1992), 'Wetland agricultural production and river basin development in the Hadejia–Jama'are valley, Nigeria', *Geographical Journal*, **158**, 1–12.

Krutilla, J.V. (1967), 'Conservation reconsidered', *American Economic Review*, **57**, 777–86.

Mäler, K.G. (1992), 'Production function approach in developing countries', in J.R. Vincent, E.W. Crawford and J.P. Hoehn (eds), *Valuing Environmental Benefits in Developing Countries*, Special Report 29, East Lansing: Michigan State University, pp. 11–32.

Narain, U. and A.C. Fisher (1994), 'Modelling the value of biodiversity using a production function approach: the case of the Anolis lizard in the Lesser and Greater Antilles', in Perrings, C.A., K.-G. Mälor, C. Folke, C.S. Holling and B.-O. Jansson (eds), *Biodiversity Conservation*, Amsterdam: Kluwer Academic Publishers, pp. 109–19.

Polet, G. and M. Shaibu (in preparation), 'Utilization of Doum Palm (Hyphaene thecaica), in the Hadejia–Nguru Wetlands', Hadejia–Nguru Wetlands Conservation Project, Mimeo.

Thomas, D.H.L., M.A. Jimoh and H. Matthes (1993), 'Fishing', in Hollis et al. (1993), pp. 97–115.

Thompson, J.R. and B. Goes (1997), *Inundation and Groundwater Recharge in the Hadejia–Nguru Wetlands, Northeast Nigeria: Hydrological Analysis*, Kano: Hadejia–Nguru Wetlands Conservation Project, and London: Wetland Research Unit, University College London.

Thompson, J.R. and G. Hollis (1995), 'Hydrological modelling and the sustainable development of the Hadejia–Nguru wetlands, Nigeria', *Hydrological Sciences Journal*, **40**, 97–116.

Turner, B. (1977), 'The *fadama* lands of Central Northern Nigeria: their classification, spatial variation and present and potential use', Unpublished PhD thesis, London.

PART II

Economic Policy Towards the Environment

6. Environmental taxation: evidence from the transport sector

Melinda Acutt[*]

INTRODUCTION

The transport sector is currently one of the most important areas of interest for environmental policy. In both developed and developing countries the transport sector is a significant contributor to a wide range of environmental problems including noise, localized air pollution, greenhouse gas emissions, traffic congestion, visual intrusion, impacts on flora and fauna and community severance. The importance of these effects has been highlighted by the British Royal Commission on Environmental Pollution (RCEP) (1994 and 1997) and road transport was singled out for particular attention.

In this chapter, I briefly outline the environmental problems related to the transport sector, highlighting their relative importance. I then discuss the valuation of these environmental problems and review a number of studies that have attempted to place monetary values on these externalities. The main part of this chapter then looks at the applicability of environmental taxation to the transport sector and assesses a number of different environmental tax policy options to reduce these externalities. I assess each option against a range of policy assessment criteria including: kilometres both by car and by public transport; fuel consumption and emission levels; car ownership; traffic congestion; government finances; administrative complexity; and equity.

ENVIRONMENTAL IMPACTS OF TRANSPORT: OVERVIEW AND TRENDS

The transport sector, as noted above, is a significant contributor to a range of environmental problems. According to the RCEP's latest report (1997, p. 105),

[*] This chapter draws on previous work carried out jointly with John Dodgson, National Economic Research Associates. I would like to thank him for all his help and comments.

For national sustainability goals to be met, transport in the UK must be radically modified . . . official forecasts for the next quarter century show road traffic continuing to increase at a similar rate to the last quarter century, with no assurance as yet that improvements in vehicle technology will bring about the required improvements in air quality. Unless this position changes, the consequences will be environmentally, economically and socially unacceptable:

- pollution from road vehicles will continue to have effects on health and the natural and built environment
- emissions of carbon dioxide from road vehicles will make a growing contribution to the greenhouse effect, and thus to climate change
- traffic noise and intrusion will have ever more extensive effects on the quality of life
- the road network will be used less efficiently because of increasing traffic congestion.

In this section I give a brief overview of these problems, taking the UK as a case study.

Global Climate Change

Air pollution problems contributed to by the transport sector can be divided into two main categories: global climate change and more immediate health problems. Considering global climate change, emissions from anthropogenic sources are increasing the atmospheric concentrations of greenhouse gases substantially. Although the exact implications of this increase in greenhouse gases in the atmosphere are still being debated, a recent review of evidence by the Intergovernmental Panel on Climate Change concludes that 'The balance of evidence suggests a discernible human influence on climate' (Houghton 1996, p. 3). Governments of developed countries are committed, under the Rio Convention on Climate Change, to reduce emissions of greenhouse gases back to their 1990 levels by the year 2000. This commitment is set to increase to an average reduction of 5.2 per cent below 1990 levels by 2010 on ratification of the December 1997 Kyoto Protocol and the UK government has already set itself a target of reducing carbon dioxide emissions to 20 per cent below the 1990 level by the year 2010.

The single most important greenhouse gas is carbon dioxide (CO_2). According to the Department of Transport (1996), the UK transport sector as a whole accounted for 26 per cent of UK CO_2 emissions in 1994, and road transport alone accounted for 23 per cent. It is important to note both the absolute and relative increases in road transport-related emissions over time. Road transport emissions rose from 26 to 34 million tonnes of carbon (Mtc) over the ten years from 1984 to 1994, while the proportion of total emissions accounted for by this sector rose from 18 to 23 per cent. The UK government forecasts increases in transport CO_2 emissions of between 23 and 36 per cent between 1994 and 2020. Hence the transport sector is becoming increasingly important for CO_2 emissions reduction policies, and it is unlikely that further abatement targets can be met without policies aimed specifically at this sector.

Air Pollution

The other main atmospheric emissions from transport are: carbon monoxide, nitrogen oxides, volatile organic compounds (VOCs), particulates and lead. These emissions are problematic primarily because of their more immediate health effects, but carbon monoxide, nitrogen oxides and VOCs are also implicated in global climate change. Health effects associated with these emissions range from impaired perceptions and reflexes, through lung irritation and respiratory illness, to angina, cancer and death. A recent study estimated that 6665 premature deaths occur each year in the UK as a result of air pollution from transport (Maddison et al., 1996, p. 75).

Figure 6.1 shows levels of total UK road transport emissions over the period 1984 to 1994 for most of the main emissions from the road transport sector. Figure 6.2 shows the percentage of total UK emissions accounted for by the road transport sector. Nitrogen oxide emissions rose in absolute terms until 1989, but have started to decline since then. All the projections are for continuing decline because of the effects of the three-way catalytic converters (CATs) that must be fitted to all new petrol cars since 1993 under EU Directive 91/441/EC. Carbon monoxide and VOC emissions are also reduced by CATs, and total emissions of these pollutants also peaked in 1989. In contrast, black smoke has increased from 136 thousand tonnes in 1984 to 248 thousand tonnes in 1994. This is due to the increasing proportion of diesel cars in the UK fleet. This increase in black smoke emissions is highlighted in Figure 6.2, which shows that the proportion of black smoke emissions accounted for by the road transport sector has increased from 29 to 58 per cent over this period. This is in contrast to the proportion of the emissions of nitrogen oxides, carbon monoxide and VOCs accounted for by road transport, which have remained roughly the same over the ten-year period to 1994. Road transport accounted for 86 per cent of total UK carbon dioxide emissions in 1984 and 90 per cent in 1994, showing some increase. The proportion of VOCs attributable to road transport rose from 41 per cent in 1984, to a peak of 46 per cent in 1989 and 1990, before falling to 40 per cent in 1994. The proportion of nitrogen oxides accounted for by road transport rose from 46 per cent in 1984, to 53 per cent in 1994.

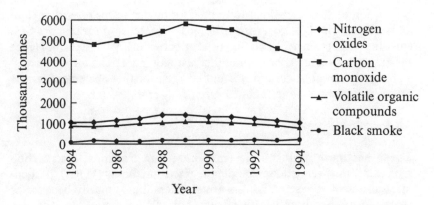

Source: Department of Transport (1996).

Figure 6.1 Total UK road vehicle emissions

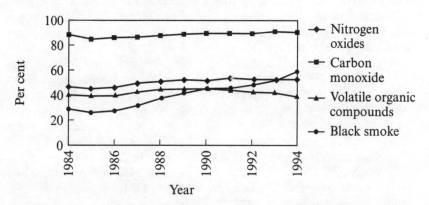

Source: Department of Transport (1996).

Figure 6.2 Road transport emissions (percentage of total UK emissions)

Noise

The road transport sector is also an important contributor to increased
noise pollution in the UK. According to the Department of the
Environment (1992) road traffic was, on average, the main source of noise
pollution outside dwellings; over the period 1986 to 1991, road transport
was responsible for 66 per cent of noise pollution. Noise pollution, especially during the night, contributes to ill health, a loss of productivity due
to sleep loss and an inability to concentrate, as well as to an impairment of
children's learning (Maddison et al. 1996).

Congestion

Traffic congestion is also a serious problem. Growing volumes of traffic lead to reduced traffic speeds, and traffic travelling more slowly contributes proportionately more per passenger kilometre to a range of environmental problems, than free-flow traffic. More fuel is consumed in stop–start traffic, leading to higher levels of air pollution, and noise pollution levels will also be higher in terms of length, if not of level. According to Maddison et al., the Department of Transport have estimated that morning peak speeds in London have fallen from 18.1 kilometres per hour (kph) in 1968–70, to 16.0 kph in 1986–90. Daytime off-peak speeds have also fallen, from 21.3 kph in 1968–70, to 18.9 kph in 1986–90, while evening speeds have fallen from 18.6 kph to 16.5 kph over the same period. A recent study by National Economic Research Associates (1997) found that congestion costs are spread throughout the day, only 22 per cent being incurred in the weekday morning and evening peaks. Congestion is an inefficient way to ration the scarce road network, as those whose time is more valuable are delayed by drivers with lower valuations of time on relatively unimportant trips.

VALUING THE ENVIRONMENTAL IMPACTS OF TRANSPORT

Excess environmental degradation occurs as a result of the underpricing of private transport to the end user. Decisions about the amount of private transport to be consumed are made which are efficient from each individual's viewpoint, but inefficient for society as a whole. Private transport is underpriced to the end user if the price does not include all the incremental infrastructure and environmental costs associated with the travel. Designing policies to correct for this price gap will require an estimate of the marginal environmental damage caused by the transport sector. As has been shown in Chapters 2 to 5, environmental effects are always difficult to value, especially where physical effects, such as those on health, may be uncertain. There will also be difficulties in predicting how emissions from vehicles affect ambient pollution levels. This may require both atmospheric dispersion models and chemical transformation models. The problem of the location and movement of pollutants is further analysed in Chapter 7.

Nevertheless, there have been a number of attempts to estimate the external costs of the transport sector. It is therefore possible to compare the results from different studies to see if a consensus is emerging. Results from five of the most recent studies are given in Table 6.1. Comparison is

Table 6.1 Summary of estimates of marginal[a] external costs of car[b] travel

Study	Estimate year	Units	Vehicle type	Global warming	Air pollution	Noise	Congestion	Accidents	Road damage	Total
Maddison et al. (1996)	1993	Pence per vehicle km (all vehicle types)	Average per *vehicle* km	0.02	4.8	0.06–0.8	4.7	0.4	0.7–2.3	11.2–12.9[c]
Peirson and Vickerman (1998)	1991	Pence per car passenger km	Inter-urban car	0.02	0.35	0.08	0.85	0.15	n/a	1.45
			London	0.03	4.34	0.39	15.06	1.5	n/a	21.32
Tinch (1995)	1993	Pence per car passenger km	Urban car	Included in air pollution	1.4	1.87	n/a	n/a	n/a	n/a
			Average car		0.25	0.34	n/a	n/a	n/a	n/a
Mayeres et al.[d] (1996)	2005	Pence per car passenger km	Large petrol car, urban	0.07	1.37	0.06	n/a	4.23	n/a	n/a
			Large diesel car, urban	0.06	1.25	0.06	n/a	4.23	n/a	n/a
Mauch and Rothengatter[e]	1991	Pence per car passenger km	Average car	0.46	0.70	0.28	n/a	1.84	n/a	n/a

Notes:

a. Figures from the Tinch study are given in terms of average external costs.
b. Maddison figures are per vehicle km and include road freight as well as passenger transport.
c. Estimates of the individual costs shown for the Maddison study were converted to vehicle kilometres by the author. These figures do not add exactly to the total external cost figure because of rounding.
d. Estimates by Mayeres were converted to £ and to passenger kilometres by the author.
e. Estimates by Mauch and Rothengatter were converted to £ by Nash and are quoted in Nash (1997).

hampered by different units of measurement. All studies, except for Maddison et al. (1996) refer to pence per passenger kilometre, but are for different car types. The figures given by Maddison et al. are for all types of road vehicles, and so include buses as well as light and heavy goods vehicles. Studies refer to marginal costs except for Tinch (1995) in which figures are for average costs.

Nash (1997) notes that variations between estimates occur both because of methodological differences and because of differences in the way in which costs are assessed. For example, Maddison et al. and Peirson and Vickerman estimate low global warming costs because they base their estimates on discounted predictions of the economic impact of global warming over the next two to three hundred years. Mauch and Rothengatter estimate a far higher level of costs for global warming as they calculate the costs of reducing the effect of global climate change (Nash 1997; Peirson and Vickerman 1998). This is an interesting difference in approach between whether the correct valuation of the externality is the cost of resources misallocated, or the costs of reducing the damage from the externality (Vickerman 1997). The general consensus in the economic literature is that the resource cost approach is more appropriate. However, damage reduction costs, such as those estimated by Mauch and Rothengatter are useful for policy makers as they highlight the potential cost of allowing the environmental problem to worsen before taking remedial action.

Considering congestion costs, a recent study by National Economic Research Associates estimates that the cost to road users in 1996 was £7 billion in terms of increased total time, fuel use and other operating costs (NERA 1997). The study also found that the problem of congestion in the biggest cities is not limited to peak hours. Only 20 per cent of these costs were incurred in the weekday morning and evening peaks, 22 per cent were incurred around the peaks, 34 per cent between the peaks, and 24 per cent in the evenings and at weekends. Congestion increased costs to other road users, impacting on bus operators and passengers. Buses suffer 10 per cent of congestion costs even though they only account for one per cent of the traffic flow (ibid).

While there are many problems in valuing the external costs of car transport, a review of the evidence to date, as given in Table 6.1, does suggest broad orders of magnitude that can be used in policy appraisal. One of the biggest problems highlighted by these estimates is that substantial differences occur between the external costs of urban (especially peak time urban) and rural or interurban traffic. According to Maddison et al. (1996) the average tax paid in the UK is 4 pence per vehicle kilometre. Looking at Table 6.1, we can see that this is significantly below the total marginal external costs for urban drivers for those studies that include all the external impacts, but could be above the level of marginal external costs imposed by rural drivers. This implies that a policy that can differentiate between drivers by time and place would be more efficient and fairer than one that covered all drivers throughout the country. However, a differentiated policy would add significantly to administration costs. These and other policy concerns are addressed in the next section, which assesses the effectiveness of a range of possible environmental tax instruments.

EVALUATION OF ALTERNATIVE ENVIRONMENTAL TAXATION INSTRUMENTS

Imposing a tax on the environmentally damaging activity will raise its price and so reduce the level of activity. The amount of the reduction will depend on a number of factors relating to the responsiveness of demand to the price rise (the price elasticity of demand). Factors such as visibility of the price rise, future expectations about price movements and availability of alternatives will all be important. A range of taxation options exist in the transport sector. For a tax instrument to be effective it must be related to the damage an extra unit of pollution imposes. This requires not only that the tax be levied on the source of the pollutant, but also that the effects of an extra unit of the pollutant are the same whenever a given amount is emitted. There are two reasons why this might not be the case. First, pollutants may have localized effects, so that costs differ in different areas. Second, marginal effects might differ from average effects; for example, at low levels of emissions, marginal costs may be low, but they may rise as the total amount of emissions rises. Directly metering emissions and other environmental impacts from all mobile sources would be financially impractical, so the difficulty is then on what to base the tax. There are a number of different bases on which taxation can be raised, which will each affect the various environmental impacts of the transport sector to a different extent. We consider taxes levied on fuel, emissions, annual vehicle ownership and road pricing.

Fuel Taxes

A tax can be levied on fuel in order to raise the fuel price. Raising the price of fuel will have direct effects in terms of reducing fuel consumption all else being equal. The power of this policy is enhanced over the long term as it will also have a number of secondary effects which will occur in the longer run. Car ownership decisions will be affected when vehicles come to be replaced – leading to some reduction in car ownership levels and the bias of new car purchases towards smaller, more fuel-efficient cars. Manufacturers will have greater incentives to design more fuel-efficient vehicles to meet consumer demand. There will also be an increased incentive to scrap the least-fuel-efficient older cars.

Fuel taxes will increase the marginal costs of motoring and so will reduce kilometres driven. Goodwin (1992, p. 159) surveys the evidence from a number of studies and suggests a short-run elasticity of about –0.15 between fuel prices and car kilometres. This is increased over the longer run, partly due to the effects on car ownership, to produce a long-run elasticity in the range of –0.3 to –0.5. The impact of fuel prices on the overall size of the car fleet was included in Newton's (1996) time-series model of UK car ownership. The effect of fuel prices was small but significant: in 1990 the elasticity of car ownership with respect to the price of fuel was estimated at -0.007. Other studies (see Goodwin 1992, p. 158; Commission of the European Communities 1995, Annex 1, p. iii) have found higher figures.

Fuel price increases will have a direct impact on the amount of fuel consumed. Estimates of the relationships between the price of fuel in the roads sector show short-run elasticities of about –0.3 and long-run elasticities of –0.7 or more (Goodwin 1992, pp. 157–9). These elasticities are greater than the associated car kilometre elasticities because additional fuel savings will be gained via improved driving habits, better vehicle maintenance, making fewer of the least-fuel-efficient shorter trips and a longer-term switch to more-fuel-efficient cars.

Fuel taxes will have an impact on CO_2 emissions via their impact on car fuel consumption because CO_2 emissions are directly related to fuel consumption. Reductions in fuel use will also affect other emissions. However, there is not a direct relationship between fuel used and emissions such as nitrogen oxides, carbon monoxide and volatile organic compounds due to the existence of end-of-pipe technology such as catalytic converters. (The impact of catalytic converters on these emissions can be seen in Figure 6.1, above. This effect will continue until all petrol cars are fitted, but will then be reduced as increased vehicle kilometres again push up emission levels.)

Acutt and Dodgson (1996a) forecast the effects of increasing fuel taxes on fuel consumption and emissions of CO_2, carbon monoxide, nitrogen oxides and VOCs from cars in the UK to the year 2025. The forecasts are derived from a price-sensitive model that disaggregates the car fleet by engine size and vintage, and disaggregates vehicle kilometres into three road types. A more detailed description of the car model can be found in

Acutt and Dodgson (1994). We modelled the impact of increases in real fuel duty by 5 per cent per annum, allowing also for increases in the net price of motor fuel based on the average of the Department of Trade and Industry's 'low' and 'high' forecasts published in Energy Paper No. 65 (Department of Trade and Industry 1995). Under the base case, where petrol prices are held constant at their 1996 levels, carbon dioxide emissions are projected to rise, although at a decelerating rate. Under the rising petrol tax scenario, emissions are forecast to peak in the year 2000 and return to their 1995 levels by 2006. Forecasts for the remaining three emission types show the dramatic effects of the fitting of catalytic converters. Taking carbon monoxide as an example, by 2006, when most of the UK car fleet will be fitted, emissions are predicted to fall by 37 per cent under the base-case scenario, before beginning to rise again as the effects of increased road traffic outweigh the effect of the catalytic converters. Under the rising petrol tax scenario, emissions will fall by 40 per cent by 2006. This shows that some reductions in carbon dioxide will result from increasing petrol taxes, but these are relatively small as compared to the effects of the fitting of catalytic converters.

As fuel taxes can be expected to reduce travel demand there will also be reductions in traffic noise, accidents and congestion, although none of these relationships are expected to be linear. In addition, if increased fuel prices cause drivers to move more slowly and carefully, this is also likely to reduce accident numbers, severities and costs. Impacts on visual intrusion and severance are likely to be small but beneficial as traffic flows fall. There may be some impacts on flora and fauna via reduced air pollution and road kills, and longer-term impacts on habitats via reduced global climate change potential (Royal Society for the Protection of Birds 1994).

Rising car fuel prices are likely to increase the demand for public transport via the cross-elasticities of demand between fuel prices and public transport demand. Acutt and Dodgson (1996b) show how the cross-elasticities are related to own-price elasticities, modal shares and diversion factors[1], and then derive cross-elasticity values between fuel prices and public transport for the six main public transport modes in Britain. These elasticities are relatively low.[2] In a recent paper, Wardman et al. (1997) review and estimate cross-elasticities for the inter-urban car–rail market. They find that while the cross-elasticities for car travel with respect to train cost are very low, rail demand is 'considerably more sensitive to variation in the times and costs of car travel' (p. 179). They suggest that this is in part due to the low market share of rail in the inter-urban leisure market. This increase in public transport use as a result of fuel price rises will lead to some relatively small increases in fuel consumption and emissions from public transport operators. Any increase must be weighed against the reductions from the private sector.

Differentiated fuel taxes can be used to encourage the use and purchase of certain types of vehicle over others. Differential taxes which affect the choice between diesel and petrol change the mix of emissions: petrol cars have higher nitrogen oxide emissions than diesel, much higher volatile organic compounds and carbon monoxide, but lower sulphur dioxide and much lower particulates.

Another example of such a fuel tax is the differential between leaded and unleaded petrol in the UK. A tax differential of 2.7 pence per litre was introduced in 1989 to encourage a switch to unleaded petrol. The differential has been increased steadily to a level of 4.8 pence from 1993 onwards. In 1989 unleaded petrol accounted for only 19 per cent of UK motor spirit (petrol) sales. This rose to 34 per cent in 1990, 53 per cent in 1993, and 63 per cent in 1995. The effectiveness of this price differential was enhanced by the ease with which cars could be converted from leaded to unleaded petrol and the high profile of green political campaigns in the UK at the time. The proportion of vehicles using unleaded petrol will also carry on increasing because of the mandatory fitting of catalytic converters on new cars, which require unleaded petrol.

Governments already tax road fuels and so while increases in tax rates are not likely to increase government costs, they will increase government tax revenue. (There is a theoretical possibility that tax revenue can fall when the rate of a tax rises because of the Laffer curve effect, where the effect of the reduction in demand for the taxed commodity outweighs the effect of the increase in the tax per unit sold. However, this requires a combination of high existing tax rates *and* medium to high price elasticities: consequently government net revenue will rise in practice.)

Transport users will be worse off as a result of a tax increase, although they do not suffer the psychological effect of a new tax. The impact on economic efficiency will depend on whether the new tax rate moves us closer to the optimum. The idea of using a fuel tax to combat the impact of global warming is that it moves society closer to the economically-efficient point where marginal benefits of activities equal the marginal social costs of those activities, although this point may be difficult to determine in practice. The increased tax will hit hardest those with the greatest use of fuel: these will tend to be the better-off members of society, although lower-income car travellers with particularly high use (such as lower-income households in rural areas with poor public transport) may be hardest hit as a proportion of income. Administrative complexity will be low because of existing fuel tax collection systems.

Emissions Taxes

A pure emissions tax represents a direct tax on the amounts of pollutants actually produced by vehicles. Such taxes are likely to encourage motorists to switch to less-polluting cars. Since they would increase the costs of car travel they could also be expected to reduce car-kilometres driven. They would increase kilometres travelled by public transport because of this decrease in car travel, but if applied to public transport modes would also increase the cost of travel by public transport if passed on in higher fares. The direction of their overall impact on public transport demand is therefore ambiguous. In so far as emissions are related to fuel used, they would also reduce the consumption of fuel. A successful emissions charging mechanism could be expected to reduce emissions by giving car owners direct incentives to change their vehicle or improve its maintenance. If the taxes increase car running costs then there would also be indirect impacts on traffic flows and hence on other environmental impacts of traffic.

The problem with pure emissions taxes is that it is difficult to devise an effective tax instrument, since similar vehicles may emit different levels of pollutants, and even the emissions of a given vehicle vary according to whether the engine is cold or has warmed up. Also the impact of emissions on health will vary with location. The German Council of Environmental Advisers proposed a system of charges that would be directly related to quantities of pollutants emitted: according to the British Royal Commission on Environmental Pollution (1994, p. 109) data on the use of a car during the year would be stored in an electronic engine management system, read out as part of the annual test on emissions and passed on to the tax authorities. The German Council had recognized that it would take a considerable time to develop the necessary technology, pass EC legislation to make it compulsory, and fit it to the fleet of vehicles. An alternative is to use differential fuel taxes to target particular emissions such as lead.

Consequently, effective emissions tax systems would be expensive to develop and implement. They should raise some revenue, although an effective system will be designed to encourage potential taxpayers to take actions, such as better maintenance and the use of less-polluting vehicles, which lower their tax liability. Therefore, the net impact on the public purse could be positive or negative. The financial impact on transport users and its impact on equity will be difficult to determine *ex ante*: higher-income households will generally own the larger cars, although there is an expectation that the older, more-polluting, vehicles may be owned by lower-income households. Economic efficiency should be improved by such schemes, although administrative complexity seems particularly high.

Variable Excise Taxes

At present in Britain the annual car licence does not distinguish between cars of different sizes, as it does in many other countries. However, the March 1998 Budget contained a proposal to reduce the annual car licence for small cars. If licence duties are to be differentiated by vehicle size their overall impact on car ownership would depend on whether or not they are revenue-neutral (a revenue-neutral tax change would involve adjusting the rates so that the total tax revenue remained unchanged although owners of larger cars paid more while owners of smaller cars paid less). Variable excise taxes are likely to encourage a shift to smaller cars. Since they do not affect marginal running costs they are not likely to have a direct impact either on car use or on public transport demand. Fuel use would be likely to decline with the switch to smaller cars.

Since these taxes are expected to reduce fuel use because of a switch to smaller cars, there will be equivalent reductions in carbon dioxide, as well as some reduction in other emissions. If overall demand for car travel is not expected to fall, there will be few other environmental consequences. Smaller cars might be quieter than larger ones, but a bit less safe for occupants in the event of an accident.

As with fuel taxes, an existing tax system will already be in place, although in some countries the system will need to be modified to distinguish between different types of car. The impact on tax revenue and hence on motorists will depend on whether the revised scheme is revenue neutral. If it is, lower-income motorists with smaller cars will benefit compared with those with larger vehicles. Economic efficiency should improve as the tax is adjusted to be more in line with the environmental consequences of different vehicles, while the administrative complexity of the scheme will be quite low, depending on how much modification is needed to the existing tax collection system.

Road Pricing

This has been recommended by economists for many years (see Newbery 1990), but despite many studies it has rarely been implemented. The area licensing system introduced in Singapore in 1975 is the major exception. By increasing the cost of car travel in urban areas congestion pricing might persuade some households to give up or reduce their car ownership. At first sight it would also reduce car kilometres travelled, although it is possible that some motorists might make longer trips to avoid charging zones. Public transport demand in urban areas is likely to increase as a result of the introduction of congestion charging schemes.

Table 6.2 Effects of environmental tax instruments

Policy	Effects on km by car	Effects on km by public transport	Effects on fuel consumed and CO_2	Effects on NO_x CO and VOCs	Effects on car ownership	Effects on traffic congestion	Effects on the public purse	Equity	Admin. complexity
Fuel tax	Reduce total	Increase total	Reduce total	Reduce total	Reduce total, move to smaller cars, possible earlier scrappage	Reduction	Increase tax revenue	Problems in rural areas	Low
Emissions tax	Small reduction	Ambiguous	Small reduction	Reduce total	Switch to less polluting cars	Very small reduction	Increase tax revenue, but high admin cost	Ambiguous	High
Variable excise tax	No direct impact	No direct impact	Reduce total	Small reduction	Shift to smaller cars	No direct impact	Unchanged if revenue neutral	Improvements	Low to medium
Road pricing	Reduction in priced area, but ambiguous in total	Increase total	Ambiguous, depends on effect on km driven	Ambiguous, depends on effect on km driven	Small reduction	Reduce in priced area, may increase elsewhere	Increase revenue, although high collection costs	Ambiguous	High

Schemes which reduce congestion (without generating extra trips elsewhere) do tend to reduce fuel use and carbon dioxide emissions, but they reduce carbon monoxide and volatile organic compound emissions by proportionately more because driving becomes smoother as congestion is reduced (Abbott et al., 1995, p. 34). Austin (1995, quoted in Maddison et al. 1996, pp.113–14) has estimated that optimal road pricing in London would lead to significant reductions in emissions. Traffic noise will be reduced in the priced areas as flows reduce and speeds improve. Accident numbers should fall as traffic flows become freer, although accident severities might increase as speeds rise. The most significant impact of road congestion charging should obviously be in reducing traffic congestion. Since congestion charging relates to urban areas it should not affect flora and fauna. Reduced traffic flows will reduce visual intrusion and community severance.

There has been considerable research work on the likely impact of road pricing, including detailed estimates of the costs of developing schemes for Electronic Road Pricing (ERP), and revenue projections (although the latter are dependent on estimates of the elasticity of demand for car travel in charged areas). These schemes are deliberately designed to improve economic efficiency, and it may be relatively straightforward to determine optimal traffic flows given engineering data on speed–flow relationships and operating cost formulae, together with estimates of the value of travel time. Given the strong political opposition to charging schemes, there have also been studies of the possible equity effects. These will depend in part on how good the alternative public transport systems are for those motorists with lower values of time who are 'tolled off' the system. The overall impact on equity will depend on the extent to which those with higher values of time actually benefit because they value the time savings from reduced congestion more than the charge they have to pay. The distribution of benefits will also depend on how the government spends its revenue surpluses. Despite the technological advances in electronic road pricing systems, administrative complexity is likely to be high.

CONCLUSIONS

This chapter has highlighted the importance of the transport sector, and road transport in particular, to UK environmental policy. Road transport is a significant contributor to a wide range of environmental problems, including global climate change, air pollution with more immediate health effects, noise, congestion and impacts on biodiversity. Valuation of these impacts is not straightforward, but is important for policy analysis. A number of studies have attempted to value these impacts, and as shown in Table 6.1, some degree of agreement regarding the ranges of values is possible. An important factor shown by these valuations is that marginal external costs differ significantly by the driver's location. This means that an instrument which could also differentiate by driver's location would be more equitable and efficient in resource allocation terms than one that cannot.

A number of policy instruments were analysed in detail against a range of policy assessment criteria, including transport-use indicators such as kilometres by car and public transport, environmental indicators and policy feasibility indicators. A summary of this analysis is given in Table 6.2. The analysis shows that the single most desirable policy discussed is fuel taxation. This is the only environmental policy which leads to an unambiguous reduction in car travel. Combined with this it also has the advantages of being relatively easy to administer, and of raising revenue, which could be used to reduce other, distortionary taxes elsewhere in the economy, and so provide a 'double dividend' in welfare terms. However, this policy is not necessarily the most effective one for all the environmental problems discussed. The fitting of catalytic converters on all new petrol cars is likely to be more effective in terms of reducing emissions of nitrogen oxides, carbon monoxide and volatile organic compounds.

Thus, it can be concluded that policies aimed at each environmental problem need to be assessed on a case-by-case basis, and that there may well be cases, such as the catalytic converter, where regulations requiring the use of certain technologies may be more effective than the broader tax instruments. Fuel taxes also have problems in terms of equity, as it would be difficult to differentiate them by location, and so could lead to problems in rural areas, especially as public transport is likely not to be a cost-effective alternative to car travel in areas of low population. Additionally, introduction of different local policy measures such as selective road pricing may be useful in order to reduce car travel in the most congested city areas. In these areas, with high population densities, public transport can provide a more cost-effective alternative to car travel.

NOTES

1. Modal shares refer to the relative share of travel undertaken on each of the two modes under consideration; and diversion factors refer to the proportion of any increase or decrease in travel on a mode, resulting from a price change, that is diverted from the other mode.
2. The estimates of the cross elasticities of demand for public transport with respect to the price of petrol for six public transport sectors are: InterCity: 0.094; Network South East 0.041; Regional Railways 0.091; London Underground 0.017; London buses 0.020; and other local buses 0.013.

REFERENCES

Abbott, P.G. et al. (1995), *The Environmental Assessment of Traffic Management Schemes: A Literature Review*, Transport Research Laboratory Report 174, Crowthorne: TRL.

Acutt, M.Z. and J.S. Dodgson (1994), 'A price-sensitive model for forecasting car emissions', Universities Transport Study Group Annual Conference, University of Leeds, January.

Acutt, M.Z. and J.S. Dodgson (1996a), 'Policy instruments and greenhouse gas emissions from transport in the UK', *Fiscal Studies*, **17** (2), 65–82.

Acutt, M.Z. and J.S. Dodgson (1996b), Cross-elasticities of demand for travel', *Transport Policy*, **2** (4), 271–7.

Commission of the European Communities (1995), *Towards Fair and Efficient Pricing in Transport: Policy Options for Internalising the External Costs of Transport in the European Union*, Com(95) 691 final, Luxembourg: Office for Official Publications of the European Communities.

Department of the Environment (1992), *Digest of Environmental Protection and Water Statistics*, London: HMSO.

Department of Trade and Industry (1995), *Energy Projections for the UK: Energy Use and Energy Related Emissions of Carbon Dioxide in the UK 1995–2020*, Energy Paper No. 65, London: HMSO.

Department of Transport (1996), *Transport Statistics Great Britain 1996*, London: HMSO.

Goodwin, P.B. (1992), 'A review of new demand elasticities with special reference to short and long run effects of price changes', *Journal of Transport Economics and Policy*, **26**, 155–69.

Houghton, J. (1996), 'Global warming: a scientific update', Royal Society Technology Lecture, 15 February.

Maddison, D., D. Pearce, O. Johansson, E. Calthrop, T. Litman and E. Verhoef (1996), *The True Costs of Road Transport: Blueprint 5*, London: Earthscan.

Mayeres, I., S. Ochelen and S. Proost (1996), 'The marginal external costs of urban transport', *Transportation Research D*, **1** (2), 111–30.

Nash, C. (1997), 'Transport externalities: does monetary valuation make sense?', in G. de Rus and C.A. Nash (eds), *Recent Developments in Transport Economics*, Aldershot: Ashgate, pp. 232–54.

National Economic Research Associates (NERA) (1997), *The Costs of Road Congestion*, London: NERA.

Newbery, D.M. (1990), 'Pricing and congestion: economic principles relevant to pricing roads', *Oxford Review of Economic Policy*, **6**, 22–38.

Newton, C.R. (1996), 'Forecasting Car Ownership', Liverpool Research Papers in Economics, Finance and Accounting 9606, Department of Economics and Accounting, University of Liverpool.

Peirson, J. and R. Vickerman (1998), 'The environment, efficient pricing and investment in transport: a model and some results for the UK', in D. Banister (ed.), *Transport Policy and the Environment*, London: Chapman & Hall, pp. 161–75.

Royal Commission on Environmental Pollution (RECP) (1994), *Eighteenth Report: Transport and the Environment*, London: HMSO.

Royal Commission on Environmental Pollution (RCEP) (1997), *Twentieth Report: Transport and the Environment – Developments Since 1994*, London: HMSO.

Royal Society for the Protection of Birds (1994), 'Transport and biodiversity: a discussion paper', RSPB, Sandy.

Tinch, R. (1995), *Valuation of Environmental Externalities: Full Report*, London: HMSO.

Vickerman, R. (1997), Personal Communication.

Wardman, M., J.P. Toner, and G.A. Whelan (1997), 'Interactions between rail and car in the inter-urban leisure travel market in Great Britain', *Journal of Transport Economics and Policy*, **41** (20), 163–81.

7. Economic incentives for the control of pollution: modelling tradeable permit systems[*]

Nick Hanley

INTRODUCTION

The purpose of this chapter is threefold. First, to introduce the idea of using tradeable permits to control pollution. Second, to review practical experience in using such systems, and to investigate why they have not been used more widely. Finally, to present some results from a modelling exercise, where we simulate the use of tradeable permits for the control of water pollution in a Scottish estuary, under both deterministic and stochastic conditions. This is the first such stochastic model in the literature. It is hoped, by the end of this chapter, that the reader will be convinced that permits offer a promising way forward in the development of environmental policy.

HOW TRADEABLE PERMIT MARKETS WORK

Pollution comes in many forms, but an important distinction for our present purposes is between uniformly and non-uniformly mixed pollutants. In the former case, the location of the pollution discharge is irrelevant in terms of polluting potential. For example, with reference to the greenhouse effect, whether one tonne of carbon dioxide is emitted in France or Britain does not really make a difference in terms of enhanced global warming. Many pollutants have this uniform mixing characteristic. In the latter case, the location of the discharge matters: for example, whether a coal-burning power station is located in the English Midlands or in Spain matters crucially in terms of the impact of SO_2 discharges into the atmosphere, and resultant acidic deposition in Scandinavia. In a more local

[*] This work is based on an Economic and Social Research Council (ESRC)-funded project 'Market mechanisms for the control of water pollution'. The project team was Nick Hanley (project leader); Professor Jim Shortle (Penn State University); Dr Alistair Munro (University of East Anglia); and Robin Faichney (University of Stirling).

context, the location of a paper mill on a river matters crucially in explaining the polluting potential of that mill, due to the effect of organic effluents on dissolved oxygen levels and fish mortality.

Uniformly Mixed Pollutants[1]

The major economic explanation for pollution is the absence of a sufficient set of private property rights in environmental resources. The main idea behind tradeable pollution permits (TPPs) is to allocate such rights, and make them tradeable. This results in the development of a market for the right to pollute, and consequently a market price for this right. Under certain conditions this price provides the correct incentive for dischargers to arrange emission levels, such that a cost-minimizing solution is reached. For a uniformly mixed pollutant, this involves an equality of marginal abatement costs (MACs) across polluters, since if one polluter could abate an additional unit more cheaply than another, then the same amount of abatement could be achieved at a lower cost. Let us see how this works out, considering first the simplest case, namely an assimilative, point-source, uniformly mixed pollutant: for example, carbon dioxide (CO_2) emissions from power stations. The control agency is concerned only with achieving a specified reduction in total emissions, irrespective of the locations of dischargers. Suppose current emissions from a region are 200 000 tonnes per year, and that the target reduction is 100 000 tonnes, leaving 100 000 tonnes of continuing emissions. The agency issues 100 000 permits, each one of which allows the holder to emit one tonne per year of CO_2. Discharges are illegal without sufficient permits to cover them.

These permits may be issued in one of two ways. First, they can be given away, perhaps *pro rata* with existing emissions. This process is known as 'grandfathering'. Second, they can be auctioned. Firms are then allowed to trade these permits. Assuming that the initial allocation does *not* conform to the least-cost one, we expect firms with relatively high MACs to be buyers, and firms with low MACs to be sellers. This is shown in Figure 7.1, where the horizontal axis measures both emissions and permits held by the firm. Before any intervention by the agency the firm is at e_p controlling no emissions. Suppose a TPP system of control is now introduced, and market price for permits of p^* is established. The firm will choose to hold e^* permits, since for any holding below this level, MACs lie above the permit price (it is cheaper to buy permits than to reduce emissions), but if the firm initially holds more than e^* (and thus can emit to the right of e^*), it will choose to sell, since the price it can get (p^*) exceeds the marginal cost of making permits available for sale by reducing emissions. A firm with higher costs of controlling pollution will wish to hold more permits given a permit price of p^*.

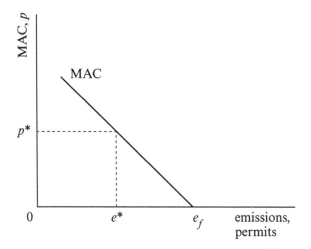

Figure 7.1 Marginal abatement costs and the efficient level of permit holding

Where does p^* come from? It is the equilibrium price in the permit market, as is shown in Figure 7.2. The agency issues a fixed number of permits, $\bar{E}$, (100 000 in this case). We know that each firm compares its MAC schedule with the permit price to decide how many permits to hold. If prices fall, the firm will hold more permits, and control fewer emissions. The MAC curve for a firm is thus its demand curve for permits, and so the aggregation of MAC curves across $i = 1, ..., n$ firms in the control region ($\sum_i MAC_i$) is the regional demand for permits. If the control agency increases or decreases the supply of permits then, given a particular demand curve, the market-clearing permit price will fall or rise, respectively.

The intuition behind the least-cost property of TPPs should now be clear. Each firm equates the permit price with its MAC schedule which, as explained above is a necessary condition for cost-minimizing abatement of a uniformly mixed pollutant. These reactions by firms move them to their cost-minimizing positions. Alternatively, we could view TPPs as a way of maximizing the reduction in emissions subject to a given total expenditure on abatement.

The total *financial burden* of the permit system to any individual firm will be composed of resource (that is, control) costs, the relevant area under MAC, plus transfer payments. In Figure 7.3, the financial burden for a particular firm is shown under three possible scenarios.

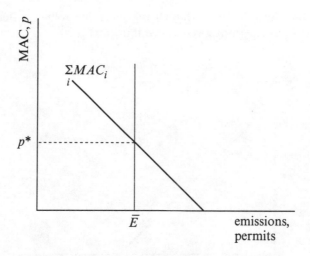

Figure 7.2 Determination of the market-clearing permit price

In (a), the firm must pay for all the permits it wishes to hold (say in an auction, where the declared single price is p^*). In (b), the firm is given some permits, but fewer than it requires for cost minimization, so it buys more from other dischargers. In (c), the firm initially receives more permits than it requires, and so sells some. It may be seen that the transfer payments (the shaded areas) for a given firm depend on the permit price and whether it is a net buyer or net seller (in all three cases, resource costs are as shown in Figure 7.3 (a)). For the industry, net transfers are zero under a grandfathering scheme, since revenue from sales cancels out permit expenditures in aggregate (unless the authority levies an administration fee). Under an auction, however, transfers leave the industry *en bloc*. Finally, in the case considered here (a uniformly mixed pollutant), it should be obvious that permits exchange at a rate of 1:1. If Bloggs sells 100 permits to Smith and Sons, then Bloggs must cut their emissions by 100 units, and Smith may increase theirs by 100. This is because control, as pointed out above, is aimed at total emissions, not their spatial location. As we shall see, this will not hold when we consider non-uniformly mixed pollutants. The main results of this section and the next are established more formally in the appendix.

Non-uniformly Mixed Pollutants

So far, it has been assumed that the pollutant of interest is uniformly mixed. Many pollutants, however, are non-uniformly mixed: for example, organic wastes discharged to a watercourse, and sulphur dioxide

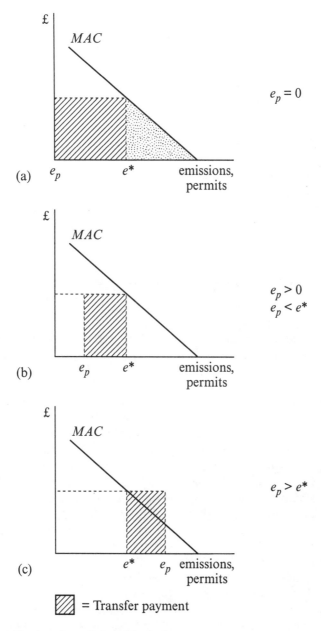

= Transfer payment

Note: e_p = Number of permits issued free to firm.

Figure 7.3 Transfer payments and resource costs under permits

discharged to the air. In this case, the control agency is interested in both the amount of discharges and their spatial distribution, since these two factors combine to determine the effect of the pollutant on ambient air or water quality at monitoring points. Using water or air quality models, transfer coefficients can be estimated which relate discharges at any point i to ambient air/water quality at some other point j. Pollution from each source i is now constrained by the maximum allowable concentrations at each monitoring point j. For the cost-minimizing solution each source's MAC will now be equal to the average of the cost of emission reductions needed to hit the various targets. Pollution from each source i is constrained by the maximum allowable concentration at each monitoring point j. This system of permits is known as an ambient permit system. For the cost-minimizing solution the MAC for each source will now be equal to the weighted average of the cost of emissions reductions needed to hit the targets.

EXPERIENCE WITH TRADEABLE POLLUTION PERMIT SYSTEMS

In many simulation studies (see, for example, the summary by Tietenberg 1994), TPP systems have been shown by economists to result in large (sometimes very large) cost savings over command-and-control regulatory alternatives. It is somewhat surprising, therefore, that greater use has not been made of TPPs in practice. By far the biggest application has been to stationary-source air pollution control in the United States. A number of schemes are in place, which might be categorized into early national schemes, recent national schemes, and local schemes.

The early national schemes followed on from compliance difficulties with the 1970 Clean Air Act, which established strict targets for improvements in a number of air quality measures throughout the USA. Partly as a means of avoiding the high costs of meeting these targets by conventional means, the US Environmental Protection Agency (EPA) initiated a number of TPP schemes, which were 'tacked on' to existing legislation. This began with the Offsets scheme in 1977, and was followed with the Bubbles, Banking and Netting schemes, known collectively as 'emissions trading'. These schemes involved trading in emission reduction credits (ERCs), which sources could acquire by reducing their emissions by more than was legally required of them at the time. The surplus reduction had to be enforceable, permanent and quantifiable to qualify as an ERC. Bubbles policies allowed trade in emission permits within an imaginary bubble created over a multiple-chimney industrial site. The success of the scheme has been debated, both in terms of cost savings and environmental improvement. Hahn (1989) found that most trades had been internal to companies, but that for the bubble policy alone savings of $435 million per annum were predicted. Tietenberg (1994), reviewing evidence on the cost savings of the schemes, states that 'the programme has unquestionably and substantially reduced the costs of complying with the Clean Air Act. Most estimates place the accumulated capital savings ... at over $10 billion' (p. 243).

The most recent national scheme to be launched in the USA is the Acid Rain Programme, announced in 1990. The goal of the programme is to reduce SO_2 emissions from large stationary sources by 50 per cent. Some 445 firms are involved in trading 'sulphur allowances', which are denominated in tons of sulphur. A free initial allocation of allowances was issued, based on historic emissions, while the EPA also holds an annual auction of surplus permits. Permit prices have now stabilized at about $100 per ton of sulphur, while emissions have fallen from about 10 million tons to about 5 million tons per year. Trading volumes were initially very small but have increased considerably. Some sources have reduced emissions by a lot more than the 'command-and-control' uniform rate, others by much less. Desulphurization equipment prices have fallen, and there is much evidence of cost-saving behaviour: overall, cost savings are estimated to be about $2 billion per annum (Burtraw 1997). However, while the scheme aims to control a non-uniformly mixed pollutant, there is no control over changes in the location of discharges due to trade. This may lead to the violation of localized critical levels for acidic deposition.

Local schemes for TPP markets in water pollution control have been much less successful in the USA. These include the now-redundant Fox River scheme for biological oxygen demand; and two small point–nonpoint trading schemes for the control of phosphate emissions. With reference to air quality, a large TPP scheme covering a number of pollutants has recently been launched in the Los Angeles district (the RECLAIM system), but no evidence is available yet on actual cost savings.

Why has wider use not been made of TPP schemes (they are largely absent outside the USA)? The answer probably lies in perceived problems in implementing permit schemes. These include worries over small markets, permit hoarding, and the exclusion of new entrants. In addition, economists have suggested that early predictions of cost savings may have been overoptimistic. Finally, some environmentalists and policy makers may be worried about leaving the allocation of pollution control responsibility to market forces (for a survey of impediments to trade in TPP markets, see Munro et al., 1995).

MODELLING TPP SYSTEMS: AN EXAMPLE

Model Construction

In this section, I present some results from a recent project concerned with modelling the use of TPPs to control biological oxygen demand (BOD) on the Forth estuary in Central Scotland.[2] BOD inputs are organic, and reduce dissolved oxygen (DO) levels in the estuary through microbial activity. DO is a crucial water quality parameter as far as fish are concerned, and a minimum DO level is necessary to permit the survival of, for example, salmon and trout. Major BOD sources in the estuary are chemical plants, paper mills, refining, yeast manufacture and sewage treatment. During the time period around which the model was constructed, summer DO levels 'sagged' below the minimum required to support salmon and trout (4.5mg/l). This sag still exists, although water quality has been slowly rising as more point sources install better control equipment.

Our modelling strategy was to combine a water quality model (MIKE 11) with a number of economic mathematical programming models to simulate a permit market in the estuary. MIKE 11 is a modelling system for rivers and channels produced by the Danish Hydraulic Institute. It has been used successfully to model estuaries and is also widely used for purposes ranging from flood prediction and control to waste water plant design. It consists of a number of modules, of which this project utilized the Hydrological (HD) and Water Quality (WQ) modules. The HD module was run first, to determine water movement, and then the WQ module, to determine the fates of the various dissolved and suspended substances. The model was calibrated using 1992 data.

MIKE 11 is a one-dimensional (cross-sectionally averaged) dynamic model, and as such was deemed suitable for this project largely because the estuary varies from being partially to well mixed, as opposed to stratified, thus one (longitudinal) dimension was likely to be sufficient. Tidal features were deemed likely to have a significant effect on water quality, requiring a dynamic as opposed to a steady-state model.

Developing the model involved the selection and testing of key parameters such as bed resistivity, diffusion coefficients and typical solar radiation, in order to calibrate it such that predicted values provided a good match to observations. The model predicts the double low and high tides characteristic of the estuary.

Given the fact that estuary DO drops significantly only during the first two-thirds of the summer, we chose a period of about three weeks during July 1992 to run the model under a 'worst-case' scenario. By cutting BOD inputs for each major point source, and holding all other inputs constant, it was possible to calculate the marginal effect of each source j's impact on water quality at defined points along the estuary (since MIKE 11 predicts water quality at a range of levels of spatial disaggregation).

In fact, these values vary to some extent over time, and we show here (Table 7.1) the mean of the daily values for each discharger at Reach 4 over the three-week period.[3] We present and use data for Reach 4 in this analysis since this reach is where the oxygen sag condition is critical for salmon migration. The values represent the milligrams per litre increase in DO resulting from a 100 kilograms per day reduction in BOD.

The economic models used were mathematical programming models. Two approaches were taken: first, where water quality is assumed to be deterministic, and second, where stochastic processes are explicitly allowed for. These two alternatives represent two different approaches to uncertainty in ecological–economic modelling. Uncertainty about the impact of BOD reductions on DO concentrations has at least two sources.[4] One is uncertainty about the physical processes governing the relationship between discharges and ambient concentrations. Hydrological models can reduce but do not completely eliminate this type of uncertainty. The second source is the inherent variability of natural processes, such as stream flow and temperature. With uncertainty about physical processes and natural variability, pollution control measures cannot be designed to achieve water quality targets exactly and continuously. Holding emissions constant, there may be times at which the targets are violated, and other times at which water quality exceeds the targets by a wide margin. Reducing the frequency or probability of violations would require tighter emission controls and higher control costs. One issue we examine is the trade-off between the probability of meeting standards and the costs of control. A second issue is the impact of the probability of meeting standards on the allocation of abatement across sources. Without uncertainty, least-cost control requires that emission reductions be allocated among sources to equalize the marginal costs of improving ambient concentrations. However, with uncertainty about the impact of emissions on ambient concentrations, the allocation of emission reductions among sources should take into account the relative risk associated with different sources. For instance, a source with low abatement costs may not be preferred to sources with higher costs if the uncertainty about the impact of emission reductions on ambient quality associated with the low-cost source is greater than the uncertainty associated with higher-cost sources (Shortle 1990).

Data required for this study are emission reduction costs and the impacts of emissions on the distribution of ambient concentrations by pollution sources in the estuary. The major anthropogenic sources of pol-

Table 7.1 Model parameters

Source	(Capacity 100 kg/day)	Marginal abatement cost (MC_i) (100 kg) $(\frac{mg}{a}/\frac{100\,kg}{day^a})$	Expected diffusion coefficient $(E(t_i))$	$\dfrac{MC}{E(t_i)}$	Coefficient of variation $(cv(t_i))$
Firm A					
(1)	$0 \leq a_b \leq 18.19$	288 800	0.0000707	4.08×10^9	2.36679
Firm B					
(1)	$0 \leq a_c \leq 1.34$	15 200	0.011775	129 0870	0.17180
(2)	$0 \leq a_c \leq 6.68$	60 800	0.011775	516 3482	0.17180
Firm C					
(1)	$0 \leq a_q \leq 35.17$	7 800	0.012326	632 808	0.16573
(2)	$0 \leq a_q \leq 70.34$	6 900	0.012326	559 792	0.16573
Firm D					
(1)	$0 \leq a_w \leq 2.60$	1 800	0.005659	318 077	0.27850
(2)	$0 \leq a_w \leq 5.20$	7 800	0.005659	1 378 335	0.27850
Firm E					
(1)	$0 \leq a_z \leq 6.85$	200	0.000419	477 324	0.93658
(2)	$0 \leq a_z \leq 17.12$	52 000	0.000419	1.24×10^8	0.93658
(3)	$0 \leq a_z \leq 34.24$	140 700	0.000419	3.36×10^8	0.93658

lution on the estuary were identified using data from the Scottish Environmental Protection Agency (SEPA). Pollution control costs from each source were obtained from a questionnaire and follow-up interviews. The BOD content of effluent is one of the most important items specified by SEPA discharge consents. The questionnaire was designed to elicit the cost of reducing BOD discharges.

The questionnaire posed a number of hypothetical situations, asking by what means, and at what cost, each firm's discharge of BOD could be reduced by given amounts over given timescales. Reductions of 10 per cent, 25 per cent, and 50 per cent over one year and five years were specified. Meetings with participating firms were used to discuss the objectives of the questionnaire and to help clarify any uncertainties. Most of the firms were very cooperative. In almost all cases, a cut within one year was not considered possible. We therefore focus on the longer time span. Even then, in some cases, not all levels of reduction were considered feasible. In two cases, levels other than those suggested in the questionnaire were given as the consequences of pollution control strategies either already being implemented, or most likely. Despite the willingness of some of the municipal authorities to cooperate, all of the sewage treatment works had to be omitted from the economic model because of insufficient economic information (these works were in any case smaller sources of BOD than the industrial sources).

Based on the survey of BOD sources in the estuary, marginal abatement costs for each step on the abatement cost function for each source are assumed to be constant, with the unit cost depending on the abatement capacity. Marginal costs and the capacities they apply to are reported in Table 7.1. Because of data limitations, only five of the eight sources are included. Total abatement cost in the actual simulation model is given by

$$c = \sum_{i} \sum_{j} c_{ij} d_{ij} a_i \qquad (7.1)$$

where

c_{ij} ≡ marginal abatement cost for source i with capacity j

d_{ij} ≡ $\begin{cases} 1 \text{ if capacity is type } j \\ 0 \text{ otherwise} \end{cases}$

a_i ≡ total abatement by source i

j = $\begin{cases} 1 \text{ if } 10\% \\ 2 \text{ if } 20\% \\ 3 \text{ if } 50\%. \end{cases}$

Model Results

The combined environmental and economic models were run under two different policy scenarios. These were uniform cuts in emissions (the regulatory approach); and a TPP market. We assume that such a market would reap all possible gains from trade between sources and achieve the least-cost solution. A range of target improvements in DO at the sag point were specified, ranging from 10 per cent to 49 per cent. This upper figure represents the largest feasible increase in DO according to our model. In each case, we present results for both the deterministic and stochastic cases. In the stochastic case, θ represents the probability of the target improvement being achieved, and it ranges in value from 50 per cent to 99 per cent. Table 7.2 gives details. Here, all costs are expressed relative to the cost of achieving a 10 per cent increase in DO under the deterministic, least-cost solution.

Economic policy towards the environment

Table 7. 2   Model results

Target[a]	Uniform regulation TC	Deterministic TC	Probabilistic	
			q (%)	TC
10%	7.35	1.00[b]	50	1.07
			75	1.08
			90	1.10
			95	1.18
			99	1.21
20%	18.23	2.04	50	2.11
			75	2.11
			90	2.13
			95	2.15
			99	2.23
30%	31.46	3.00	50	3.04
			75	3.05
			90	3.06
			95	3.08
			99	3.14
40%	47.26	3.92	50	3.96
			75	3.97
			90	3.98
			95	3.99
			99	4.04
45%	55.17	4.42	50	4.95
			75	4.99
			90	5.09
			95	5.19
			99	5.63
49%	61.49	7.07	50	7.35
			75	7.36
			90	7.38
			95	8.08
			99	29.56

Notes:
a. Increase in the three-week daily average DO level relative to the maximum feasible increase.
b. Costs are expressed relative to the cost of the least-cost allocation for 10% increase in the expected DO. The cost for this case is £120 256.2.

Four main points emerge from these results:

- The least-cost solution is significantly cheaper than uniform regulation in all cases. This is because, as Table 7.1 shows, existing MACs vary widely across sources.
- As the target improvement in DO increases, the cost savings implicit in the TPP alternative increase.
- The stochastic scenarios all imply higher costs than the deterministic scenarios.
- As the probability of hitting the target is increased, the cost of doing so rises also.

We have noted elsewhere (Shortle et al. 1997) that the least-cost solution under the stochastic case involves a different distribution of permits to that of the deterministic case. Moreover, differences in the reduction in the variance of DO achieved can also be noted between uniform regulation and the TPP market.

However, three very important caveats must be attached to these results. First, as noted above, we have assumed a perfectly competitive, full information permit market, which captures all gains from trade. In practice, actual costs under a TPP system will be higher than those shown, as imperfections will prevent the market from achieving all possible cost savings. These impediments include competition in the product market, transaction costs, sequential rather than simultaneous trading, and asymmetric information (see Munro et al. 1995, for further details). Second, we have not been able to formulate realistic trading rules which would mimic the outcome of the probabilistic TPP market, since this outcome is achieved by trading according to MAC differences, relative variances and co-variances between sources. Third, the actual regulation in the UK of discharges to water (under the consent system) is not a mirror image of uniform regulation; rather, regulators have been more flexible in their setting of discharge limits. This flexibility takes on board both differences in polluting impact (as measured here by transfer coefficients), and costs of achieving reductions in emissions. However, one should bear in mind that regulators do not aim to achieve the least-cost outcome through the consent system: their primary legislative duty is to achieve the greatest practicable improvement in water quality.

CONCLUSIONS

This chapter has outlined the basic theory of tradeable pollution permits (TPPs), and shown how they can achieve pollution control more efficiently than regulatory alternatives. We have also reviewed evidence of the operation of a few such schemes in practice. Two points emerged here: first, there are very few such schemes worldwide, and most that do exist operate in the USA for the control of air pollution; and second, that while cost savings seem to have definitely occurred, they are perhaps less than environmental economists were hoping for prior to the schemes' introduction. Finally, I presented some results from a modelling study which looked at the potential cost savings of introducing a TPP system for the control of BOD in the Forth estuary. This study includes the first explicit treatment of uncertainty within the environmental system in the literature. Results showed that potential cost savings were high, but until actual pilot schemes are set up to test out TPPs for water pollution control in the UK, the extent to which these potential cost savings can actually be realized remains uncertain.

NOTES

1. This section is adapted from Chapter 5 of *Environmental Economics in Theory and Practice*, by Nick Hanley, Jay Shogren and Ben White (Macmillan, 1996).
2. For full details on this modelling exercise, see Shortle et al. (1997).
3. The water quality model divides the estuary into stretches; each stretch is known as a reach. Reaches are of unequal length and are decided on hydrological and morphological grounds.
4. A third source of uncertainty is stochastic discharges. Discharges are often partly stochastic. Although stochastic emissions have received some attention in the literature (for example, Beavis and Walker 1983; Brannlund and Lofgren 1996), we do not address this issue here.

REFERENCES

Beavis, B. and M. Walker (1983), 'Achieving environmental standards with stochastic discharges', *Journal of Environmental Economics and Management*, **10**, 103–11.
Brannlund, R. and K. Lofgren (1996), 'Emission standards and stochastic waste-loads', *Land Economics*, **72**, 218–30.
Burtraw, D. (1997), 'A review of cost savings and performance in the US Acid Rain programme', Paper to the workshop on tradeable permits and joint implementation, University of Sussex, 1997; forthcoming in S. Sorrell and J. Skea (eds), *Tradeable Permits, Tradeable Quotas and Joint Implementation*, Cheltenham: Edward Elgar.

Hahn, R. (1989) 'Economic prescriptions for environmental problems', *Journal of Economic Perspectives*, **3**, 95–114.

Hanley, N., J. Shogren and B. White (1996), *Environmental Economics in Theory and Practice*, Basingstoke: Macmillan.

Montgomery, W. (1972), 'Markets in licenses and efficient pollution control programmes', *Journal of Economic Theory*, **5**, 395–418.

Munro, A., N. Hanley, R. Faichney and J. Shortle (1995), 'Impediments to trading in tradeable permit markets', Discussion Papers in Ecological Economics 95/1, University of Stirling.

Shortle, J. (1990), 'The allocative efficiency implications of water pollution control', *Water Resources Research*, **26**, 792–7.

Shortle, J., R. Faichney, N. Hanley and A. Munro (1997), 'Least cost pollution allocations for probabilistic water quality targets to protect salmon in the Forth Estuary', Paper to the workshop on tradeable permits and joint implementation, University of Sussex, 1997; forthcoming in S. Sorrell and J. Skea (eds), *Tradeable Permits, Tradeable Quotas and Joint Implementation*, Cheltenham: Edward Elgar.

Tietenberg, T. (1984), 'Marketable emission permits in principle and practice', Discussion Paper 123, Resources for the Future, Washington, DC.

Tietenberg, T. (1994), *Environmental Economics and Policy*, New York: Harper Collins.

APPENDIX 7A   PROOF OF THE LEAST COST PROPERTY OF TRADEABLE POLLUTION PERMITS FOR UNIFORMLY AND NON-UNIFORMLY MIXED POLLUTANTS

The original proof of the least-cost property of TPPs is due to Montgomery (1972), but our proof draws on Tietenberg (1984). Suppose that A represents the level of carbon dioxide (a uniformly mixed pollutant) emitted from the control region, and is given by:

$$A = \alpha + \sum (e_{fi} - x_i) \tag{7A.1}$$

where α is emissions from other sources including natural sources, e_{fi} are 'uncontrolled' emissions from $i = 1, ..., n$ polluting firms, and x_i are reductions in emissions. Firms face control costs C_i which depend solely on the level of emission reduction:

$$C_i = C_i(x_i) \tag{7A.2}$$

where $C_i(x_i)$ is a continuous, twice-differentiable function, with $C' > O$ and $C'' > O$. The control agency wishes to hold total emissions at or below some level $\bar{A}$, which is assumed to be less than the current total of discharges. The agency's problem is thus to:

$$\underset{(x)}{\text{Min}} \sum_i C_i(x_i) \tag{7A.3}$$

subject to:

$$\alpha + \sum (e_{fi} - x_i) \le \bar{A} \tag{7A.4}$$

and

$$x_i \ge 0. \tag{7A.5}$$

Constraint (7A.4) says that the sum of background emissions plus firm emissions net of reductions must be no greater than the desired maximum amount. Forming the Lagrangian:

$$L = \sum C_i(x_i) + \lambda [\bar{A} - \alpha - \sum (e_{fi} - x_i)]$$

Differentiating with respect to x_i yields the Kuhn–Tucker conditions for an optimum:

$$C'_i (x_i) - \lambda \geq 0 \tag{7A.6a}$$

and:

$$x_i [C'_i(x_i) - \lambda] = 0, i = 1, ..., n \tag{7A.6b}$$

$$\alpha + \sum (e_{fi} - x_i) \leq \overline{A} \tag{7A.6c}$$

$$\lambda [\alpha + \sum (e_{fi} - x_i) - \overline{A}] = 0 \tag{7A.6d}$$

$$x_i \geq 0; \lambda \geq 0 \; i = 1, ..., n. \tag{7A.6e}$$

From the above we can see that λ is the shadow price of the pollution constraint, which is only positive if the pollution constraint (equation 7A. 4) is binding. All firms MACs (given as $C'_i (x_i)$) must be equal to this value, although some sources may have control costs that are too high for them to enter into the least-cost solution (so that for this source, we would have $x = 0$).

For a permit market to achieve this outcome, we need to issue a permit supply of $\overline{E} = \sum(e_{fi} - x_i)$, since this is the permitted level of emissions. Permits will then trade at 1:1 rate between dischargers. This is known as an *emissions permit system* (EPS). Suppose each firm is given an initial allocation of $e^o{}_i$ permits, where $\sum e^o{}_i = \overline{E}$, and that a price of P is initially (arbitrarily) set for permits. The representative firm's problem is now to:

$$\underset{x_i}{\text{Min}} \; C_i(x_i) + p (e_{fi} - x_i - e^o{}_i). \tag{7A.7}$$

The solution to this problem implies:

$$C'_i (x_i) - p \geq 0 \tag{7A.8a}$$

$$x_i [C_i(x_i) p] = 0 \tag{7A.8b}$$

$$x_i \geq 0. \tag{7A.8c}$$

Comparing these equations with (7A.6a–6e) we can see that the least-cost solution will be replicated if the price p is equal to λ, which it will be if the permit market is competitive (see Montgomery 1972).

Admitting non-uniformly mixed pollutants changes the nature of the cost-minimization problem, by changing the pollution constraint. Ambient pollution concentration at any point j is given by:

$$A_j = \alpha_j + \sum d_{ij} (e_{fi} - x_i) \qquad (7A.9)$$

where α_j is pollution from other sources arriving at point j; and the d_{ij} terms are the transfer coefficients. The problem now is to:

$$\text{Min} \sum C_i (x_i)$$

subject to:

$$\alpha_j + \sum d_{ij} (e_{fi} - x_i) \leq \bar{A}_j$$

where A_j are the maximum allowable pollutant concentrations at each point j. Assuming for simplicity that all sources do some controlling (that is, that $x_i > 0$, $\forall i$), then the Kuhn–Tucker condition of interest is:

$$C'_i (x_i) - \sum d_{ij} \lambda_j = 0 \qquad (7A.10)$$

so that each source's MAC is equal to the weighted average of the shadow cost of emission reductions needed to hit the targets. Put another way, there is now a shadow price (λ_j) at each monitoring point, so that we have moved away from the simple 'equalize MACs' rule that was relevant in the uniform mixing case.

8. Environmental policy, firm location and green consumption

Michael Kuhn

INTRODUCTION

The problem that firms may relocate from countries with relatively strict environmental regulation has become a top priority on the agenda of policy makers, executives and economists. In many European countries suffering from high unemployment this issue is considered to be of crucial importance since the emigration of firms would cause a further reduction in employment. On the other hand, it is feared that countries may loosen their environmental regulation in order to retain their local industry and attract foreign investment. As this incentive prevails in all countries, the outcome is likely to be a so-called race to the bottom: countries undercut each other's environmental standards or taxes down to the lowest possible levels, implying a deterioration of environmental quality everywhere. The trade-off between a healthy environment and a flourishing economy seems to become a huge stumbling block on the way towards effective environmental policies and the obvious question is: is there any reason to believe that the prospect of firms relocating as a result of environmental policies and environmental regulation racing to the bottom is less serious than it looks at first sight?

Let us begin with the observation that by relocating from one country to another a firm usually incurs a substantial cost. If this is greater than the net cost of complying with the stricter environmental policy a firm will not relocate. However, the compliance cost reduces profitability. In the extreme, the firm is forced to leave the market and so is a loss to the regulating country in any case.

Yet this is not the end of the story. In recent years, more and more markets have witnessed the advent of environmentally benign variants of products. Given the existence of green consumption behaviour, a firm may use the employment of clean production methods as a selling argument. By serving the 'green' share of the market the firm effectively differentiates its product from the traditional variants, which are produced in a polluting manner. The firm then enjoys a monopolistic margin, allowing it to set a mark-up on price. This in turn offsets at least part of the higher production cost and thereby mitigates the loss of competitiveness and/or profitability. The firm may then remain in the market even when complying with the relatively strict regulation. If governments take into consideration the preferences of green consumers, the tendency towards a race to the bottom is also reduced, creating a potential for unilateral environmental policy action.

The rest of the chapter is organized as follows. The next section takes up the issues of firm relocation in reaction to asymmetric environmental regulation and the race to the bottom problem by briefly reviewing some theoretical and empirical results. The third section deals with green preferences, how they may be motivated and how they influence firms' strategies. In the fourth section, I outline a model which shows the conditions under which firms maintain a clean production technology rather than relocate in reaction to unilateral regulation and under what conditions environmental regulation is feasible. The final section concludes.

ENVIRONMENTAL POLICY AND FIRM LOCATION: A BRIEF OVERVIEW

The questions as to how firms' location choices are affected by environmental regulation and how this feeds back into policies has been discussed extensively in the theoretical literature (for example, Markusen et al. 1993 and 1995; Motta and Thisse 1994; Ulph 1994; Kanbur et al. 1995; Rauscher 1997a; Bouman 1997).[1] The following is a summary of the main spirit of the literature rather than an exhaustive review.

Markusen et al. (1993) develop a two-firm–two-country model, in which the number and location of the firms' plants is determined endogenously. One country's environmental tax rate is varied unilaterally to study the effect on market and location structure. The results show that firms adjust their output and location to changes in the tax rate. Numerical results show that the trade-off between environmental damages and the domestic firm's profits in the welfare function requires a deviation of the welfare-maximizing tax rate from the Pigovian level.[2]

Motta and Thisse (1994) incorporate set-up costs into a similar setting. Their argument is that firms usually are not 'footloose' in their location decision but rather have a plant located in one of the countries before a revision of environmental policies occurs. Opening a new plant in the course of relocation gives rise to the set-up cost which is already sunk for the abandoned plant in the former host region.[3] If the set-up cost is sufficiently large, the firm will refrain from relocating in reaction to a regulatory measure which increases marginal cost. Additionally, Motta and Thisse consider a trading cost or a barrier to trade blocking the export of products back to the former home market, which can essentially be interpreted as implicit costs of relocation. In any case the cost increase due to regulation reduces the home firm's competitiveness and market share and – if strong enough – drives the firm from the market.

How do these results relate to the race to the bottom problem? In Markusen et al. (1995), two regional governments non-cooperatively set emission tax rates.[4] Thereby they influence the decision of a monopolist on the number and location of plants. The governments maximize domestic welfare depending on domestic consumption, the tax revenue and local pollution damage. The outcome depends on the marginal disutility of pollution. If it falls short of some boundary value, governments have an incentive to mutually undercut each other's tax rates, trying to induce the monopolist to open a single plant in their region only. A race to the bottom occurs, where tax rates are too low and pollution levels are too high *vis-à-vis* the cooperative outcome. Yet, if disutility of pollution is sufficiently high the so-called 'not in my backyard' (NIMBY) result obtains, where regions engage in a 'race to the top'. By trying to keep out the polluting firm they overbid their tax rates. In equilibrium, the firm does not enter the market at all, and welfare is lower than in the cooperative case. Both the race to the bottom and the NIMBY result can be seen as a prisoner's dilemma situation, where the regions' failure to cooperate leads to Pareto-inefficient results. By cooperatively setting their taxes, both regions would increase their welfare. Rauscher (1997a) arrives at a similar result, adding the insight that the race to the bottom result is due to a second-best setting. Governments try to tackle two goals, attraction of the firm and internalization of pollution damage, by means of only one instrument, the emission tax rate. Rauscher shows that the first-best policy involves using a subsidy to attract the firm and charging the Pigovian tax rate. However, in the real world, where free trade institutions such as the General Agreement on Tariffs and Trade (GATT), the World Trade Organization (WTO) or the European Union (EU) or North American Free Trade Agreement (NAFTA) treaties limit the use of direct subsidies as a means of trade policies, environmental policies can be seen as a second-best alternative. Rauscher also shows that in the case of transboundary pollution a race to the bottom will be more likely. Since pollution becomes external to a region's welfare, attracting the firm remains the sole objective.

A general shortcoming of the above models is that they do not allow for the possibility that some consumers may be willing to pay a premium on environmentally friendly methods of production. The opportunity to sell a green variant may serve as an important counterbalance to reloca-tion.[5] We will come back to this in the fourth section. Finally, it is worth mentioning that the race-to-the-bottom result is very sensitive to the objective function being maximized by local governments. In particular, the weights attached to the different interest groups' welfare components will govern the outcome.[6] This brings to the forefront the public choice issue of regulatory capture: how do different interest groups influence a self-interested politician's or bureaucrat's choice of environmental poli-cies.[7] The old insight that production side interests are usually better organized and thus more influential than consumption side interests sug-gests that regulatory levels may be too low, a fact only recently highlighted by Krugman (1997).

Are these arguments backed up by empirical facts? This question is not easily answered, since the available evidence covers only the effect of environmental regulation on firms' plant locations within the USA. Jaffe et al. (1995) survey a number of studies, most of which find no significant effects of environmental regulation on domestic (US) siting choices. These results hint at the fact that wage rates, general tax rates, the supply of public services and agglomeration economies as determinants of siting choices by far override the importance of environmental regulation. Hence, the US data on the firm level does not support concerns about firms' evasion of environmental policy by means of relocation.[8] In a study on the impact of environmental policies on direct foreign invest-ment (DFI) by German industry, Bouman (1996) arrives at a different conclusion. He estimates the impact of German and foreign wage rates, the real exchange rate and two alternative measures of emission-abatement cost on German DFI. He uses sectoral data and a Seemingly-Unrelated-Regressions model, which allows for differences in the sectoral coefficients. Bouman reports a significant and positive impact of abate-ment cost on DFI for a number of sectors, for example, mechanical engineering, chemicals, and food and beverages.'[9] This seems to indicate that in a number of important sectors firms relocate in reaction to a tightening of regulation. In the light of our question a shortcoming of the study is that the aggregated data conceal individual firms' behaviour as well as the destination of DFI. In summary, empirical evidence does not suggest a definite conclusion on whether environmental regulation induces relocation. Nor is it possible to conclusively evaluate whether races to the bottom are a relevant phenomenon.[10] At the least it seems fair to say that there are forces counterbalancing firms' tendency to relo-cate from countries with relatively strict regulation, so that a massive outflow of capital does not occur. On the other hand, environmental regulation may simply not yet have become sufficiently strict so as to induce substantial relocation.

CAUSES AND CONSEQUENCES OF GREEN CONSUMERISM

Let us start with the trivial observation that households' utility depends positively on environmental quality. This immediately brings up two questions which are less trivial. How do consumption goods relate to environmental quality, and why do consumers engage in green consumption behaviour? The former question can be restated in the following way: what constitutes 'environmental friendliness' of a consumption good? As we do not require an exact definition, we are content with describing a good as (relatively) environmentally friendly if it is associated with (relatively) low levels of negative externalities (pollution) during the stages of its life: production, transportation, consumption, recycling and disposal. Acknowledging that this description lacks an appropriate aggregation of externalities and does not relate them to the lifetime of the product, thus ignoring the important notion of durability, we observe that it captures one central aspect with regard to the motivation of green consumption behaviour: 'environmental friendliness' relates to low levels of negative externalities.[11]

This has a crucial implication for green consumerism, as it gives rise to a social dilemma: an individual can, in general, not expect to noticeably influence the aggregate pollution level by his or her consumption behaviour.[12] Thus a consumer will not take into consideration the impact of his or her consumption choice on pollution. Suppose that the private net benefit (marginal utility less price) derived from consuming one unit of an environmentally friendly product is lower than the net benefit derived from consuming one unit of its harmful counterpart. This assumption seems justified in many cases, as quite often the environmentally friendly variants of products are more expensive or provide less benefit.[13] In this case no consumer will engage in green consumption. However, when this private loss from green consumption is less than the loss in welfare associated with pollution from the non-green good, this outcome is inefficient. If green consumption took place as collective action the aggregate pollution level would fall measurably and everybody would enjoy a benefit in excess of the 'cost' of green consumption.

The individuals' failure to cooperate justifies a political solution. For example, an appropriate subsidization (taxation) of green (non-green) products would create a net gain from green *vis-à-vis* non-green consumption and thus enhance green consumption. However, our aim is to explain why green consumerism takes place even in the absence of governmental policies. Recall the assumption that consumption of a green product yields a lower net benefit to the individual than consumption of a non-green product. While this assumption is crucial for the existence of a social dilemma, it can by no means be taken for granted. Suppose that consumption of an environmentally friendly product generates an extra benefit large enough to turn the net loss of green *vis-à-vis* non-green consumption into a net gain. Then there exists a private incentive to engage in green consumerism and the social dilemma is overcome.

Just what does this extra benefit look like? Recall that it has to be unrelated to a reduction of the externality, which consumers do not expect to influence. Being necessarily private, the benefit may be of a physical, monetary or psychological nature. Examples for the former two types of benefit are abundant. Many goods produced in an environmentally benign manner are also of a higher physical quality. For example, food or textiles originating from organic farming are not only characterized by comparatively low externalities in production but also by a low content of harmful substances. Handcrafted as compared to manufactured products are often associated with relatively low degrees of emissions and/or energy intensity as well as with a relatively high quality in a general sense. The use of energy-efficient consumer durables adds the private benefit of a reduced energy bill to the public benefit of saving energy.

The psychological benefits from green consumption relate to intrinsic motivation or social rewards. An intrinsically motivated individual derives benefit from behaving in what he or she perceives to be the morally correct way.[14] The individual will exhibit such behaviour independent from the attitudes or actions of others. In the case of social rewards the benefit from consuming green products depends on whether the individual complies with or deviates from a social norm.[15] Green consumption behaviour will then occur only if it is honoured by society or at least by the social group to which the individual belongs.

Usually only a certain proportion of consumers are willing or able to buy an environmentally friendly product. If a trade-off exists between environmental friendliness and some other quality feature of a given product, the green variant will be bought only by consumers who rank environmental friendliness – or the psychological benefit from green consumption behaviour – higher than the other quality feature. Thus, there exists no unambiguous ranking of product variants, giving rise to horizontal product differentiation. For both a green and a non-green variant there would be a positive demand if they were offered at an equal price not greater than the consumers' reservation price. On the other hand, if environmental friendliness is an additive feature to a product, with all other quality features being fixed, consumers unambiguously rank the green variant higher. This is the case of vertical product differentiation: if both variants were offered at the same price only the green variant would be bought. However, whenever the green variant is offered at a higher price than the non-green variant, some consumers with a relatively low income or a low benefit from environmental friendliness buy the latter.[16]

In a setting of product differentiation firms compete not only by setting prices or quantities but also by choosing the degree of environmental friendliness of their product. As each consumer has a most preferred degree of environmental friendliness according to his or her preferences (horizontal or vertical differentiation) and his or her income (vertical differentiation) the differentiated variants are only imperfect substitutes. Substitutability is therefore greater the closer variants are in terms of environmental friendliness. Conversely, the producers' monopolistic profit margin increases with the degree of product differentiation. Thus firms have an incentive to differentiate products in order to avoid the erosion of profit due to price competition. This is why in an unregulated market one would expect to find green and non-green variants of products, which conforms to reality. A literature has developed that applies models of vertical differentiation to environmental economics (Motta and Thisse 1993; Cremer and Thisse 1994; Constantatos and Sartzetakis 1995; Moraga-González and Padrón-Fumero 1997), with the general message that environmental policies have side effects on market structure and market size.[17] These secondary effects may enhance, neutralize or even reverse the intended impact of environmental policies.[18] Moreover, an evaluation of welfare must now include the extra benefit derived from green consumption, as well as profits, basic consumer surplus and disutility from pollution. The choice of welfare-maximizing environmental policies must allow for a trade-off between the above components of welfare, so that environmental policy instruments will usually not be set to Pigovian levels. Again this is due to a second-best setting, where two inefficiencies – the externalities and the monopolistic profits – are tackled with a single environmental policy instrument.

While 'green' preferences are revealed by the existence of 'eco' variants on a number of markets, evidence is scarce as to the importance of green consumerism. A study by Couton et al. (1996) on the French car market reports a significant positive influence of quality and environmental characteristics on prices, which reflect consumers' valuation of these characteristics. Survey data reported in Hemmelskamp and Brockmann (1997) seem to indicate that a relatively small proportion of consumers is indeed willing to pay a surcharge for environmentally benign products. However, the authors express some scepticism on the importance of this green market potential. In any case, there is a need for further empirical studies on green consumption behaviour in order to evaluate its importance.

A MODEL OF ENVIRONMENTAL POLICY, FIRM LOCATION AND GREEN CONSUMERISM

Linking the issues discussed in the previous two sections, I shall now outline a model that studies the effects of environmental policies on duopolists' location and technology choices, while it allows for green consumption behaviour.[19] Additionally the feedback on countries' environmental policy choices is analysed. To keep matters as simple as possible, what follows is an informal presentation of the model. A formal version is presented in Kuhn (1997).

The Model

Two firms choose their location in one of two regions. The regions form a single market in which the firms sell a single commodity.[20] Production takes place either with a clean (green) or a polluting (non-green) technology. Employing the green technology causes an additional fixed cost *vis-à-vis* the non-green technology, which for instance, relates to some fixed end-of-pipe technology or Research Development (R&D) in low emission technologies. The pollution caused by non-green producers harms households and possibly other firms located in the same region, but there are no transboundary spillovers. Local governments are assumed to have the legislative power to control pollution by setting an environmental standard, which effectively prohibits the non-green technology.

Consumers, evenly partitioned between the two regions, may buy either one or zero units of the commodity according to the price charged. Thereby, a certain share of (green) consumers, exhibit a willingness to pay (WTP) for environmentally friendly methods of production. The WTP amounts to an extra benefit from green consumption which is unrelated to pollution damage. It may be of a psychological (social rewards or intrinsic motivation) or physical nature (higher overall quality of the green product). The green consumers' WTP for environmental friendliness is reflected in their readiness to pay a higher price for the green variant. None the less, they only buy the green variant if the price surcharge *vis-à-vis* the non-green variant does not exceed their WTP. Non-green consumers, who are not willing to pay a premium for clean production,[21] always buy the cheaper variant, given that its price falls short of the utility derived from consumption, which is assumed to be equal for all consumers. The heterogeneous behaviour of consumers determines consumer surplus and the demand functions faced by the firms. Both consumer surplus and demand are dependent not only on the prices charged by the firms but also on the technologies employed. Note that with regard to the green variant, consumer surplus not only contains the surplus from consumption but also the extra benefit obtained by green consumers. Obviously, these features constitute the vertical differentiation character of the model.

Consider the following game, which captures the interdependence of environmental policy and the firms' location and technology choices.[22]

In the first stage of the game the local governments revise their environmental policies so as to maximize local welfare, consisting of the aggregate profits of firms located in the region and local consumers' surplus less local environmental damage. Thereby, each government takes into consideration the decision of the other region and the expected reaction of firms.

The next two stages of the game concern firm competition. Each firm maximizes profit by choosing a strategy that consists of technology, location and price. The choice is contingent on the regions' policies and the competitor's strategy.

In stage two of the game, firms simultaneously choose their location and technology. Thereby, we assume that at the outset each region hosts one firm. As the set up cost, net of the fixed cost of green production is sunk at the historical location, relocation will, other things being equal, reduce a firms profit.[23] A firm's choice of technology has a double impact on profit. On the one hand, the fixed cost may be saved by choice of the non-green technology. On the other hand, the technology chosen has an impact on operating profit via demand, market price and variable cost. Note that the rival's technology affects a firm's operating profit also, by having a likewise influence on demand and market price.

In the third stage of the game, the stage of market competition, firms maximize operating profit by setting prices, while taking as given their own and competitor's technology as well as the demand functions they face. The game can be solved recursively by applying the criterion of subgame perfection and working by backward induction.[24]

Equilibrium Quality and Location Structure

The equilibrium of stages two and three can be derived contingent on the environmental policies and the structural parameters as given by the share of green consumers, their WTP for green production methods, the fixed cost of green production and the relocation cost. Let us assume values for the structural parameters which, in the absence of regulation, would give rise to the equilibrium in which both firms produce with the polluting technology and maintain their location from the outset. With firms' optimal strategies so defined, we may ask how firms react to different constellations of environmental policies. The two cases of bilateral *laissez-faire*, that is, neither region having a standard, and bilateral regulation are trivial. In the first case, both firms choose the polluting technology and in the second, the standards enforce clean production in both regions.[25] Relocation occurs in neither of the cases.

Now let us consider unilateral regulation. We find that a firm will not relocate if, other things being equal:

1. the relocation cost is sufficiently high relative to the fixed cost of clean production,
2. the share of green consumers is positive, albeit not too large, and
3. their WTP for environmental friendliness is sufficiently high.

The economic intuition behind the result is as follows. The firm in the region without a standard always maximizes its profit by choosing the polluting technology. The firm which is confronted with a domestic standard has the following choice. It may either relocate, switch to the non-green technology and thus become a competing non-green producer or it may stay, maintain the green technology and thus become a monopolistic green producer. The firm chooses the strategy that yields the greater profit. First, consider the profit realized when the firm decides to relocate. It decreases in the cost of relocation, and increases in the fixed cost, which is saved when switching to the non-green technology. This relationship determines condition (1). Now consider the profit realized when the firm decides not to relocate. As a monopolist the firm is able to take full advantage of green consumers' WTP. Thus the green monopolists profit unambiguously increases in WTP, which determines condition (3). According to the various influences just described the profit realized by relocation is smaller than the profit realized by becoming a green monopolist whenever conditions (1) to (3) are satisfied.

A positive level of relocation cost and a strictly positive share of green consumers turn out to be necessary conditions for the non-relocation result. If relocation were absolutely costless a firm could maximize profits by relocating and switching to the polluting technology, while becoming a green monopolist is always second best.[26] As the existence of green consumers is a prerequisite for product differentiation and thus the monopolistic margin, it is evident that a positive share of green consumers is a necessary condition for non-relocation. Surprisingly, a strictly positive WTP for environmental friendliness is a necessary condition for non-relocation only if the relocation cost is small relative to the cost of clean production. This can be explained as follows. If relocation is very costly relative to green production, even an infinitesimal margin will prevent the firm from relocating. We may summarize with:

Result 1: Relocation from a region with unilateral regulation will be less likely the greater the cost of relocation and the greater the green market potential.

Finally, we should notice that history may play an important role in determining the equilibrium technology and location structure. If at the outset of the game neither region has imposed a standard both firms produce with the non-green technologies as their first-best. The game then proceeds as described above. However, things may look different if both regions have historically imposed a standard. Then, both firms have introduced the green technology at the outset of the game. Now, the outcome depends on whether the fixed cost of the green technology is sunk or not. If it is not sunk the game proceeds as before. However, there are good reasons to believe that the cost of green production is sunk, for example in the case of R&D in clean technologies or investment in some long-term abatement capital. In this case neither a switch back to the non-green technology nor relocation take place under unilateral or bilateral deregulation. In a type of hysteriesis incumbent firms continue to produce with the green technology even though they would not do so when entering the market. In a setting in which entry does not take place, a readjustment of environmental policies then becomes irrelevant. To make the following section on policies interesting let us thus suppose that neither region has imposed a standard at the outset so that relocation may occur.

Equilibrium Environmental Policies

Let us now turn to the two regional governments' environmental policy decisions, which are contingent on the above-mentioned market parameters, the cost of relocation and the (negative) impact of pollution on household utility. The general conclusion is that bilateral *laissez-faire* is, other things being equal, less likely

1. the greater the damage impact,
2. the greater the share of green consumers,
3. the greater their WTP for environmental friendliness,
4. the smaller the fixed cost of the green technology, and
5. the greater the cost of relocation.[27]

Our finding that *laissez-faire* by both regions is less likely the greater the disutility of pollution, corresponds to the results found in the homogeneous good models of Markusen et al. (1995) and Rauscher (1997a). We find that the green market potential has an additional limiting effect on the likelihood of bilateral *laissez-faire* in that a government accounting for the private benefits from green consumerism will consequently be less in favour of such a policy. Note that for sufficiently low levels of pollution impact, bilateral *laissez-faire* is, however, the efficient outcome. We must be careful not to interpret this case as a harmful race to the bottom. If disutility from pollution is at a minor level and consumers do not care too much about the existence of green products, there is no reason for governments to prevent firms from using the cheaper, albeit non-green, technology. For relatively high levels of pollution impact, both regions impose a standard. Asymmetric equilibria, in which a single region regulates, exist only if a firm does not relocate to the region without a standard.[28] This is intuitively clear, since a unilateral standard would imply a substantial loss of welfare if the firm relocated. The existence of asymmetric equilibria, which are always Pareto efficient, is highly policy relevant. This finding strongly qualifies any general claim as to the infeasibilty of unilateral environmental regulation in a global economy. Finally, for intermediate values of damage impact and certain combinations of the other structural parameters, both inefficient bilateral regulation and inefficient races to the bottom are possible. We may summarize with:

> *Result 2*: Green market potential has a negative impact on the likelihood of bilateral *laissez-faire*. If relocation does not occur, unilateral regulation may be an equilibrium for intermediate values of damage impact. Inefficient bilateral regulation and races to the bottom cannot be excluded.

Let us conclude with a caveat. When deciding on environmental policies governments trade-off the interests of producers, consumers and pollution victims, all of which are included in the regional welfare function. This takes us back to the welfare weights involved. While this issue has not been addressed in the model, a public choice view may also suggest a bias towards deregulation in this framework too.

CONCLUSIONS

We have enquired into the issues of whether firms have an incentive to relocate into regions with relatively lax environmental regulation and whether this may lead to a race to the bottom in environmental policies. A look into the literature shows that neither problem can be dismissed on theoretical grounds, while there seem to exist some forces counterbalancing firms' incentives to relocate (set-up costs, trading barriers) and governments' tendency to engage in a race to the bottom (disutility of pollution, availability of a second instrument). A public choice perspective hints at a certain likelihood of suboptimal levels of regulation. The empirical evidence is ambiguous. Whereas US studies mostly reject the hypothesis that environmental regulation has an important influence on firms' plant location (within the USA), a recent European study concludes that sectoral German DFI can be explained by pollution-abatement expenditures.

So far the literature on firm location has ignored the existence of a green market potential which may have a limiting effect on producers' tendency to evade environmental regulation. In order to make this case, I identify some motivations for green consumerism. Since an individual consumer does not expect to influence the aggregate pollution level, he or she does not account for it in his or her consumption decision. Hence it becomes crucial that a physical, monetary or psychological extra benefit goes along with green consumption in order to offset the associated cost. In reality we should expect a certain, albeit small, share of consumers to exhibit green consumption behaviour. This gives rise to product differentiation on behalf of firms, where environmentally benign product variants are introduced into the market in order to achieve a monopolistic margin. In such an 'environmentally differentiated' oligopoly environmental policy necessarily not only has direct effects on environmental targets but also affects market structure and aggregate demand. Empirical evidence as to the relevance of green consumerism is too scarce to be considered conclusive.

Finally, I outline a two-country–two firm game that integrates the issues of firm location, green consumerism and environmental policy. The results indicate that green market potential serves as a counterbalance to a firm's incentive to relocate from a region with unilateral regulation. However, existence of a relocation cost becomes a necessary condition for relocation not to take place. Green market potential also reduces the regional governments' incentive to engage in mutual deregulation and, if sufficiently large, opens a potential for unilateral regulation.

NOTES

1. While the literature dealing with firms' location choices is microeconomic in spirit there exists a parallel macroeconomic line of literature on capital movements and environmental policies. For an overview, see Kuhn and Tivig (1996).
2. Readers not familiar with environmental economics may observe that the Pigovian rate of an environmental tax must be set so as to equalize marginal damage (cost) of pollution = marginal cost of abatement = tax rate. In this case an (economically) efficient level of pollution will be obtained, where the cost of abating a further unit of pollution just equals the damage avoided.

3. The sunk cost relates to any type of irreversible investment, such as investment in specific equipment, in R&D or in the creation of goodwill. In the given case it is important to separate sunk costs on the firm and on the plant level, where relocation implies only the latter.

4. The tax rate may be differentiated between goods for domestic consumption and export goods.

5. Markusen et al. (1993) and Bouman (1997) allow for product differentiation but not with regard to the method of production which is the relevant characteristic in this case.

6. In this context it is interesting that even though the issue of unemployment plays a dominant role in the debate on environmental policy and relocation, this has not fed back into models, which are most prominently of a full-employment type. For an exception, see Rauscher (1997a).

7. To the best of my knowledge this issue has not been discussed in connection with firms' location choices. For a model of regulatory capture involving trade and the environment, consult Rauscher (1997a).

8. For Germany, anecdotal evidence suggests that long-lasting regulatory decision making and stringent standards have had a vast negative impact on the siting decisions of biotechnical firms.

9. Surprisingly, he also finds significant negative coefficients, for example for mineral oil refining, non-ferrous metal production or mining. He suggests that in highly concentrated sectors the abatement-cost figures may reflect *ex-post* rather than *ex-ante* measures, which would give rise to the negative dependency.

10. Anecdotal evidence for Germany indicates that in the last few years the government has postponed or abolished a number of ambitious environmental policy projects by referring to their negative impact on Germany's competitiveness and attractiveness for foreign investment. Reference was also made to the low regualtory levels in other European countries, for example, the UK.

11. This is not quite in line with ecological economics, which would refer, rather, to a low throughput of natural resources and/or energy as being central for 'environmental friendliness'. See, for example, Daly (1991).

12. Neither can he or she expect to influence aggregate material or energy flows in the ecological economics scenario. The consequences for green consumption behaviour are the same, so that environmental and ecological economics are reconciled at least in this respect (see note 1).

13. For example fuel-efficient cars generally have a lower top speed, environmentally friendly garments are not so colourful, and reusable food containers have to be collected and carried back to the shop.

14. For a survey on such forms of (impure) altruistic behaviour, see Rose-Ackerman (1996).

15. For a general model, see Holländer (1990), for an application to environmental economics, see Rauscher (1997b).

16. For an introduction into models of product differentiation, consult Tirole (1988).

17. This literature is based mainly on the older and in a sense more mature literature on the effects of minimum quality standards, for example, Ronnen (1991).

18. For a discussion on how policies which are designed to limit the emissions caused by a consumption good may increase the aggregate emission level, see Moraga-González and Padrón-Fumero (1997).

19. The model is based on a framework by Ecchia and Mariotti (1994).

20. Since an integrated market requires neither trading costs nor barriers to trade there are no spatial price differences. Hence, neither firm enjoys any sort of spatial monopoly power.

21. This is not to say that non-green consumers do not care about pollution. However, they have no incentive to engage in green consumption since they derive no extra benefit from it.

22. Readers not familiar with game theory may consult Gibbons (1992) or Tirole (1988) for an introduction. I shall restrain my reference to specialist language to a minimum, making the argument accessible for outsiders. Game theory is the apppropriate tool for modelling strategic interaction between players. In our case we look at strategic interaction between three pairs of actors: the two governments – the setting of optimal

environmental policies contingent on the policy choice of the other government, the governments and firms – the location and technology choices contingent on environmental policies, and the firms – competition by choice of location, quality and price.

23. Indirect types of relocation cost may also be considered. Assume, for example, that a non-green producer causes pollution damage not only to households but also to other firms located in the same region. The damage incurred by a firm that relocates into a region hosting a polluter; can then be interpreted as the cost of relocation. In Kuhn (1997) this type of relocation cost is considered too.

24. Define a (Nash) equilibrium as a set of strategies from which no player has an incentive to deviate, when taking as given the strategies of the other players. Then subgame perfection essentially means that an equilibrium of the overall game requires equilibrium behaviour for all subgames, that is for all possible contingencies in the successive stages of the game, whether actually realized or not.

25. Note that negative profit levels are ruled out by appropriate assumptions. While the case of a firm leaving the market because of a loss of profitability is thus excluded from analysis, the results found for the case in which both firms are in the market, are unaffected.

26. In the case of set-up costs, relocation would occur if the set-up cost were not sunk in the former host region. This corresponds, for example, to plant-siting decisions coming along with an expansion of production activity or with the replacement of economically or technologically obsolete equipment.

27. Condition (5.) is relevant only if firms would actually relocate in reaction to unilateral regulation.

28. There exist two symmetric equilibria with unilateral regulation.

REFERENCES

Bouman, M. (1996), 'Do pollution abatement costs induce direct foreign investments? Evidence for Germany', Mimeo, Tinbergen Institute and University of Amsterdam.

Bouman, M. (1997), 'Fixed pollution abatement costs, market structure and the location of industries', Mimeo, Tinbergen Institute and University of Amsterdam.

Constantatos, C. and E.S. Sartzetakis (1995), *Environmental Taxation when Market Structure is Endogenous: The Case of Vertical Product Differentiation*, Milan: Fondazione ENI Enrico Mattei: nota di lavoro 76.95.

Cordella, T. and I. Grilo (1995), '"Social dumping", and delocalization: is there a case for imposing a social clause?', Louvain: Center of Operations Research and Economics (CORE) Discussion Paper 9504, Louvain.

Couton, C., F. Gardes and Y. Thepaut (1996), 'Hedonic prices for environmental and safety characteristics and the Akerlof effect in the French car market', *Applied Economic Letters,* **3**, 435–440.

Cremer, H. and J.-F. Thisse (1994), *On the Taxation of Polluting Products in a Differentiated Industry*, Milan: Fondazione ENI Enrico Mattei: nota di lavoro 31.94.

Daly, H.E. (1991), 'Elements of environmental macroeconomics', in R. Costanza (ed.), *Ecological Economics. The Science and Management of Sustainability*, New York: Columbia, pp. 32–46.

Ecchia, G. and M. Mariotti (1994), *Market Competition and Adoption of 'Green' Technologies in a Model with Heterogeneous Consumers*, Milan: Fondazione ENI Enrico Mattei: nota di lavoro 52.94.

Gibbons, R. (1992), *A Primer in Game Theory*, Hemel Hempstead: Harvester Wheatsheaf.

Hemmelskamp, J. and K.L. Brockmann (1997), 'Environmental labels – the German "Blue Angel"', *Futures*, **29**, 67–76.

Holländer, H. (1990), 'A social exchange approach to voluntary cooperation', *American Economic Review*, **80**, 1157–67.

Jaffe, A.B., S.R. Peterson, P.R. Portney and R.N. Stavins (1995), 'Environmental regulation and the competitiveness of U.S. manufacturing: what does the evidence tell us?', *Journal of Economic Literature*, **33**, 132–63.

Kanbur, R., M. Keen and S. van Wijnbergen (1995), 'Industrial competitiveness, environmental regulation and direct foreign investment', in I. Goldin and A. Winters (eds), *The Economics of Sustainable Development*, Paris and Cambridge: OECD and Cambridge University Press, pp. 289–302.

Krugman, P. (1997), 'What should trade negotiators negotiate about?', *Journal of Economic Literature*, **35**, 113–17.

Kuhn, M. (1997), 'Going "green" or going abroad? Environmental policy, firm location, and green consumerism', in H. Folmer and N.D. Hanley (eds), *Game Theory and the Environment*, Cheltenham: Edward Elgar, (forthcoming).

Kuhn, M. and T. Tivig (1996), 'Ecological dumping and environmental capital flight: the economics behind the propaganda', Universität Konstanz: Sonderforschungsbereich (SFB) 178 Working Paper, Series II, No. 324.

Markusen, J., E.R. Morey and N. Olewiler (1993), 'Environmental policy when market structure and plant locations are endogenous', *Journal of Environmental Economics and Management*, **24**, 69–86.

Markusen, J., E.R. Morey and N. Olewiler (1995), 'Competition in regional environmental policies when plant locations are endogenous', *Journal of Public Economics*, **56**, 55–77.

Moraga-González, J.L. and N. Padrón-Fumero (1997), 'Pollution linked to consumption: a study of policy instruments in an environmentally differentiated oligopoly', Madrid: Universidad Carlos III de Madrid, Working Paper 97–06, Economics Series 02.

Motta, M. and J.-F. Thisse (1993), *Minimum Standards as Environmental Policy: Domestic and International Effects*, Milan: Fondazione ENI Enrico Mattei: nota di lavoro 20.93.

Motta, M. and J.-F. Thisse (1994), 'Does environmental dumping lead to delocation?', *European Economic Review*, **38**, 563–76.

Rauscher, M. (1997a), *International Trade, Factor Movements and the Environment*, Oxford: Clarendon Press.

Rauscher, M. (1997b), 'Voluntary emission reduction, social rewards, and environmental policy', University of Rostock: Thünen-Series of Applied Economic Theory, Working Paper No.10.

Ronnen, U. (1991), 'Minimum quality standards, fixed costs, and competition', *RAND Journal of Economics*, **22**, 490–504.

Rose-Ackermans, S. (1996), 'Altruism, nonprofits, and economic theory', *Journal of Economic Literature*, **34**, 701–28.

Tirole, J. (1988), *The Theory of Industrial Organization*, Cambridge, MA: MIT Press.

Ulph, A. (1994), 'Environmental policy, plant location and government protection', in C. Carraro (ed.), *Trade, Innovation, Environment*, Dordrecht et al.: Kluwer, pp.123–63.

9. Environmental regulation: uncertainty and threshold effects in the case of biodiversity

Purificación Granero Gómez[*]

INTRODUCTION

The aim of environmental policy is to deal with environmental degradation processes which result from activities such as resource extraction, production, consumption, waste disposal, and so on. Environmental policy tries to influence agents who carry out these activities, with the use of a wide range of instruments. The conventional economic approach of environmental policy requires the authority to control environmental externalities up to the point at which the marginal control cost equals the marginal damage. As explained in Chapter 7 of this book, economic instruments offer incentives for polluters to equalize their marginal abatement costs. This achieves pollution reduction at the lowest aggregate cost.

In order to achieve the optimal level of externality, an authority may choose among the available instruments. In a context of perfect knowledge the choice is arbitrary, since the optimal level can be attained precisely by emission taxes, emission subsidies, tradeable permits (economic instruments[1]) or emission standards (a command-and-control regulation). The former class tries to influence behaviour indirectly by altering the incentive structure the economic agents or the polluters face in the market. The latter, on the other hand, specifies mandatory action such as placing limits on certain activities, or use of specific technologies. In the case of more than one agent, this specification has to be 'tailored' for the emission standard to be efficient.

In the real world, environmental policy must be designed and implemented under conditions of uncertainty. In this setting, the objective of

[*] For his very helpful comments on earlier versions of this chapter, the author owes a special debt to John Bowers. The author also thanks Melinda Acutt, Pamela Mason, Diego Azqueta and an anonymous referee for their valuable comments and suggestions. The usual disclaimer applies.

environmental policy is not the theoretical optimal level of externality, but rather a predetermined target. Moreover, the choice of policy instrument is no longer arbitrary, but can influence the effectiveness of policy.

Uncertainty is a fundamental feature of most, if not all, environmental problems, in that the effects of actions upon the environment and the costs of environmental degradation are imperfectly known. An additional factor is the existence of cumulative or stock effects and threshold values, which may cause degradation processes which leading to irreversibilities. The accumulation over time of flow externalities (such as CO_2, SO_2 emissions, excessive resource exploitation, and so on) results in stock externalities (greenhouse gases accumulation, acid rain, resource depletion, and so on). When the stock reaches the threshold level, then irreversible and possibly unacceptable damage can be incurred, such as climate change, resource exhaustion and species extinction. The implications of ecological discontinuities are discussed in detail in Chapter 11.

The regulation of environmental problems is subject also to uncertainty regarding the performance of the various instruments. Instruments may fail to attain the objectives because of imperfect detection where regulations are violated, and because of inadequacy of the administrative and legal infrastructures which support implementation and enforcement.

Hitherto, the literature has treated environmental and instrumental uncertainty separately, and moreover has treated these uncertainties separately from the existence of stock externalities and threshold effects.[2] The purpose of this chapter is to analyse how the joint presence of both uncertainties and the existence of threshold effects will affect the design of environmental policy and the choice of appropriate instruments. This chapter relates to the problem of biodiversity loss to illustrate the analysis, since biodiversity conservation suffers from both uncertainty and threshold effects. The second section briefly reviews a set of criteria commonly used to appraise environmental policy instruments. The third addresses the role of efficiency and cost effectiveness for instrument choice under uncertainty and threshold effects. The following section extends the analysis to the environmental effectiveness criterion and examines the implications of instrument failure. The implications for instrument choice derived from uncertainty over time and its problems are then analysed, and a final section concludes.

CRITERIA FOR INSTRUMENT CHOICE

The literature on the choice of instruments has been concerned mainly with the relative advantages and disadvantages of economic instruments and direct controls. Within economic incentives, the literature has focused on the relative merits of price controls versus quantity controls. There are various criteria (Bohm and Russell 1985; Panayotou 1994; Barde 1995) according to which choices among instruments can be made. These can be applied both to targets identified as being economically optimal, and to those set on scientific or political grounds.

Cost effectiveness

If agents under regulation are cost minimizers, then economic instruments will lead to the least (abatement) cost in achieving the environmental objective by allowing the market to allocate the given target among the polluters. This allocation takes place according to the varying abatement costs so that those with higher costs abate less and those with lower costs abate more (Montgomery 1972; Baumol and Oates 1988). For direct controls to be cost-effective the regulator has to do what the market does in the incentive approach, and this requires complete information about abatement costs.

Both taxes and tradeable permits are cost-effective instruments and under perfect information, ought to produce equivalent results. However, under a criterion of informational requirements, permit systems will be preferred to charge systems since a correctly set charge would have to be at the precise level which equates marginal abatement costs at the required level of abatement (Tietenberg 1990). Under a charge system, the regulatory authority either must have perfect information regarding control costs, or must initiate a *tâtonnement* process in which the initial charge level is adjusted in response to the reactions of regulatees. Likewise, while under perfect information taxes and permits have no advantage over direct controls, under uncertainty, the establishment of direct controls may involve delays. These result from the time lag between the establishment of a regulation and the observation of its effects, and could impose large costs on regulatees.

In general, informational requirements for designing cost-effective instruments increase when the damage caused to the environment varies across the sources of pollutants, when different pollutants are regulated and where pollution damage varies across sites. This is true for direct controls as well as for economic incentives.

Flexibility

There are two respects in which a policy instrument can be flexible. The first relates to the freedom of regulatees to choose the most cost-effective way to comply with the regulation, and is an intrinsic characteristic of economic instruments. The flexibility of direct controls varies, with emissions standards being more flexible than technological standards. The second relates to the ease with which, in the face of exogenous changes (economic and/or natural), instruments can adjust automatically in order to keep environmental targets unaltered. Under this criterion when, for example, changes in abatement costs are likely, quantity instruments are preferred to price instruments. Under variations in the number of regulated agents, only the quantity instrument of tradeable permits can maintain environmental quality. On the other hand, instruments such as environmental quality standards reflect changes in environmental conditions. For instance, when natural conditions worsen, but the environmental standard remains unchanged, regulatees are subject automatically to more stringent requirements.

Dynamic Incentives

Instruments can be judged on the extent to which they provide incentives to develop and to adopt more efficient abatement technologies. Instruments which allow firms to choose how to comply with regulations may induce agents to innovate, particularly where compliance is costly. Under this criterion, charges and permit systems are favoured over direct controls since compliance costs are constituted not only by the costs of abatement, but also by payment for the actual level of emissions. Under direct controls, the only compliance cost is that of abatement, so there is no incentive to innovate in order to reduce emissions further. However, if designed carefully, direct controls could also encourage innovation. For example, if the object of regulation is the overall environmental quality of a product or process, this could induce more innovation than a requirement to install a certain technology.

Cost of Implementation

Implementation of regulation necessitates transaction costs, so that the adequacy of an instrument should be judged on both compliance costs and implementation costs (administrative, monitoring and enforcement costs).[3] Different instruments involve different basic monitoring and enforcement costs. However, regulation expenses are also largely determined by the nature of the problem in question, the regulator's administrative capacity and characteristics of the regulatees (Panayotou 1994). Nevertheless, consideration of this criterion will favour those instruments that imply self-compliance and decentralization of monitoring and enforcement activities (for example, deposit refund systems where purchasers have an incentive to return containers and retailers an incentive to monitor returns).

Revenue Capacity

The main purpose of policy instruments is the correction of market failures. However, their revenue-generating capacity can contribute to their desirability. Revenues may be used to cover administrative costs, avoiding the need for government support. They may also be used to generate a welfare gain by reducing the distortions of non-lump-sum taxes. This is the double-dividend hypothesis. Under this criterion, economic instruments such as charges and non-granted tradeable rights are preferred to direct regulations, whose revenue-generating capacity is limited to administrative fines and penalties.

Equity

The distributional effects of instruments may also be assessed, in terms of the allocation of costs and benefits among involved agents. If there are socially regressive impacts, measures to mitigate and/or compensate for them should be adopted. The problem, however, cannot be treated *ex post* when future generations are affected. In setting policy objectives, problems involving intergenerational equity should be handled *ex ante*.

Environmental Effectiveness

The most important criterion on which an instrument must be judged is its ability to attain the environmental objective. The effectiveness criterion will therefore favour those with the minimum risk of failure, while acknowledging that no instrument will achieve the objective with certainty. This criterion is particularly important in cases of irreversible damage where deviations from the objective are unacceptable.

Other criteria mentioned in the literature are: acceptability, conformity with international agreements, predictability, simplicity of implementation, and ease of integration with other policies affecting the same economic sectors. The above discussion has shown that while some criteria may lead to the same choice of instrument, others may involve trade-offs. The assessment of economic and command-and-control instruments does not, therefore, give an unambiguous conclusion. Their relative desirability has to be established on a case-by-case basis. The relative weights given to each criterion in the selection of instruments will usually be politically motivated, at least in part.

UNCERTAINTY, THRESHOLD EFFECTS AND ENVIRONMENTAL IRREVERSIBILITIES: THE CASE OF BIODIVERSITY

Biodiversity refers to the variety of genes, species and ecosystems. The extent of current loss of biological resources and the existence of multiple pressures on them are putting their diversity at risk. The irreversible loss of biological resources may impose a high cost if they are crucial components of the life-support system. This loss can be particularly serious if the resource performs a unique function. In defining a policy aimed at avoiding the risk of such loss, the particular characteristics of biodiversity have to be considered.

Two main characteristics of biodiversity are its intertemporal nature and uncertainty. The uncertainty surrounds both its economic value and its ecological characteristics. These factors contribute to a problem of intergenerational equity since the uncertain costs of biodiversity use will be borne, to a great extent, by future generations. Two factors which are central to the problem of biodiversity loss are, as noted by Hanemann (1988), the degree of risk aversion and intertemporal preferences, both of which can be expressed by the discount rate. The tendency towards excessive depletion of biological resources is enhanced by the fact that future costs are either highly discounted, or not considered. The degree of risk aversion is important because a more risk-averse attitude would cause greater weight to be attached to potentially irreversible losses. This would lead to more conservative use of biological resources. Since uncertainty relating to biodiversity may be reduced over time, there is a (risk) premium attached to activities which allow for the possibility of new information. Therefore one can assume, as in the following analysis, that a higher degree of risk aversion will favour conservation.

Biodiversity Uncertainty and Instrument Choice: The Criterion of Efficiency

The first implication of uncertainty is that the regulator will have imperfect, if any, information about costs and benefits of biodiversity loss. In this situation, price- and quantity-based instruments may not produce equivalent outcomes. Weitzman (1974) shows that if policy is set when environmental damage costs are uncertain then neither type of policy will produce the desired level of environmental protection. In this case, however, each policy will be wrong to the same degree, as the relevant economic agents will equate the price or quantity imposed by the regulator with their marginal abatement cost (MAC) schedules; so provided the agents are economic optimizers, either policy will produce the same outcome.

However, if it is control costs that are uncertain then the outcomes from the two policies will differ. This is because, as in the case of environmental uncertainty, firms know their own MAC schedules and equate the imposed price or quantity with their true MAC – rather than the MAC estimated by the regulator. In this situation a quantity-based instrument will result in the given level of biodiversity use, whereas the price (or control costs) will be uncertain and will depend on the location of the true MAC. Implementation of a price-based instrument, on the other hand, will determine prices, while the quantity will vary, again depending on the location of the true MAC. The preferable instrument can be identified by the relative slopes of the MAC and marginal environmental cost (MEC) schedules. Price-based instruments are preferred to quantity-based ones when the slope of the MAC curve exceeds that of the MEC curve. Likewise, quantity-based instruments are preferred to price-based ones when the slope of the MAC curve is lower than that of the MEC curve.

Weitzman's analysis adopts an *efficiency* criterion by minimizing the expected welfare loss from deviations from the realized or *ex-post* optimum. It also assumes that both instruments are cost-effective[4] and, once in place, are not easy to revise on the basis of new information. If biodiversity use is mainly subject to uncertainty about its environmental costs, then neither instrument is preferred to the other. When, on the other hand, control costs are uncertain, the implications for instrument choice are not clear since Weitzman's findings apply when uncertainty represents an information gap between the regulator and the regulatee (that is, a case of asymmetric information) rather than a lack of information faced by both (Laffont 1977). This second situation, where neither party has the relevant information, can be argued to be closer to the case of biodiversity, where control costs must include both the costs from taking specific actions and the uncertain forgone benefits from controlling its current use.

When both environmental and control costs are simultaneously and correlatively uncertain, the preferred instrument depends on a number of factors, among them environmental cost uncertainty. This may alter the previous result which was based solely on the relative slopes (Stavins 1996). This reinforces the implications of the previous paragraph and, therefore, no a *priori* statement can be made about the most appropriate instrument for biodiversity conservation. In sum, the efficiency criterion gives no clear guidelines regarding instrument choice in an uncertain setting. This conclusion is strengthened when the threshold characteristic of biodiversity is considered below.

Threshold Effects and Irreversibility: The Cost-effectiveness Criterion

The potential irreversibility of biodiversity loss comes from the existence of thresholds or critical values for populations of organisms and biogeochemical cycles beyond which the ecosystem loses its resilience and self-organization. See Chapter 11 for a more detailed discussion of resilience and other ecological constraints. A marginal change in the quantity or quality (mix of species) of the existing diversity in the neighbourhood of the threshold may generate irreversible losses, for example species extinction, which imposes a social cost. Even in the case of certainty, the existence of thresholds and thus the risk of irreversibilities, affects the definition of the optimal policy for biodiversity conservation. This is depicted in Figure 9.1, which shows the marginal environmental cost of biodiversity use (MEC) and its marginal net private benefit (MNPB). The MNPB can be interpreted as the marginal control cost since, for biodiversity loss, the only way to reduce damage is to reduce its use, so control costs are simply the benefits forgone.[5] The MEC curve has a point of discontinuity reflecting the existence of a threshold (q_d^*).

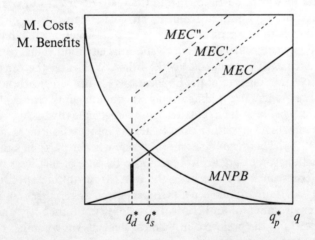

Figure 9.1 Optimal use of biodiversity and threshold

At the optimal biodiversity use (q^*_s), the marginal net private benefit is equal to the marginal environmental cost or, in other words, the marginal social cost and the marginal social benefit are equal. This takes place on the left of the optimal private use (q^*_p), but on the right of the threshold. This is caused in part by the fact that the MEC curve does not include the future costs from irreversibilities, which will be suffered mainly by future generations. Therefore, the *efficient* solution does not guarantee the conservation of biodiversity.[6] Since the cost of passing the threshold is, although uncertain, assumed to be enormous, the maximization of the net social benefit by a high risk averse agency implies a biodiversity use defined by the point of discontinuity (q^*_d). Figure 9.1 depicts the case in which the threshold value is known with certainty. The solid MEC curve represents the worst-case scenario, in which the optimal or efficient policy does not guarantee sufficient biodiversity conservation, when this requires not crossing the threshold value. It could be that increased knowledge means that crossing the threshold implies a larger perceived increase in current costs. If this results in the marginal cost curve becoming MEC' or MEC" in Figure 9.1, then the application of the efficiency criterion does result in sufficient conservation. However, the conclusions regarding the potential inadequacy of this criterion still hold in the case in which the threshold value is itself uncertain.

The case in which the true value of the threshold is unknown will be referred as *static uncertainty*. In this case, biodiversity conservation requires a target for restriction on its use so that given existing knowledge, the minimum stock and diversity necessary for safeguarding ecosystem resilience are maintained. This is not necessarily an argument in favour of command-and-control instruments. The standards may be achieved either by direct controls or indirectly by economic incentives. The preferred policy depends only on the marginal control costs or, in our case, the marginal net private benefits. If these are known with certainty then, as noted above, either instrument can achieve the target cost-effectively. However, if they are imperfectly known then either the target is not achieved or it is achieved at a cost greater than the least cost. The former occurs when a price instrument is set and the latter in the case of quantity constraint.[7] If actual control costs or benefits from biodiversity use are greater than expected, a tax system will lead to higher use of biodiversity than required by the target, although the outcome will be produced at minimum cost. If actual control costs become lower than expected, on the other hand, a tax system will guarantee a greater control of biodiversity use at minimum cost. Given the uncertain value of the threshold and the risk of irreversibilities from passing it, the fact that a tax system can lead to biodiversity use exceeding the target, becomes a strong argument for preferring a direct control (or other quantity instrument). Indeed, the certainty of the effects of direct regulations is one of their most important advantages (see Nicolaisen et al. 1991). It derives from the fact that restrictions are directly imposed instead of, as with economic instruments, left to the cost-minimizing behaviour of regulatees.

STATIC UNCERTAINTY AND RISK OF INSTRUMENT FAILURE: ENVIRONMENTAL EFFECTIVENESS

Certainty regarding the outcome of direct regulation rests implicitly on the assumption that all instruments are effective. However, the fact that all instruments, even if properly implemented, have a risk of failure means that the result may not hold. We have already identified one source of instrument failure, namely uncertainty about the threshold value or static uncertainty.[8] Static uncertainty requires the design of a constraint which incorporates a safety margin, allowing for the possibility that the threshold value is at a lower level of use than is currently thought.

Even when the threshold value is perfectly known, instruments may fail if compliance is imperfect because of flaws in monitoring and enforcement activities (Russell et al. 1986). This means that the risk of passing the threshold comes both from uncertainty surrounding its value and from the risk of instrument failure. Because of the potentially high costs associated with irreversibilities, *environmental effectiveness* becomes the crucial criterion in the establishment of a policy for conservation of biodiversity. Since the effectiveness of a policy can only be checked *ex post*, this criterion is required to minimize the risk of failure. This risk can be reduced by using *safety margins* (Bowers and Young 1995) in the setting of both the target (standard or constraint) and the level of the control instrument.

To sum up, static uncertainty and risk of instrument failure provide an essential criterion for the choice of instruments for biodiversity conservation: the *minimum risk of failure criterion*. This criterion is none other than the cost-effectiveness criterion when a new meaning is attached to cost in the presence of risk of failure. If the chosen instrument fails to meet the standard and irreversibilities take place, high costs would be incurred. Assuming that no instrument is 100 per cent effective and treating the cost of failure as large, the allocatively efficient measure is that with the lowest risk of failure (Bowers 1994).

The argument (for example, Perrings and Pearce 1994, p. 23) that direct (quantity) controls are safer than economic (price) incentives because the penalty imposed on those resource users who exceed the standard changes the shape of the private cost function, is not clear. This is because the use of *ex post* measures such as penalties or administrative fines is not intrinsic to command-and-control instruments. 'The fact that no single instrument is perfect as a policy tool suggests the possibility that efficiency may be enhanced through the simultaneous use of multiple instruments' (Segerson 1996, p. 154). These multiple instruments may encompass not only direct regulations and liability, but also economic incentives and liability and even direct controls and economic incentives. The successful implementation of both economic and direct control or *ex-ante* instruments requires some kind of sanction to enforce their compliance.

Command and Control: Risk of Failure and Safety Margins

The control system under direct regulation consists of the announcement of a maximum use level of biological resources (q_{st}) plus a penalty (F) in the case of non-compliance. Assuming that (i) the penalty is an administrative fine, so that there is need for neither prosecution nor conviction, and (ii) it is a uniform function (f) of the violation size, the regulatees under the system will face the following payment structure:

$$0 \quad \text{if} \quad q < q_{st}$$
$$p(M)p(D)f(q - q_{st}) \quad \text{if} \quad q > q_{st}$$

where q is the actual use level, $p(M)$ is the probability of monitoring and $p(D)$ is the probability of detection conditional on the committal of a violation. The payment is zero in the case of compliance and in the case of non-compliance the expected penalty $E(F)$ is equal to the total penalty (F), times the probability of monitoring $p(M)$ times the probability of detection $p(D)$. The total penalty is the penalty per unit of resource use (f) times the violation size ($q - q_{st}$).

Once the standard or consented level of biodiversity use has been declared, the control variables of the regulatory system are $p(M)$, $p(D)$ and the penalty per unit of violation f. The authority can set them so that the desired degree of compliance and safety margin are reached. Since monitoring is not costless and instruments and techniques for violation detection are imprecise and imperfect (Bohm and Russell 1985), there exists a practical constraint to setting those probabilities at one. This means that the expected penalty is likely to be lower than the actual penalty, that is $E(F) < F = f(q - q_{st})$. Despite this constraint, the system has some degrees of freedom given by all other possible values of monitoring and detection probabilities and those allowed for the penalty by the legal system.[9] To ensure compliance the expected penalty must exceed the net private benefit for each level of biodiversity use above the permitted level.

$$p(M)p(D)f(q - q_{st}) > NPB(q), q > q_{st}.$$

The safety margin of the command-and-control instrument, SM_{cc}, is defined by the difference between the two terms:

$$SM_{cc} = p(M)p(D)f(q - q_{st}) - NPB(q)$$

which can be raised indirectly by reducing the consented use level q_{st}, that is, by increasing the margin of safety of the target. The safety margin may be expressed in marginal terms by differentiating the above equation:

$$MSM_{cc} = ME(F) - MNPB.$$

Where $ME(F)$ is the marginal expected fine, and $MNPB$ is the marginal net private benefit. For a specific value of the control variables, the safety margin of the system increases as $q_d^* - q_{st}$ gets bigger.[10] Figure 9.2 shows, in marginal terms, how such a direct control system would work. MEC and MNPB curves are depicted, together with the $ME(F)$ function. The marginal safety margin is the distance between the marginal expected penalty and the MNPB curve, which increases as q increases. For the threshold value, the instrument works with a safety margin given by the extent to which the $ME(F)$ exceeds the MNPB at that value. This difference, together with the difference between the threshold and the permitted use level (the safety margin of the target) determine the composite safety margin of the system.

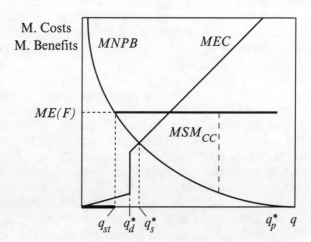

Figure 9.2 Safety margin under command-and-control instruments

Economic Instruments: Risk of Failure and Safety Margins

The control variables for economic instruments vary according to whether the instrument is price or quantity based. Suppose a tax is levied on the use of biological resources. Assuming that, as in the previous case, some kind of sanction is necessary to enforce tax compliance, the control system consists of a tax per unit of resource used (t^*) and a fine (f) per unit of resource which is found to have been used and not declared for tax. Under this system, any user will face payments on each unit of the resource used that is taxed t^* if they comply and expected payments of $p(M)p(D)f$ if they do not, that is:

$$t = t^* \text{ if compliance}$$
$$t = p(M)p(D)f \text{ if no compliance}$$

where the variables in the second equation are those described above. The system will minimize the instrument's risk of failure when it is unprofitable not to pay the tax, that is when:

$$p(M)p(D)f > t^*.$$

The instrument's safety margin, which guarantees compliance, is given by:

$$SM_t = p(M)p(D)f - t^*.$$

Monitoring and detection probabilities and the penalty are control variables common to both systems. The difference with respect to the direct control case is that the consented use level (q_{st}) is not imposed directly, but reached through the tax. The tax rate t^*, therefore, is the variable to adjust in order to get the total desired safety margin. Figure 9.3 shows again the *MEC* and *MNPB* curves in marginal terms, with the *MEC* curve having a point of discontinuity at the threshold level. The intersection point between the two curves gives rise to the static socially optimal level of private use of biodiversity (q_s^*). If this level was desired, a tax could be imposed to achieve it by setting the tax rate equal to the MEC at that optimal level. That is, the classical Pigouvian tax: $t_s^* = MEC(q_s^*)$. However, since this level does not guarantee biodiversity conservation a more restricted use level has to be set. The control authority must set the tax rate at the value of the MNPB corresponding to the desired level of biodiversity use. So, to get the use level corresponding to the threshold, the tax rate has to be $t_d^* = MNPB_d = MNPB(q_d^*)$.

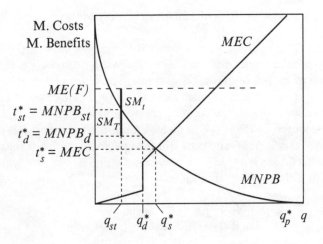

Figure 9.3 Safety margin under economic instruments

Having set the permitted use at q_{st}, the tax rate necessary to reach it is equal to the marginal net private benefit corresponding to that desired standard: $t_{st}^* = MNPB_{st} = MNPB(q_{st})$. The target safety margin is, then, given by $t_{st}^* - MNPB_d$ or $MNPB_{st} - MNPB_d$, the distance SM_T in the figure. The larger the difference, the safer the control. The instrument safety margin is $ME(F) - MNPB_{st}$ and is shown in Figure 9.3 as the distance SM_t. The composite safety margin of the tax system is the sum of SM_T and SM_t. The argument that command-and-control instruments are preferred because of their implications for the shape of the private cost function does not hold, since a tax combined with a non-payment sanction will also change the shape of the private cost function.

Summarizing, under high-risk aversion, the presence of static uncertainty and the risk of instrument failure do not rule out the use of certain instruments. Instead, they change the design from rules which efficiently allocate resources to those which ensure a *desired safety margin*.[11] Neither economic instruments nor command-and-control mechanisms are free from risk of failure. The existing restrictions on the control variables of the penalty function make the consented use level or the policy target (q_{st}) the most important variable in a biodiversity conservation policy.

DYNAMIC EFFECTS, STOCK EFFECTS AND EXOGENOUS CHANGES

Biological resources and ecosystems have an intertemporal and dynamic dimension. Effects of the current use of biodiversity will extend over time. If we are uncertain about present effects of current actions and uses, even more uncertainty may surround future consequences. This is not only because of the uncertainty generally attached to the future, but also due to the *inherent dynamic* or variability of biological diversity (Hanemann 1988). This means that a biodiversity conservation policy cannot be based on a dynamic framework, which incorporates all effects.

As a source of uncertainty, the inherent dynamic becomes even more important when the *stock* characteristic of the externalities attached to biodiversity use is considered. Each unit of flow externality at any time will generate in any future period an additional effect because of its contribution to the cumulative or stock externality. Further consequences may take place if this stock is such that the own dynamic of the system is altered. The worst outcome arises when a distortion makes the threshold move to a lower level. The risk of irreversibility increases because of the intrinsic variability and stock effects to which biodiversity is subject.[12]

Additionally, biodiversity may be subject to alterations due to exogenous factors, resulting in temporary shocks or more permanent changes. In both cases, the risk of irreversibility can emerge again if the system carrying capacity is modified. Finally, the knowledge about and understanding of biological diversity may progress over time varying indirectly the threshold value or, more precisely, what was thought to be the minimum value necessary to keep the resilience of the system.

All these dynamic factors can alter the initial conditions under which a policy for biodiversity conservation is established. These include not only natural but also economic conditions. The first, as already mentioned, refers to the estimated threshold value, and the second to the range of activities subject to regulation. Regarding this, two cases may appear: (i) existing activities or uses which were not harmful to biodiversity at the initial conditions become so, and (ii) new activities or uses are introduced which were not running when the policy was set up because, according to the information available then, they were either unprofitable or unknown.

Dynamic uncertainty refers to the possibility that, once a policy has been implemented, the threshold value varies or is passed because of changes in the initial conditions and information set on which the policy was based. Dynamic uncertainty generates additional problems in the setting of a policy for conservation of biodiversity. These are the *first mover problem* and the *moral hazard problem*.

Dynamic Uncertainty and the First Mover Problem

Over time, the change in initial natural conditions and knowledge of biodiversity may alter the threshold value, as well as the range of activities or uses that can be exploited from biological resources. As a consequence, both environmental costs, in the first case, and net private benefits, in the second case, increase. The increase in costs is due to the fact that, after the change, some use levels imply a higher cost. On the other hand, net private benefits increase because new economic opportunities exist. *The first mover problem* (FMP) refers to the possibility that those who can benefit from the new circumstances will be the first to perceive the opportunities and will exploit them before the control authority can act (Bowers 1994).

The FMP may also refer to the case where existing harmless activities or uses become harmful after the change, to the extent that affected users may continue with their unregulated activities before the control authority acts. In both cases, the result may be to get closer to the threshold level. A policy designed with safety margins may prevent these changes from putting biodiversity at risk; but the margins may fall to a lower level.

If the changing conditions lead directly to irreversibility (for example, when the net private benefit shifts above the expected penalty making it profitable to surpass the threshold) corrective measures cannot be taken. The solution requires the adoption of preventive measures to cut the root of the problem before it appears. For examples of such policies, see Bowers and Young (1995).

Dynamic Uncertainty and the Moral Hazard Problem

The damage caused to biodiversity or its irreversible loss depends not only on the magnitude of users' actions but also on the *state of nature*. That is, it depends on variables beyond the control of those directly involved: the control authority and the users. As mentioned above, external shocks such as diseases or meteorological changes may reduce the carrying capacity of the ecosystem. The limits on the magnitude and content of the allowed activities which are acceptable under usual (initial) conditions can become, under other circumstances, insufficient to prevent biodiversity loss.

The existence of uncertainty about the state of nature leads, among other consequences discussed in the previous sections, to the *moral hazard problem* (MHP). This refers to the fact that, since an adverse outcome can be blamed on an adverse state of nature, a controlled user has no incentive to keep his or her actions within the defined limits and/or to take the appropriate measures to prevent biodiversity losses. This problem may appear only if the control authority cannot know accurately the state of nature and cannot distinguish whether the damage done is because of adverse conditions or deliberate actions. A risk-averse authority can attempt to prevent the MHP by ensuring that users will benefit from their conservation uses. Benefits can be derived from *direct payments* and/or *defined property rights* over biodiversity services. Positive instruments are preferred to negative or sanction-based ones.

CONCLUSIONS

The theoretical analysis of the relative advantages of different environmental policy instruments does not give an unambiguous response, but instead suggests the need for a case-by-case analysis. This chapter has presented an analysis of instrument choice under static and dynamic uncertainty, threshold effects and policy failure, with a particular application to the problem of biodiversity loss. The potential irreversibility of biodiversity loss implies the need for a high degree of risk aversion in the choice of instruments.

Under uncertainty, the efficiency approach for instrument choice may not be useful. This is because uncertainty about environmental and control costs leaves undetermined the most appropriate instrument, and also because its application may not guarantee conservation in the presence of a threshold value. As a consequence, a cost-effective approach is needed to maintain the minimum stock and diversity necessary for maintenance of ecosystem resilience. When control costs or private benefits from biodiversity use are perfectly known, then under the cost-effectiveness criterion no instrument is preferred to another. When they are unknown, however, a highly risk-averse regulator will prefer quantity instruments to price instruments. This conclusion, however, does not necessarily hold when one recognizes that all instruments have a risk of failure. Static and dynamic uncertainty and imperfect monitoring and enforcement are sources of instrument failure. Under the threat of potential irreversibilities, environmental effectiveness can be enhanced by minimizing the risk of instrument failure through the establishment of safety margins. In other words, the instrument choice should be according to the minimum risk of failure criterion.

The application of this criterion under static uncertainty is not relevant for instrument choice, but rather for instrument design since it provides new rules by which to set the level of the control instruments. Efficiency rules are not sufficient to ensure the desired safety margin. Economic instruments, as with command and control, can guarantee the desired level by adjustment of the control variables.

Finally, the problems derived from dynamic uncertainty (FMP and MHP), which take place once the policy has been implemented, offer a more complete criterion for the choice of instruments. Under a high degree of risk aversion, the adjustment of safety margins and/or other *corrective measures* are not sufficient to cope with these problems. Instead, they require the adoption of a *preventative strategy*. Given that the penalty function cannot be implemented without limits, the prevention of these problems requires the adoption of positive instruments, that is, instruments which increase the profitability of biodiversity conservation. Therefore, the move from static to dynamic uncertainty problems changes the most effective strategy for reducing biodiversity loss. Instead of negative or sanction-based instruments, which affect the private cost function, positive instruments or those that affect the private benefits are preferred.

NOTES

1 'Price' instruments (taxes and subsidies) have to be set equal to the marginal costs at the optimum. 'Quantity' instruments (tradeable permits and standards) have to reflect the optimal level.
2. The effect of uncertainty about environmental and control costs on the choice of policy instruments is analysed in the seminal article of Weitzman (1974) and, more recently, in Stavins (1996). On imperfect enforcement, see, for example, Polinsky and Shavell (1982), Linder and McBride (1984), Russell et al. (1986) and Huang (1996). For a recent article on when environmental regulation should be adopted in the presence of uncertainty about environmental damage and stock effects, see Kolstad (1996).
3. Tradeable right systems incur in addition licensing and trade-registration costs.
4. Because of this assumption, the quantity instrument can represent either a command-and-control instrument or a tradeable rights system.
5. The figure is based on Figure 2 in Perrings and Pearce (1994), where costs and benefits are presented in total terms.
6. The marginal approach to this problem does not guarantee biodiversity conservation whenever the threshold falls at a point where the MEC is lower than the MNPB, unless the problem is constrained by allowing a use level no greater than the threshold. In the case shown in the figure, this constraint of the maximization problem would be binding at the optimum.
7. Only a tradeable permit system, which combines both approaches, secures the least-cost attainment of the target – of course, provided it works properly and it is not subject to transaction costs and other market failures.
8. Strictly speaking, this is not an instrument failure, but a failure in the establishment of the target. However, since the target level directly determines the level of the control instrument it can also be termed instrument failure.
9. For a case where prosecution and conviction are considered and a discussion about the limits of the penalty, see Bowers (1994).
10. Since the true value of the threshold is unknown, q_d^* actually refers to the minimum stock and diversity necessary for maintaining ecosystem resilience according to the current knowledge.
11. Since the establishment of safety margins implies a social cost, there will be a socially optimal degree of safety. The marginal costs of implementation should be set equal to the marginal costs of exceeding the threshold times the probability of the event occurring.
12. Even in a situation without uncertainty, the existence of stock externalities has implications for the design of an optimal environmental policy. From a dynamic framework, the optimal policy control differs from that set in a Pigouvian (static) framework. Indeed, the Pigouvian policy would lead to a lower control of the externality. This is so since the optimal policy requires, for each period, a level of control such that its marginal cost is equal to the marginal damage of the flow externality at the corresponding period plus the marginal damage arising in every future period for raising the externality stock (Farzin 1996).

REFERENCES

Barde, Jean-Philippe (1995), 'Environmental policy and policy instruments', in H. Folmer, H.L. Gabel and H. Opschoor (eds), *Principles of Environmental and Resource Economics*, Aldershot, UK and Brookfield, US: Edward Elgar, pp. 201–27.

Baumol, William J. and Wallace E. Oates (1988), *The Theory of Environmental Policy*, 2nd edition, Cambridge, US: Cambridge University Press.

Bohm, Peter and Clifford Russell (1985), 'Comparative analysis of alternative policy instruments', in A.V. Kneese and J.L. Sweeney (eds), *Handbook of Natural Resource and Energy Economics* Vol. 1, Amsterdam: North-Holland, Elsevier Science Publishers, pp. 395–460.

Bowers, John (1994), 'Incentives and mechanisms for biodiversity: observations and issues', Working Document 94/4, Assessment and Management of Natural Resource System (AMNRS) Program, Commonwealth Scientific and Industrial Research Organisation (CSIRO), Canberra.

Bowers, J. and M. Young (1995), 'Biodiversity instruments and the first mover problem', unpublished paper.

Farzin, Y.H. (1996), 'Optimal pricing of environmental and natural resource use with stock externalities', *Journal of Public Economics*, **62** (1–2), 31–57.

Hanemann, W. Michael (1988), 'Economics and the preservation of biodiversity', in E.O. Wilson (ed.), *Biodiversity*, Washington, DC: National Academy Press, pp. 192–9.

Huang, C.-H. (1996), 'Effectiveness of environmental regulations under imperfect enforcement and the firm's avoidance behaviour', *Environmental and Resource Economics*, **8** (2), 183–204.

Kolstad, C.D. (1996), 'Learning and stock effects in environmental regulation: the case of greenhouse gas emissions', *Journal of Environmental Economics and Management*, **31**, 1-18.

Laffont, J.-J. (1977), 'More on prices vs. quantities', *Review of Economic Studies*, **44**, 177–82.

Linder, S.H. and M.E. McBride (1984), 'Enforcement costs and regulatory reform: the agency and firm response', *Journal of Environmental Economics and Management*, **11**, 327–46.

Montgomery, W.D. (1972), 'Markets in licenses and efficient pollution control programs', *Journal of Economic Theory*, **5**, 395–418.

Nicolaisen, J., Andrew Dean and Peter Hoeller (1991), Economics and the Environment: A Survey of Issues and Policy Options, *Economic Studies* No. 16, Paris: OECD.

Panayotou, T. (1994), 'The use and application of economic instruments for environmental management and sustainable development', Environmental Economics Series Paper No. 12, United Nations Environment Programme (EEU)–Harvard Institute for International Development.

Perrings, C. and D. Pearce, (1994), 'Threshold effects and incentives for the conservation of biodiversity', *Environmental and Resource Economics*, **4**, 13–28.

Polinsky, A.M. and S. Shavell (1982), 'Pigovian taxation with administrative costs', *Journal of Public Economics*, **19**, 385–94.

Russell, Clifford S., Winston Harrington and William J. Vaughan (1986), *Enforcing Pollution Control Laws*, Washington, DC: Resources for the Future.

Segerson, Kathleen (1996), 'Issues in the choice of environmental policy instruments', in J.B. Braden, H. Folmer and T.S. Ulen (eds), *Environmental Policy with Political and Economic Integration*, Aldershot, UK and Brookfield, US: Edward Elgar, pp. 149–74.

Stavins, R.N. (1996), 'Correlated uncertainty and policy instrument choice', *Journal of Environmental Economics and Management*, **30**, 218–32.

Tietenberg, T.M. (1990), 'Economic instruments for environmental regulation', *Oxford Review of Economic Policy*, **6** (1), 17–33.

Weitzman, M.L. (1974), 'Prices vs. Quantities', *Review of Economic Studies*, **41**, 477–91.

PART III

Environmental Sustainability

10. The economics of environmental sustainability

Pamela Mason

INTRODUCTION

The purpose of this chapter is to examine the debate, both within and beyond the economics profession, about the relevance of sustainability. In particular, it aims to provide an easily accessible explanation of the economic arguments against the relevance of sustainability, while providing counter arguments to the effect that the conditions under which sustainability could be relevant are not implausible.

For sustainability to be defined in a meaningful way, there are various factors which must be specified, some of which are examined in the next section. The following section examines the arguments against the adoption of an explicit sustainability policy. These consist, in short, of the demonstration that, assuming that the market correctly rations stocks of environmental and other goods, then if people want sustainability (for example, of consumption or well-being) the market will provide it. If they do not, then there is no reason to be concerned about it, indeed, imposing a sustainability constraint would result in a suboptimal growth path. Together, these arguments imply that a sustainability policy will be either superfluous or inefficient. Having illustrated these arguments with the help of a simple optimal growth model, the various counter arguments are then examined. These note that the first set of arguments use assumptions which are too unrealistic to provide reliable policy conclusions, and also omit significant factors such as the environmental and social costs of economic growth. It is argued that inclusion of these factors may alter the conclusions both as to the nature of the optimal growth path, and as to whether or not the market is capable of identifying this path.

This chapter is not intended to provide either a comprehensive review of the literature on sustainability or suggestions as to how sustainability might be implemented. Rather, it is intended to provide a rough guide as to the identification of a sustainable path under various circumstances, and to demonstrate that there are plausible circumstances under which sustainability could be a useful concept. The aim is not therefore to provide answers to the problem of sustainability, but to justify asking the questions.

WHAT IS SUSTAINABILITY?

The fact that sustainability is fairly easy to define in an abstract sense makes it initially surprising that a standard operational definition appears to be so difficult to identify.[1] In a theoretical model, one need decide only which factors contribute to wellbeing, and the extent to which they can be traded off among each other. If, as is usual, sustainability is then defined as non-decreasing well-being into the indefinite future, then given production technology and stocks of productive assets, the best available sustainable path can be identified. In practice, however, it becomes very much harder to determine whether or not an economic path is sustainable. For instance, in a simple two-country model, an agricultural state could be importing its energy from the other, oil-producing state, paying with exports of food. If its export revenues are consistently lower than the cost of its imports so that it is accumulating debt then, other things being equal, the consumption path is probably unsustainable. If its external trade is balanced, then whether or not the consumption path is sustainable will depend, among other things, on whether or not the energy-exporting country is investing in alternative technology to maintain the supply of energy once the stock of oil is exhausted. This simple example illustrates the fact that the sustainability of an economy usually cannot be measured simply by examining the economy itself. It will be affected by its ties with the rest of the world, and becomes very complicated when there are many such ties. This makes the issues surrounding sustainability very much easier to analyse in theoretical models in which the number of variables can be restricted.

The precise implications of sustainability, therefore, vary according to the context. Two of the most important factors are as follows. First, what are the aspects of welfare which should be sustained? Is it simply the rate at which marketed goods are consumed which determines well-being, or do the state of the environment and societal factors such as a sense of community and security also contribute? In particular, where these three factors conflict, to what extent is it possible to trade off one against another? Second, on what scale (for example, local, national or global) is a policy of sustainability to be implemented? This determines the problems which can be tackled feasibly, as opposed to those which must be treated as exogenous. It also determines the extent to which the policy must account for the maintenance of specific assets.

As an example, suppose that an individual's wealth consists of ownership of a forest, in a global economy in which production is dependent on timber, and humanmade capital. An objective of maximum sustainable well-being may well be achieved by cutting down the forest immediately and investing the proceeds at the going rate of interest. This would be the optimal strategy if the (present) value of the forest were maximized by immediate harvesting, and the owner does not attach sufficient value to the existence of the forest to compensate for the difference between this value and that of a sustainable harvesting strategy. However, if such a strategy of depletion and investment of the proceeds were followed by forest owners in aggregate, it may not deliver the anticipated path of consumption. Quite apart from the ecological services provided by global forests, the eventual reduced supply of timber, and increased supply of humanmade capital would cause the return to the invested capital to fall. This means that the return on the invested capital would not support the anticipated path of consumption. This phenomenon could become a problem if many economies were to follow resource depletion paths which would be feasible for a small economy, but not for the global economy, and is discussed more explicitly in Chapter 12.

It must be acknowledged that in any context, and whatever factors a policy of sustainability aims to maintain, it cannot aim for sustainability of all things. If that were the case then, for instance, no non-renewable resource could ever be used and all species would have to be preserved regardless of development opportunities forgone. In effect everything would have to remain exactly as at present, causing the economy to grind to a halt.[2] It is plain that a policy of sustainability of welfare must account for trade-offs between various components of welfare, so that at low levels of output, it may be worthwhile to trade off some natural assets for increased production. It also requires, however, recognition that sooner or later as natural resources become more scarce the balance will move in favour of their conservation. Moreover, either before or after this point, the physical limits of the environment to provide inputs and absorb waste will limit the scale of output. A framework for accounting for these limits in the optimal use of ecological resources is analysed in Chapter 11.

IS SUSTAINABILITY SUPERFLUOUS?

The case in the non-formal literature against the use of sustainability as a policy goal tends to be based on two main arguments. The first is that sustainability is simply a description of the technical characteristics of certain economic paths and does not imply that such paths ought necessarily to be followed. For instance, Beckerman (1994, p. 193) maintains that 'the concept is flawed because it mixes up together the technical characteristics of a particular develoment path with a moral injunction to follow it'. This argument is based on the fact that optimal consumption and investment decisions must be taken on the basis of some criterion of optimality, usually the maximization of the present discounted value (PV) of utility or consumption. The attraction of this criterion is that as long as one can borrow and lend at the going rate of interest, then maximization of the present value of assets means maximization of wealth. In the absence of non-market values this is sufficient for the achievement of maximum intertemporal welfare, no matter how one prefers to spread well-being over time. Hence, the argument is that if a path is identified which is optimal under the chosen criterion, it is perverse to then alter the path by imposing an extra constraint.

The second argument is that sustainability as a distinct goal is superfluous since markets will anyway provide an inexorably rising standard of living, as they have done over the last two hundred years of market capitalism. For instance, Barnett and Morse (1963, p. 249) maintain that 'by devoting itself to improving the lot of the living, therefore, each generation, whether recognising a future-orientated obligation or not, transmits a more productive world to those who follow'. The implication of both of these arguments together is that any intervention to alter the market's intertemporal allocation of resources, either will be superfluous, or will result in inefficiency and will make people worse off both currently and in the future.

There are two assumptions necessary for the second argument to hold. First it assumes, since the actual economic path reflects the choices of economic agents, that they do desire that paths of well-being should be generally increasing over time. This is not controversial, reflecting only the expectation that the economic system will provide us with increasing rather than decreasing standards of living. Second, however, it assumes that the market will be able to reflect these objectives and ensure that the desired paths of increasing well-being will actually be forthcoming. If these assumptions are satisfied there will be no conflict between sustainability and optimality. A sustainability constraint would not change the optimal path, and would therefore be superfluous. If, however, the assumption that people do desire sustainable paths of welfare is correct, but the assumption that the market will necessarily deliver these desired paths is not, then the first argument is actually reversed. In other words, if it is thought that actual unsustainability does not necessarily imply that people desire an unsustainable path, then a policy of sustainability which would correct a sub-optimal path would become desirable.

A Simple Model

The arguments against recognition of sustainability, and some of the related issues, can be demonstrated by describing a simple, but standard, optimal growth model. In this model the environment plays no role, and population is constant. The aim of the consumer is to maximize the present value of utility, with a constant discount rate, given that the capital stock grows by the difference between output and consumption. Production technology is assumed to have the standard properties by which output increases with increased capital stock, but at a decreasing rate.

Setting up the dynamic optimization framework yields the optimal path of consumption, while the path of the capital stock is already given by the set-up of the problem. In short, if on the optimal path the rate of interest is greater than the rate of discount, then it will be optimal to invest in the capital stock and for both consumption and the capital stock to be rising. If, on the other hand, the rate of interest is less than the discount rate, it will be optimal to consume capital. The optimal paths of capital and consumption can be used to depict the optimal growth path on the simple dynamic diagram shown in Figure 10.1.

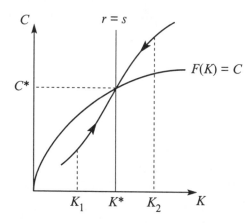

Figure 10.1 Optimal investment strategy

Figure 10.1 depicts the optimal investment strategy. The line labelled $F(K) = C$ depicts the production function, showing all the points at which the capital stock is constant, since consumption equals output. The vertical line shows the level of capital at which it is optimal for consumption to remain constant, since the rate of interest is equal to the discount rate. The intersection of the two lines, where consumption and capital are C^*

and K^*, respectively, is the steady state of the economy at which all variables are constant. At all points to the left of K^* the rate of interest, r, is greater than the discount rate, δ, since the interest rate is greater, the steeper the output curve.

This model can be used to illustrate both of the major arguments against sustainability. If the initial capital stock is greater than the equilibrium steady-state level, for example K_2 in Figure 10.1, then the optimal strategy is to consume capital, and for both consumption and the capital stock to decrease towards the steady-state level. This path maximizes the net present value of utility and so is optimal under the specified criterion. It is not optimal simply to limit consumption to the return on the initial level of capital, because the rate of discount is higher than this initial return. Consumption of some of this capital in the short term contributes more to the discounted value of utility than does a higher long-term level of consumption. This case illustrates the first argument in that a sustainability constraint would result in a suboptimal solution, since net present value could be gained by consuming some capital in the short term, and having a lower long-run level of consumption.

If the initial level of capital is less than K^*, for example K_1 in Figure 10.1, it is worthwhile to consume less than total output and invest in the capital stock. Both consumption and capital increase until the equilibrium is reached. At the equilibrium, although further investment would increase the steady-state consumption level, the future gain is outweighed by the cost of delaying consumption, as expressed by the discount rate. This illustrates the second argument, being a case in which the imposition of a sustainability rule would be superfluous, since on the optimal path, consumption is first increasing and then stationary.

Neoclassical Resource Economics and Sustainability

The aim of this section is to relate the conclusions of the seminal neoclassical models to the conceptual arguments against a sustainability policy. For a broader survey of the mainstream natural resource literature, see Toman et al. (1995).

The above optimal growth model is simplified in that it contains only one type of capital and excludes the role of natural resources. However, this type of analysis is used in the influential mainstream economic models on natural resources, growth and sustainability, in which production is dependent on humanmade capital and natural resources. They assume a production technology which is used regularly in economic modelling, the Cobb–Douglas production function, which implies that although the resource input must be positive, it is feasible for output levels to be maintained even if r becomes very small, provided that the capital stock increases sufficiently.

Two of the original articles in this literature are Dasgupta and Heal (1974) and Solow (1974). The Dasgupta and Heal model shows that, in the absence of technical progress, the PV-optimal path is sustainable only if the return to capital never falls below the discount rate. Solow shows that as long as the contribution of capital to output is greater than that of natural resources, non-decreasing consumption is feasible. This result is quite distinct from the PV-optimal result of the Dasgupta and Heal model (which often results in optimal unsustainability) in assuming that consumers wish for non-decreasing utility. The Solow result is extended by Hartwick (1977) to the 'Hartwick rule' which, arguably, is the fundamental result in mainstream sustainability theory. The rule requires that the share of capital in output be greater than that of resources, and that there be no depreciation of humanmade capital. Then, if profits from the depletion of the non-renewable resource are invested in humanmade capital, output and therefore consumption can be maintained for all time. This is also known as the 'invest resource rents' rule.

One could think of these models as constituting formalizations of the conceptual arguments against the imposition of sustainability. The Dasgupta and Heal model shows that, where production is dependent on non-renewable resources, it may or may not be optimal to follow a path of sustainable consumption. If it is not then, although people are aware of the eventual unhappiness experienced on this path, this is more than compensated for in terms of the present value criterion by the higher levels of utility in the shorter term. This illustrates the first argument against sustainability policies. The literature on the Hartwick rule shows that, if it so happens that people do desire paths of non-decreasing welfare, that is sustainability of welfare, then the economic system is capable, at least in theory, of delivering such a path. All that is necessary is adequate investment in humanmade capital. This illustrates the second argument against a policy of sustainability. This theory does admit the possibility that people may wish for non-declining utility and therefore represents a departure from the standard theory which assumes that maximization of PV will always be the objective. However, in terms of the assumptions regarding substitutability between humanmade capital and natural resources, and the presence in the market of sufficient foresight to actually deliver the desired path, the framework is the same.

IN DEFENCE OF SUSTAINABILITY

The arguments in defence of sustainability can be split into two main groups. First of all, one can criticize the models on their own terms by pointing out that their conclusions are not feasible, even in theory. The second group of comments concerns the factors, both positive and negative, which are missing from the analysis outlined above, inclusion of which could change the nature of the optimal path of consumption and resource use.

A Theoretical Defence of Sustainability

The first theoretical criticism of the above conclusions is that attainment of the optimal or sustainable path requires that the market be able to calculate the paths of resource flow, capital stock and prices for all time periods. When the objective is sustainable consumption, the market must be able to ration the finite supply of the resource over infinite time. Failure to value the resource sufficiently highly will result in too high a level of extraction in early periods, eventual depletion and unsustainability. The implication of the Hartwick rule is that, as long as the theoretical assumptions as to substitutability of capital for resources hold, then investment of resource rents will guarantee sustainable consumption. However, it is demonstrated by Pezzey (1994) and Asheim (1994), that the Hartwick rule results in non-decreasing consumption only if the economy is already on the sustainable path. What this apparent catch-22 means is that, as discussed in Asheim (1994), investment in humanmade capital of resource rents is a *feature* of a sustainable path, but not a *prescription* for the attainment of one. This is because prices of both natural resources and humanmade capital depend on the actual path followed, and on the unsustainable PV-optimal path the resource will initially have a lower price than on the sustainable path since it is not valued at its full sustainability value. On the unsustainable path, therefore, investing resource revenues in capital will mean a lower level of actual investment than it would on the sustainable path. This means that for sustainability to be realized, the Hartwick rule still depends on the extremely strong assumption of market omniscience into the infinite future.

Even in the context in which there are renewable resources and potential technical progress which can reduce the throughput of resources in production, sustainable resource use will require substantial foresight by the market. If individuals desire non-decreasing well-being, the market must ensure that as a resource becomes more scarce its price rises, encouraging research into substitutes. A potential problem with this is that the market price of a resource may be insufficiently developed to reflect scarcity of future supply. Moreover, if supply of the resource exceeds the sustainable level, this will tend to lower its price, making both conservation and research into substitutes less likely. Barnett and Morse (1963) analysed the time series of certain natural resource prices, finding that they had hitherto failed to show an increasing trend. They concluded from this that resources were not becoming more economically scarce, and that the market must be providing price incentives either to explore for new supplies, or to develop substitutes. Norgaard (1990), however, points out that the findings could result from a failure of the market to reflect scarcity rather than an absence of scarcity.

A second set of theoretical criticisms, described comprehensively by Victor (1991), relates to the fact that the conclusions of the models described above are based on assumptions which violate the laws of physics. The major problem is the assumption that humanmade capital can substitute for natural resources since, first, much production involves capital and natural resources as complements, with humanmade capital being used to transform natural resources into output. Second, not only does humanmade capital (for example, machinery) consist of transformed natural resources, it also requires natural energy resources to operate. These criticisms imply that even in the narrow theoretical context in which utility depends only on consumption, the assumptions used to conclude that the market will necessarily reflect any objective of non-decreasing well-being are too strong for the theoretical conclusions to be sufficiently reliable to inform policy. They support the argument that it is possible for sustainability to be desired, but for the economic system not to deliver it.

A 'Real World' Defence of Sustainability

Hitherto we have remained more or less within the framework of the neo-classical models and argued simply that the assumptions necessary for the solutions to hold are too strong for the conclusions to be applicable. One can also examine factors omitted from this analysis, which may be sufficiently important to justify altering the actual path of economic progress. One argument is that distorted measures of wellbeing mean that we over-value growth of consumption relative to other important factors, some of which conflict with increased production.[3] Second there is the argument that, whether or not we are happier with ever higher levels of output and consumption, finite sources of natural resources and limited capacity of the environment to absorb waste, mean that indefinite growth is impossible. The picture of economic growth could be made more complete by including the environmental inputs to, and emissions of waste from, the economic system, and by accounting for the costs of economic growth as well as the benefits.

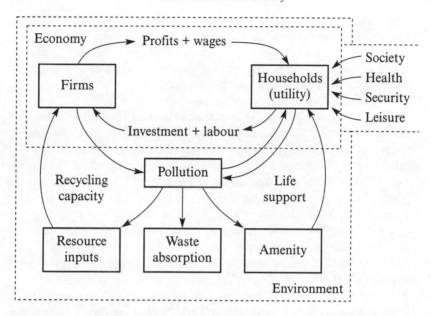

Figure 10.2 Economy, environment and society

Figure 10.2 includes not only the 'circulatory system' of the economy, but also its 'digestive tract', of inputs and emissions. Depicting the dynamics of the system involves accounting for the capacity of the environment to recycle wastes using solar energy, maintaining the supply of environmental inputs to production, and generally maintaining the atmospheric, climatic and soil productivity services necessary to support human life. This capacity is a stock resource, which may be run down by destroying global ecosystems. While not all ecosystems are essential to the maintenance of these services, it is possible that their continued destruction increases the risk of triggering threshold effects. Chapter 11 contains a detailed description of threshold effects and their impact on the sustainable use of environmental resources. As ecosystems are exploited, there may be a period during which ecosystems can be destroyed with relatively little noticeable effect, followed by a collapse in environmental services once a certain level of destruction is passed. Ehrlich and Ehrlich (1981) compare the continued destruction of ecosystems to the ongoing removal of rivets from the wings of a plane. While no particular rivet is essential, a crash becomes increasingly likely as more are removed. Their argument is that, as few rational individuals would knowingly fly in a plane undergoing such a process, so we should not allow the analogous process of ecosystem destruction to put our own habitat at risk. That is, limits ought to be placed on economic growth so that the economic system stays within the 'carrying capacity' of the global environment. (Arrow et al. 1995).

A comprehensive economic model of optimal growth accounts for the complex interplay between different stocks and flows in the economy, the environment and society. Development of a simple conceptual version of such a model should at least demonstrate the dangers of measuring economic progress by means of narrow indicators such as output levels, and of excessive faith in the powers of the market to price essential stocks correctly and to reflect the total costs of economic growth. The danger is that economic indicators will signal neither when further growth in the scale of output is no longer desirable, nor when it is no longer sustainable.

One can conceive of an economy characterized by the relationships depicted in Figure 10.2, in which production is a function of both humanmade capital and natural resources. Well-being is positively related to consumption, the level of 'societal goodwill', environmental assets, health, pollution and equality. Pollution has a negative impact on health, while leisure is assumed to have a positive effect.[4] Environmental assets are represented by the stock of the environmental resource and pollution is a byproduct of resource use in production. The stock of the natural resource performs several functions. It provides well-being directly as well as natural resource inputs, it recycles pollution, and performs life-support functions. The stock is assumed to have a threshold level, below which there is a risk of ecological collapse. Finally, for each of consumption, society, the environment, health and equality, the more there is already, the less will be the contribution to well-being of an extra unit.

Without making these relationships explicit, the optimal level of production cannot be identified. However, the qualitative effects of economic growth can be described, and are depicted in Figure 10.3. At low levels of output when the scale of the economy is small, environmental stocks are high, and consumption and pollution are low. Increasing output will add more to utility, via increased consumption, than it removes through effects on the environment and so on. However, as consumption and pollution increase, and stocks of other goods decrease, the significance of an extra unit of consumption is less, while the significance of the loss of other goods becomes greater. There will come a point at which the negative effects of increased output outweigh the benefits. This level will be the optimal scale of the economy. At the point Q^*, the marginal benefits and the marginal costs are equal, so that a further increase in scale adds more to costs than it does to benefits.

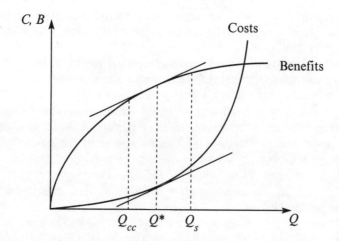

Figure 10.3 Optimality and sustainability

Daly (1991) complains that while in microeconomics there is a well-defined optimum scale of production beyond which an extra unit of output adds more to costs than it does to benefits, there is no recognition of a corresponding optimum level of aggregate output in macroeconomics. This can be explained in part by the fact that the standard system of measuring progress, that is GNP, measures only the direct costs and benefits of output and not the indirect costs. Costs such as damage to health and the environment are not accounted for, risking the possibility that the scale of output might exceed the optimal level.

There are in fact commentators who question the very idea that higher consumption is necessarily a good thing.[5] For instance, Boulding (1949) maintains that well-being is determined by stocks (such as buildings, consumer durables and so on) which provide ongoing services. He distinguishes between consumption and use and maintains that consumption ought to be minimized as a cost, rather than maximized. Consumption in his terminology is the throughput of materials necessary to maintain stocks of welfare-providing assets. By this reasoning it is the *possession* of, for instance, a refrigerator, which ought to be counted as providing well-being, rather than its *purchase*. A decrease in the quality of consumer durables so that they need to be replaced every five years rather than every 15, will increase measured consumption and the associated costs, but will not increase well-being. This implies that not only do the indicators of economic well-being which we currently use (GNP) not reflect the total costs of economic growth, but they may also overestimate the benefits.

A second scale which is significant for sustainability, labelled Q_s in Figure 10.3, is the maximum level of output for which the environment will be able to provide inputs indefinitely. This could be either above or below the optimal economic scale. It is determined by the rate at which the environment can produce inputs, and the extent to which production requires land that would otherwise accommodate the resource stock. It also depends on the efficiency with which resources are used in production, so that technical progress could shift this threshold to a higher level of production.[6] In the case shown in Figure 10.3, the sustainable resource provision constraint is at a higher level of output than the optimal one. There is a range of output levels, therefore, for which the environment could sustain input provision, but which are greater than optimal.

It is possible that the capacity of the environment to sustainably provide inputs exceeds its capacity to absorb waste without disrupting life-support services. For instance, it is thought that current fossil fuel reserves far exceed the quantities which could be used without significantly affecting the world's climate. Therefore, our assumption that life-support services are fundamental to the continued existence of the economy means that there is a third significant level, Q_{cc}, reflecting the environmental carrying capacity. This level reflects the stock of ecosystems and species biodiversity which one can be reasonably sure will be sufficient to maintain essential life-support services.

The optimal and sustainable, or in Pezzey's (1994) terminology 'opsustimal', level of output will be dictated by whichever constraint binds first. The question for the relevance of an explicit policy of sustainability is, to what extent can one assume that the market will recognize these constraints? Sustainability of input provision would require the market to value natural resources at their full sustainability value. Recognition of the optimal level of production would require that all the direct and indirect costs of production be internalized. In fact, as demonstrated in Part I of this book, it is not straightforward to place a value on costs, even when they are experienced directly. Where the costs of increased production have very long-term and global implications, which in the above model means approaching or exceeding the life-support system constraint, it is unlikely that they could be internalized accurately.

It is difficult to estimate at what point on Figure 10.3 the global economy might be. However, it is argued by ecologists that the scale of the economy relative to the environment is already sufficiently large for substantial damage to have been inflicted. An oft-quoted statistic is the finding of Vitousek et al. (1986) that 40 per cent of the earth's net primary product of photosynthesis is already consumed, directly or indirectly, by humans. This leaves an ever smaller proportion of resources available for the sustenance of all other species. Beckerman (1995) dismisses this as a 'photosynthesis fairytale', maintaining that the 60 per cent not currently used by humans is effectively 'wasted'. This assumes that the existence of species other than those which we consume, does not contribute at all to our well-being. However, while current knowledge as to the precise way in which the continuing functioning of global ecosystems maintains our life-support systems is limited, it is generally accepted that they perform fundamental services. Ecosystems depend on the continued survival of a variety of species, which in turn require for survival a certain share of the net primary product of photosynthesis. This proportion of the earth's primary energy production is not, therefore, 'wasted', even in purely anthropocentric terms.

CONCLUSIONS

The first aim of this chapter has been to demonstrate that, under assumptions of perfectly working markets and limited environmental externalities, the concept of sustainability ought to be irrelevant. However, the second aim was to argue that the assumptions required for this conclusion to hold are very strong. The market is unlikely to identify the optimal scale for the economy, since the costs of economic growth are outside the economic system. It is unlikely to stay within the limits of the biological carrying capacity of the environment, for similar reasons.

The possibility that the maximum present value of utility is achieved by an unsustainable path has to be recognized. Consumption could be increased in the short term by increasing flows of resources at the expense of lower long-term output, and possible environmental or social collapse. In this case, if the current generation wishes for such a path, then arguably, such a path has to be accepted. However, there are two provisos. First, one has to be sure that individuals are aware of the direct and indirect consequences of their actions on society, the environment, and therefore on the future. It could be argued that the interlinkages are so complicated and far-reaching that it would be difficult for them to be internalized. Second, there is the question of whether, even if a certain path is optimal under the criterion preferred by the current generation, if this results in 'asymptotic misery' for future generations, this is morally acceptable? This is an ethical problem which is beyond the scope of this discussion.

Let us assume that in the main, individuals do wish the economic system to deliver increasing rather than decreasing well-being. Is it possible that the market could internalize all of these factors into the costs of producing output so that the optimal and sustainable level of output could be identified? Or is it more likely that there are crucial determinants of well-being which are outside the economic system, and which, moreover, could eventually conflict with those indicators which are within the system, so that the anticipated path may not be delivered? If one accepts that the latter argument is at least plausible, then it is difficult to deny that sustainability is a problem worthy of some consideration.

NOTES

1. See Pezzey (1989) and Pearce et al. (1989) for a range of alternative definitions of sustainability.
2. Beckerman (1995) maintains that sustainability does indeed imply maintenance of all current stocks, and is thus 'morally repugnant' in denying much needed development opportunities. However, this would be a particularly strong definition of sustainability.
3. Several studies, for example, Easterlin (1974) have found that, despite measured standard of living having risen over time, people do not perceive themselves as being happier.
4. A more complex model would account for the effects of unemployment, which could constitute excess leisure and have a negative effect on health.
5. See Boulding (1949), Mishan (1967).
6. However, note that technical progress can increase production either by increasing efficiency with which a given level of the resource is used, or by increasing the speed with which the resource is used. For the sustainability threshold to be increased, the technical progress would have to be of the first variety, and this would require the correct market incentive.

REFERENCES

Arrow, K., B. Bolin, R. Costanza, P. Dasgupta, C. Folke, C.S. Holling, B.-O. Jansson, S. Levin, K.G. Mäler, C. Perrings and D. Pimentel (1995), 'Economic growth, carrying capacity, and the environment', *Ecological Economics*, **15** (2) 91–5.

Asheim, G.B. (1994) 'Net national product as an indicator of sustainability', *Scandinavian Journal of Economics*, **96**, 257–65.

Barnett, H.J. and C. Morse, (1963), *Scarcity and Growth: The Economics of Natural Resource Availability*, Resources for the Future, Baltimore: Johns Hopkins Press.

Beckerman, W. (1994), 'Sustainable development: is it a useful concept?', *Environmental Values*, **3** (3), 191–209.

Beckerman, W. (1995), *Small is Stupid: Blowing the Whistle on the Greens*, London: Duckworth.

Boulding, K.E. (1949), 'Income or welfare', *Review of Economic Studies*, **17**, 77–86.

Daly, H.E. (1991), 'Towards an environmental macroeconomics', *Land Economics* **67** (2), 255–9

Dasgupta, P.S. and G. Heal, (1974), 'The optimal depletion of exhaustible resources', *Review of Economic Studies*, Symposium, 'Economics of exhaustible resources', pp. 3–28.

Easterlin, R.A. (1974), 'Does economic growth improve the human lot?', in P.A. David and M.W. Reder (eds), *Nations and Households in Economic Growth: Essays in Honour of Moses Abramovitz*, New York: Academic Press, pp. 89–125.

Ehrlich, P.R. and A.H. Ehrlich (1981), *Extinction: the causes and consequences of the disappearance of species*, New York: Random House.

Hartwick, J.M. (1977), 'Intergenerational equity and the investing of rents from exhaustible resources', *American Economic Review*, **67** (5), 972–4.

Mishan, E.J. (1967), *The Costs of Economic Growth*, London: Staples Press.

Norgaard, R.D. (1990), 'Economic indicators of resource scarcity: a critical essay', *Journal of Environmental and Resource Management*, **19** (1), 19–25.

Pearce, D.W., E.W. Barbier and A.M. Markandya (1989), *Blueprint for a Green Economy*, London: Earthscan.

Perrings, C. (1991), 'Reserved rationality and the precautionary principle: technological change, time and uncertainty in environmental decision making', in R. Costanza (ed.), *Ecological Economics: The Science and Management of Sustainability*, New York: Columbia University Press, pp. 153–66.

Pezzey, John (1989), 'Economic analysis of sustainable growth and sustainable development', Environment Department Working Paper No. 15, World Bank, Washington, DC.

Pezzey, J. (1994), 'The optimal sustainable depletion of non-renewable resources', Paper presented at the 5th Annual Conference of the European Association of Environmental and Resource Economists, Dublin.

Pezzey, J. (1995), 'Non-declining wealth is not equivalent to sustainability', Department of Environmental Economics and Environmental Management, University of York (manuscript).

Pezzey, J. (1997), 'The tension between sustainability and optimality when defining income', Draft Manuscript, Department of Environmental Economics and Environmental Management, University of York.

Solow, R. (1974), 'Intergenerational equity and renewable resources', *Review of Economic Studies*, Symposium, 'Economics of exhaustible resources', pp 29–45.

Toman, M., J. Pezzey, and J. Krautkraemer (1995), 'Neoclassical economic growth theory and "Sustainability"', in D.W. Bromley (ed.), *Handbook of Environmental Economics*, Oxford: Blackwell, pp. 139–65

Victor, P. (1991), 'Indicators of sustainable development: some lessons from capital theory', *Ecological Economics*, **4** 191–223.

Vitousek, P.M., P.R. Ehrlich, A.H. Ehrlich and P.A. Matson (1986), 'Human appropriation of the products of photosynthesis', *Bioscience*, **36** (6), 368–73.

11. Ecological resilience and economic sustainability

Silvana Dalmazzone[*]

INTRODUCTION

A major theme of ecological economics research in recent years has been the role of ecological resilience in the sustainability of economic activities. Resilience is an ecological concept that refers to the capacity of the environment to repair itself in the face of pollution, exploitation or other sources of disturbance. Two main definitions exist. One is concerned with the time taken for a disturbed ecosystem to return towards some initial state (Pimm 1984; O'Neill et al. 1989). The second is concerned with the magnitude of disturbance that can be absorbed before a system crosses the threshold that causes it to undergo radical changes in its structure (Holling 1973; Holling et al. 1995). In both variants, resilience is a measure of the capacity of a system to retain productivity following a disturbance, and it is this which makes it relevant to the sustainability of the activities that are sources of disturbance (Common and Perrings 1992). This chapter considers how the concept of resilience changes the way we address standard allocation problems in environmental and resource economics. These issues are fundamental to the analysis of optimal and sustainable development outlined in Chapter 10.

The set of problems for which the notion of resilience is particularly helpful includes those in which the dynamics of the joint ecological–economic system are affected by growth in the level of economic activity. As economic activity grows relative to the ecological processes that constitute its environment, it is intuitive that the dynamics of each will change in some way. The nature of this change depends both on the degree of interdependence and on the relative scale of the two systems. In general, the more highly connected ecological and economic systems are,

* This chapter is largely based on a more technical paper, Dalmazzone and Perrings (1997). The author acknowledges helpful comments by two anonymous referees on parts of that work relevant also to the present chapter.

the more change in one implies change in the other – the more they 'co-evolve' in Norgaard's terms (Norgaard 1984). The same is true of the relative scale of the economic and ecological components of the joint system. At some activity levels, growth in economic activity may have little or no apparent impact on the regenerative functions of the environment. However, where the scale of economic activity threatens the 'assimilative' or 'carrying' capacity of the environment, economic growth may provoke sudden and far-reaching change. Daly, for example, has persistently argued that economic growth beyond the carrying capacity of the biosphere will necessarily lead to environmental collapse, and that this will not be anticipated by price signals (Daly 1968, 1973, 1991). In this chapter we also consider why this should be so.

The chapter is in four sections. The first elaborates on the concept of resilience, and considers its application to the stability of renewable resources. The second discusses how the demands the economy imposes on ecosystems, in terms of pollution burden and flow of harvested resources, reduce the resilience of the system (by either measure). They may also induce profound, although often unobservable, changes in the structure of the ecosystem and consequently in its behaviour when subject to stress. In the third we address the economic problems associated with a reduction in the resilience of systems. A final section offers our conclusions and draws out the implications of the analysis for both the economics and management of renewable resources.

THE RESILIENCE AND STABILITY OF RENEWABLE RESOURCES

As already observed, the ecological concept of resilience has two main variants. The first, often associated with Pimm's work (1984), focuses on the time taken for a perturbed system to return towards some initial state. Pimm defines resilience as 'return time', or time taken for a perturbation inflicted upon the environment to diminish to a given fraction of its initial value.

The second definition, due to Holling (1973), focuses on the size of the stability domain. The measure of resilience by this definition is the perturbation that can be absorbed before the system converges on another equilibrium state. It is therefore particularly helpful when considering the properties of multiple equilibrium systems. These are systems which, when subject to persistent degradation, are not necessarily drawn towards the original equilibrium, but may instead undergo radical changes and tend towards a new state. The existence of two or more alternative states, which may differ with respect to their species composition, ecosystem functioning or ability to provide certain services, in fact, is a common occurrence in nature. Each state may appear stable because modest perturbations have small or short-lived effects (Perrings 1995, p. 314). Resilience in the sense of Holling is concerned with the size of the perturbation that would be needed to cause the shift of an ecosystem in its 'healthy' state to a degraded, undesirable equilibrium. Being based on a measure of the limits of local stability of each state, this definition of resilience tells us how far the ecosystem is, in its present state, from the threshold that would trigger fast and sometimes irreversible changes.

We are not arguing that all environmental systems undergo sudden and unanticipated collapse if subject to overexploitation. Indeed, there exist situations in which a resource responds to stress with a smooth degradation process and, as long as it has not been completely exhausted, retains its capacity to recover when the source of stress ceases. What we intend to emphasize, however, is that natural ecosystems are complex systems, involving nonlinear interactions and feedbacks between a very large number of interrelated parts and that one of the typical features shared by most complex systems is the possibility of an abrupt change in overall quality resulting from smooth changes of a parameter.

An important example of threshold effects of this sort is offered by the diversity of species within ecosystems; there may be a range of population sizes for the different species over which the system remains stable, but if any one population falls below its critical threshold level the self-organization of the ecosystem as a whole may be radically and irreversibly altered (Pielou 1993). Another example is given by the balance between grass and woody vegetation in ecosystems subject to grazing: semi-arid grasslands, in particular, can remain productive when the grazing pressure is modest; however, when cattle density rises above a threshold, the ecosystem may shift rapidly to a state of degradation (a shrub-dominated semi-desert) and the process cannot be halted even by removal of the animals. The recovery to a productive state may require not only sustained reductions in exploitation and restoration policies, but also long periods of time during which economic benefits are forgone. Threshold values exist for the biomass of most harvested resources; the reaction of aquatic ecosystems to nutrient loads; forest and savannah fires, and so on (Shaeffer et al. 1988). The resilience of an ecosystem is related to its ability to resist the processes which would lead towards the often irreversible change involved in crossing such thresholds.

The concept is easily linked to conventional notions of assimilative or carrying capacity. The most widely used definition of assimilative capacity in ecology refers to the capacity of an ecosystem to absorb pollution without degrading some notion of biological integrity (Cairns 1977). In this definition, assimilative capacity is identical to 'critical load'; it defines the waste burden that can be absorbed before provoking a biological impact that, for that particular ecosystem, is considered unacceptable. In fact, this is the sense in which the term has generally been used in environmental economics (see, for example, Barbier and Markandya 1990; Pearce and Warford 1993; Pethig 1994a). The concept of resilience given above helps to define the response we are looking for. More particularly, the *waste resilience* of a system in some state is the maximum pollution burden the system can absorb without losing the capacity to return to the equilibrium associated with that state.

The ecological definition of carrying capacity, like that of assimilative capacity, refers to the burden that can be placed on a system before provoking responses that either involve a change in the equilibrium of the system, or are associated with some defined set of costs in the neighbourhood of a given equilibrium. It is defined, as is assimilative capacity, for a given equilibrium. Hence it is contingent on technology, the structure of production, consumption, preferences and the interactions between the economic and ecological components of the system. The *harvest resilience* of a system in some state is the maximum harvest of resources it can stand without losing the capacity to return towards the equilibrium associated with that state. For many renewable resources, the maximum perturbation from which the resource may recover is the carrying capacity of the system less some minimal viable stock size.

IMPACTS OF HARVEST AND EMISSIONS ON SYSTEM DYNAMICS

Two distinct effects on the resilience of natural systems can be considered. The first is the effect of direct depletion of the stock due, for example, to a reduction at a given point in time in a resource biomass or in a population size, as a consequence of harvesting or pollution. The second is the indirect effect of changes in environmental conditions, due to the fact that harvest and/or pollution may slow down the resource regeneration rate. Environmental quality, in other words, may decline not only because of the direct impact of the waste discharged by a polluting firm or the clearing of a forest for commercial or agricultural purposes, but also because of the subsequent effects such events may have on the self-purification and recovery capacity of the ecosystem in the face of further disturbances.

Let us consider a prototype, single-species system, whose dynamics can be described by a logistic growth function.[1] This amounts to saying that we are considering resources whose regenerative capacity is bounded by a density-dependent upper limit. This is a simplified but not unrealistic description of the behaviour of many species, whose growth, usually fast at low levels of density, slows down and eventually ceases because of competition over vital resources or disease as the population density nears its upper limit. For such resources, therefore, the rate of regeneration will be increasing at low levels of stock, reaching a maximum, and then decreasing until the limit is reached, imposed by the environmental carrying capacity (K) for that resource. This is described by the dashed curves in Figure 11.1, where the resource stock x is measured on the horizontal axis, while the vertical axis measures the regeneration rate dx/dt (the rate at which the resource stock varies over time).

The Effect of Harvesting

The rate of harvest will also depend on the available resource stock. Figure 11.1 illustrates two examples (dotted curves) of functional relationships between harvest rate and resource stock. They imply that the level of harvest increases with the available stock of the resource, within the limits imposed by the capital and other factors invested in the activity (size of the fishing fleet, number of animals in the herd or cattle, labour force and machinery employed by a logging firm, and so on). By increasing the scale of the activity, the decision maker shifts the harvest curve upwards.

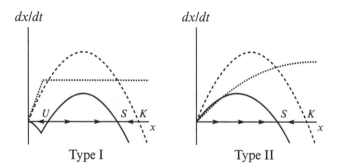

Type I   Type II

Figure 11.1 Natural regeneration in the presence of harvesting

In the presence of harvesting, then, the net regeneration rate of the natural resource will be given by the residual growth after the harvest has been subtracted. This is illustrated in the diagrams by the solid curve obtained as the difference between the regeneration and the harvest curves. The intersections between this net regeneration curve and the x

axis define the steady states of the system, that is, levels of stock for which the speed at which the resource stock changes is zero. In the vicinity of equilibria the rate at which the stock increases (or decreases) slows down, and it stops once the equilibrium is reached. The equilibrium can be stable (in which case small perturbations pushing the stock level away from the equilibrium will tend to die out) or unstable (small perturbations away from the equilibrium will tend to amplify).

In all cases in which harvesting functions take the forms shown, the system will be characterized by a locally stable equilibrium at S, which defines the net carrying capacity of the system. This means that if a perturbation causes the resource stock to decrease below (or indeed exceed) such an equilibrium level, the stock will tend to return to its original state S. Depending on the shape and level of the harvest function, then, there may be one or more additional (alternate locally stable and unstable) steady states. In Figure 11.1, Type I, for example, the equilibrium at U defines the net critical minimum stock or population size and is unstable. Thus, if a perturbation that causes a departure from the normal ecosystem functioning is large enough to force the resource stock below U, the self-compensating mechanisms that would bring the system back towards S no longer operate. The ecosystem's ability to recover is lost, and the resource stock will collapse completely, falling abruptly (and irreversibly) to zero.

For low levels of depletion, S approximates the original carrying capacity of the system, K, and the critical minimum stock U, if present, is close to zero. However, increasing levels of depletion will cause the stability domain (that is, the distance separating S from the origin if there is a single equilibrium, or the distance $S–U$ in the case of multiple equilibria) and the rate of regeneration of the system to decrease.

The Effect of Pollution: The Case of Marginal Damage Declining with the Level of Stock

Pollution affects ecosystems in different ways. The discharge of waste into the environment may, for example, directly reduce the level of environmental quality. It may also indirectly affect environmental quality by impairing one or more ecosystem functions and processes, and reducing the capacity of the system to regenerate itself. The combination of effects contributes to the complexity of system responses to pollution. We consider two alternative effects, the distinguishing feature being whether the impact of pollution on the size of the stock is positively or inversely related to the level of that stock. The resilience implications of an inverse relation will be dealt with first.

Many natural systems are structured in such a way that the marginal damage imposed by emissions is higher when the system stocks are small. This fits the intuition that ecosystems may be more fragile when their assimilative capacity has already been reduced. In the case of water pollution from organic matter, for instance, it is generally assumed that the rate at which available dissolved oxygen is depleted is directly proportional to the size of the water body. The higher the load already carried by the water body, the faster its 'health' or 'productivity' deteriorates as a consequence of further disturbance.

To see the effects of this, let the effect of polluting emissions be described by the dotted curves in Figure 11.2. The three diagrams show how increasing the level of emissions or the toxicity of the pollutant which will cause the pollution curve to shift upwards.

Pollution will reduce the natural resource regeneration rate. Consequently the ecosystem dynamics, once the effect of emissions has been taken into account, are represented by the solid curves obtained by subtracting the impact of pollution from the natural regeneration rate.

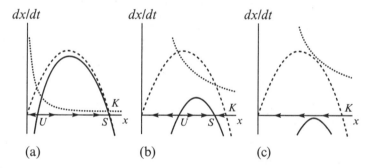

Figure 11.2 Net regeneration in the presence of pollution: inverse density dependence

Once again, the system will be characterized by two equilibria, and again the resource stock, damaged by pollution, will decrease and tend to settle at the new equilibrium level S, which is locally stable. The equilibrium at U defines the net critical minimum stock or population size and is unstable. For very low levels of emissions, S approximates the original carrying capacity of the system, K, but increasing emissions will cause it to fall. At the same time, increasing emissions cause an increase in the critical minimum stock or population size U: that is, they increase the minimum level to which the resource stock can be reduced without jeopardizing its capacity to regenerate. Emissions accordingly have two effects: to reduce the stability domain, S–U; and to slow down the systems' recovery after disturbance, measured by the rate of regeneration, dx/dt, over the relevant domain (that is by the height of the solid curve).

Both in the simple depletion and the present case, further increases in the level or toxicity of emissions will eventually cause a qualitative change in the structure of the system, including the disappearance of the steady state S (Figure 11.2c). That is, there exists a threshold level of stress at which the system loses its ability to recover towards a stable state, and the stock converges to zero.[2]

This may be illustrated by constructing a diagram that shows how the location and number of equilibria for the resource stock depend on different levels of emissions (Figure 11.3). In this way, it is possible to see the values of the control parameter for which the dynamical system undergoes qualitative changes in its stable states ('bifurcations'). The equilibrium level of stock x^* is measured on the vertical axis, and emissions e on the horizontal one. For levels of emissions lower than the

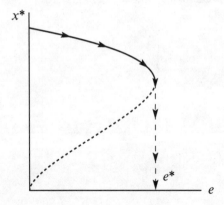

Figure 11.3 Impact of pollution on the steady states of the resource stock (I)

critical value e^*, the system exhibits two equilibria – one on each of the two branches of the diagram. The upper branch of the bifurcation diagram represents the locally stable equilibrium points, and hence it describes the condition, in terms of resource stock, at which the ecosystem will settle for each level of emissions. The lower branch of the diagram illustrates how the unstable equilibrium (the minimum critical stock size) moves as emissions increase. When pollution increases, the stable and the unstable equilibria move closer to each other, progressively reducing the stability domain. The resource stock initially decreases in a smooth, continuous fashion. However, eventually a critical level of emissions e^* is reached, at which the equilibrium level of the resource stock suddenly falls to zero. In other words, increasing emissions, even very slowly, might trigger an irreversible process, leading to an abrupt, unexpected collapse of the system. Specific consequences will depend on the scale of the natural system involved, and on the strength of the link between the environment and the socioeconomic system relying upon it.

It is particularly important that for environmental damage functions of this form, increasing emissions will affect the (unobservable) critical minimum stock or population threshold more than the observable steady state. In other words as the stress increases, all that is observed is a slow reduction in the equilibrium size of the resource stock. However, the stability domain of the system may actually be shrinking in quite a dramatic fashion. This can be seen from Figure 11.2 which shows the critical minimum stock or population size, U, moving further to the right as the carrying capacity, S, moves to the left. Similarly, in Figure 11.3 the branch representing the unstable equilibria (dotted portion of the diagram) turns out to be steeper, on average, than the branch representing the stable ones. The implications for the predictability and hence for the management of the system are of evident importance, and will be explored further in the later sections of this chapter.

The Effect of Pollution: The Case of Marginal Damage Increasing with the Level of Stock

An inverse relationship between impact of pollution and resource stock is not, however, general. In many cases it is claimed that the opposite is true. Mature systems, for example, may tend to be more easily disturbed than those in the early stages of growth (Holling 1986). Let us now consider, therefore, the case where the damage caused by pollution is an increasing function of biomass. The functional form described by the dotted curve in Figure 11.4 represents emissions which erode the regenerative capacity of the natural resource in a way similar to that in which a herbivore grazes upon plants: the impact of pollution is positively related to the size of the resource stock, but with a 'saturation' process that progressively slows down the increase in the marginal damage. A description of this kind is adopted in studies on the uptake of dissolved chemicals by micro-organisms (Lassiter 1986), on the consumption of nutrients by algae and on the biological decomposition of organic matter (Jørgensen 1994).

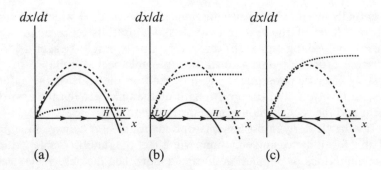

*Figure 11.4 Net regeneration in the presence of pollution: positive
              density dependence*

As in the previous case, for low emissions there is a unique equilibrium at $x = H$, which is locally stable; once again, if a perturbation
causes the stock to move away from such a level the system will automatically return to the original state. What distinguishes this case, however,
is that increasing emissions may bring about a change in the qualitative
dynamics of the system. This is visualized in the Figures 11.4b and 11.4c
by the additional intersections between the curve describing the negative
impact of emissions and the logistic curve. A new possible steady state
will appear, corresponding to a lower stock size. While the system dis-
plays a unique equilibrium state, it is always possible for the resource
(unless it has been driven to extinction) to recover towards its initial condition if the source of disturbance is removed. But if increasing stress
can cause such qualitative changes in the behaviour of the ecosystem,
and in particular the appearance of new potential stable states, this is no
longer guaranteed. The original domain of stability of H is now frag-
mented into two narrower basins, and hence the effect of pollution has
been to cause a loss of Holling resilience. Specifically, the reduction in
stock size that the system can stand without ratcheting down to a much
lower level of productivity has been dramatically reduced. In Figure
11.4b, once across the threshold at $x = U$, the resource converges instead
towards a degraded state L. This illustrates the fact that not only
normal, but also degenerated states of ecosystems can in fact be self-sus-
taining (Carpenter and Cottingham 1997).

As before, this implies an increased uncertainty as to the ecosystem's
capacity to bear stress, since it is not possible to observe the underlying
structure of the dynamical system. Unless this is properly understood,
structural changes may be masked by the relatively small reduction in the
equilibrium level of the stock.

Notice that the fragmentation of the stability domain is not the only effect brought about by the structural change. The loss of resilience in terms of size of the stability domain is associated with longer return times. As before, the rate of regeneration is slower for the system in general, and in particular around $x = H$. Longer return times after displacements from the equilibrium might be considered an indication that structural changes have occurred.

To illustrate the consequences of this qualitative change in the system, consider, as in the previous case, the diagram generated by plotting equilibrium values of the resource against emissions.

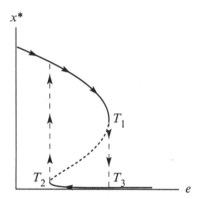

Figure 11.5 Impact of pollution on the steady states of the resource stock (II)

As e increases the equilibrium values of x follow the upper branch. Pollution is causing a slow, smooth decline in the resource stock. If the level of pressure keeps increasing indefinitely, however, a limit point T_1, is reached where the resource stock x falls by a jump on to a degraded state, characterized by a very low level of stock. At such threshold a qualitative change takes place: an ecosystem that could exist in only one stable state suddenly becomes a multiple equilibrium system – that is, a system which can settle in states other than its original state.

The breakdown, in this case, is not irreversible (as it was in the case of inverse density dependence), since the resource has not become completely extinct. By reducing emissions it is possible to set the system on the return path. The recovery, however, takes place along a path different from that followed by the resource in its degradation process. Only when levels of emission smaller than T_2 are achieved can the system make the inverse transition towards the earlier, more desirable state. Reducing the pressure upon the ecosystem by the same amount that caused the switch will not help. The original state can be restored only by means of an external intervention, and at the cost of a major reduction in emissions levels. The width of the loop that the recovery path must follow offers an indication of the economic costs associated with the fall of the resource stock. It describes, in fact, the extent to which it will be necessary to abstain from the economic activities that caused the collapse in order to allow the ecosystem to regain its former productivity.

ECOLOGICAL DYNAMICS AND ECONOMIC DECISIONS

We have discussed the impact of depletion and pollution on resource dynamics in the context of a specific set of functional forms in the previous section. It turns out, however, that the impact of stress on the velocity of recovery after disturbance, and on the stability domain of the resource, extends to a much more general class of functions. In fact, it extends to all resources that have a capacity to self-regenerate, and an upper limit to such capacity (or carrying capacity) that is negatively affected by some form of increasing human-induced stress. For the arguments in the previous sections to hold, in fact, all that is needed is that the regeneration and depletion functions be continuous and cross at least once at a level of stock within the system carrying capacity.

Moreover, we based our discussion on a simplified single-stock system; but if our arguments are a warning about the effects of non-linearities in the response of natural resources to stress, they may well be relevant in the context of ecosystem-scale models, where the addition of more feedbacks and interrelationships is quite likely to result in an even more strongly nonlinear system. They will hold, in other words, whenever it is reasonable to assume the existence of an ecosystem equilibrium that suffers a negative impact from exploitation. The concept of equilibrium we have in mind here is not that of a system whose components do not change, but rather that of a natural environment 'in balance', capable of offering a steady flow of services (Pimm 1991).

For all such resources, it has been shown elsewhere (see Dalmazzone and Perrings 1997) that increasing stress through depletion or pollution will always cause the rate at which the ecosystem recovers after a disturbance to decrease. When we consider discrete perturbations that take the system away from the vicinity of the equilibrium, this implies longer recovery times, that is, a lower Pimm-resilience.[3]

Moreover, increasing stress through depletion or pollution will always cause a decrease in the Holling-resilience of the system, that is, a decrease in the maximum perturbation that can be sustained without causing the natural system to leave the domain of attraction of its original state. In other words, it will cause the stability domain of the original equilibrium to shrink, and eventually to collapse if the stress upon the system is indefinitely increased.

It follows that for a wide class of depletion functions, including the most commonly used in the literature, increasing stress necessarily weakens the stability of the system, in terms of both the stability domain and the recovery rate. The negative effect will act in the same direction on both Holling- and Pimm- resilience.

Furthermore, a loss of resilience may result in sudden, catastrophic changes in environmental quality. This depends on the relative shape of the regeneration and depletion functions. If the system converges on a unique equilibrium, increasing pressure causes a progressive shrinking of the stability domain and slows down the self-repair process, but the resource stock declines in a continuous fashion as the level of stress is increased. The existence of multiple equilibria, however, opens up the possibility of sudden, discontinuous environmental changes.[4]

Consider now the implications of this for the exploitation of renewable resources. Let us take the simple case of a natural system that provides a flow of economic services in the form of harvest of a given resource.

The analysis conducted so far has two main sets of implications for the resilience of such systems. The first concerns the implications of an economically optimal harvest rate on the resilience of the system (irrespective of whether there are emission-induced changes in the natural rate of regeneration of the resource). As the optimal stock size in a harvested system is less than the equilibrium stock size in an unexploited system, the Holling resilience of the harvested system will be lower than that of the unexploited system. The magnitude of the disturbance required to drive the resource below its critical minimum stock size will be reduced.

The second set of implications concern the effects of emission-induced reductions in the rate of regeneration of the resource. Toxic emissions tend to reduce both the system stability domain and its recovery rate. If the decision maker ignores the impact of pollution on the resource, environmental degradation will have no effect on the privately optimal stock size. This, however, will contribute to further reduce the Holling-resilience of the system, increasing the inherent risk of triggering fast and irreversible responses. The collapse of fisheries subject to the simultaneous demands of a level of harvest inattentive to environmental conditions, and to the assimilation of increasing wastes, provide a number of examples of these dynamics (see, for example, Knowler et al. 1997).

The alternative possibility is, however, that the economic agent does take the effect of emissions into account in determining the optimal level of harvest. In this case, the functional relationship between the damage caused by pollution and the stock level matters. In the case of an inverse relationship between impact of emissions and stock or population size, in the presence of pollution the optimal harvest will be lower than in the absence of pollution. This will happen regardless of conservation concerns on the part of the economic agent. However, the effect on the size of the perturbation required to destabilize the system is ambiguous. It is possible that the steady state size of the resource stock is increased at the same time as the critical minimum stock size.

The situation is slightly different if the relationship between the impact of pollution and stock size is positive. In this case the combination of the two forms of pressure on the environment has the most severe effects. Again, the optimal rate of harvest falls (even more than in the previous case), as does the system's recovery time. Even so, the equilibrium level of the harvested resource stock will fall with respect to the unpolluted case.

To summarize, the effect of pollution on the resilience of an economically exploited natural resource depends on the form of the environmental damage function. Pollution will always decrease the rate at which the ecosystem recovers after a disturbance. Pollution will also reduce the size of the perturbation required to destabilize the system if the impact of pollution is positively related to the resource biomass, or if the change induced by emissions on the optimal equilibrium state of the resource is smaller than the effect induced on the critical minimum stock size.

A NEW APPROACH TO THE POLICY PROBLEM

Finally, consider how this view of the problem affects the way in which we would approach both management and policy. We focus on the policy and management implications of changes in the stability domain as a result both of environmental conditions and of harvest. The stability domain of a renewable resource whose conservation is a policy objective may be thought of as the relevant 'policy region', that is, the region within whose boundaries management choices should be made. The resilience of the resource, in the sense of Holling, is a measure of the distance to the boundary of the stability domain given the current value of the resource stock. While the maximum such distance in a logistic model is given by the carrying capacity of the resource, a similar measure can be constructed for any other value of the stock, including the value corresponding to the optimal level of harvest.

The analysis in this chapter highlights how the main reason for concern over the resilience of exploited resources is the existence of uncertainty. In many cases, neither the system dynamics nor the measurement of data are free from uncertainty. Both in an undisturbed and in a managed natural system, it is possible to observe only the stable equilibrium: the prevailing state of the system. Other equilibria are not observed. Yet the closer the system is brought to the boundaries of the stability domain, the higher is the risk of irreversible, or only slowly reversible, change.

The kind of knowledge it would be important to obtain concerns the relative shape of the self-regeneration and depletion functions. It would be important to know whether any damage function intersects the natural growth function as the stock size decreases. If it does not, the stock will recover from any level of stress (even though the recovery rate may depend on the extent of the loss). But if there are signals about the existence of further intersections, then the possibility of discontinuities and irreversibilities arises. The problem is that critical minimum stock sizes are unobservable, and our knowledge of the dynamics of ecological systems is limited. The observable level of environmental quality does not generally offer a reliable indicator of the system's relative position with respect to such thresholds. Moreover, as we have shown, the conditions under which ecosystems respond to increasing stress without suffering an irreversible or near irreversible loss appear to be fairly restrictive. Under more general circumstances, the risk of causing a collapse of the natural system by overstepping critical thresholds is a necessary consequence of continuously increasing levels of pressure on the environment. It is these factors which necessitate the use of policy instruments incorporating safety margins, as discussed in Chapter 9.

Much environmental policy is focused on the identification of bounds on allowable activities, through instruments such as standards, emission permits, harvesting quotas, water quality requirements, hunting seasons and so on. While the efficiency properties of different instruments in achieving target levels of protection is a legitimate area of economic interest, so is the target level of protection. In most cases target levels of protection are identified outside economics, by reference to health and safety criteria deriving from the natural sciences. Indeed, the establishment of bounds on economic activity is the way in which the natural sciences generally intervene in environmental policy.

Studies such as the one outlined in this chapter, however, suggest that there is also scope for an economic analysis. Because the thresholds of the policy region are not observed, they are generally not protected or protectable through regular market transactions. Under the right circumstances prices may in fact react to the decline in a resource stock and increase to reflect scarcity, thus providing incentives for conservation.[5] Unlike the case of a smooth decline in resource stock, however, the presence of critical thresholds does not send any explicit, continuous signal to the market. It does not, therefore, influence economic activities. Protection from unwanted breakdowns of exploited natural systems, accordingly, requires a conscious and specific management effort. The boundaries to exploitation need to be designed so as to be responsive to the warning signals detected by monitoring authorities, and to take into account the level of pressure already imposed on the system. The setting of the bounds is not independent of the economic activities they are designed to limit. In a harvested system, the critical minimum population size, and hence the size of the perturbation in stocks needed to force the system across that threshold, depends directly on the optimal rate of harvest. The cost of the reduction in the resilience of the system is therefore part of the economic problem of optimal resource utilization. Symmetrically, since a reduction in resilience is an essential datum in the identification of the bounds on economic activity, it is part of the problem of environmental protection.

By enabling us to identify the change in the capacity of exploited systems to recover, this approach aims at providing a way of evaluating the protection of critical environmental thresholds. We believe that such a shift of focus can help us see the forces at work, as well as the available options and possible outcomes, in a new light.

NOTES

1. The discussion is based on particular, albeit widely used, functional forms. A more general set of implications are drawn in the following section.
2. Such dynamic behaviour can be described, in mathematical terms, as a saddle-node (or tangent) bifurcation.
3. It is important to notice, however, that estimates of the return time used in the empirical literature, such as the inverse of the slope of the regeneration function at the equilibrium, may not register such decreases in the ability to recover. Being based on a linear approximation of the recovery curve, these empirical measures may fail to detect a loss in resilience, if the slope of the recovery curve happens to be higher around the new equilibrium than around the original one. In such cases, the commonly used measures of return time would convey misleading indications on the state of the ecosystem.
4. Multiple equilibria would arise whenever the regeneration and depletion functions cross at least twice in the positive quadrant in correspondence of a value of the resource stock within the system carrying capacity.
5. Although it must be noted that the existence of uncertainty and discontinuities is not the only reason for which the price system may fail to appropriately reflect resource scarcity. A comprehensive discussion of this issue can be found in Perrings (1987).

REFERENCES

Barbier, E. and A. Markandya (1990), 'The conditions for achieving environmentally sustainable development', *European Economic Review*, **34**, 659–69.

Cairns, J.J. (1977), 'Aquatic ecosystems assimilative capacity', *Fisheries*, **2**, 5–24.

Carpenter, S.R. and K.L. Cottingham (1997), 'Resilience and restoration of lakes', *Conservation Ecology* [online], **1** (2), URL: http://www.consecol.org.

Clark, W.C. and R.E. Munn (eds) (1986), *Sustainable Development of the Biosphere*, Cambridge: Cambridge University Press.

Common, M.S. and C. Perrings (1992), 'Towards an ecological economics of sustainability', *Ecological Economics*, **6**, 7–34.

Dalmazzone, S. and C. Perrings (1997), 'Resilience and stability in ecological economic systems', Paper presented at the 8th European Association of Environmental and Resource Economists (EAERE) Annual Conference, Tilburg, 26-28 June.

Daly, H.E. (1968/1973), *Towards a Steady State Economy*, San Francisco: W.H. Freeman.

Daly, H.E. (1991), 'Ecological economics and sustainable development', Environment Department Divisional Working Paper 1991–24, World Bank Environment Department, Washington, DC.

Hallam, T.G. and S.A. Levin (eds) (1986), *Mathematical Ecology*, Berlin: Springer-Verlag.

Holling, C.S. (1973) 'Resilience and stability in ecological systems', *Annual Review of Ecological Systems*, **4**, 1–24.

Holling, C.S. (1986), 'The resilience of terrestrial ecosystems', in Clark and Munn (1986), pp. 292–315.

Holling, C.S., D.W. Schindler, B.W. Walker, and J. Roughgarden (1995), *Biodiversity in the Functioning of Ecosystems*, Cambridge: Cambridge University Press.

Jørgensen, S.E. (1994), *Fundamentals of Ecological Modelling*, Amsterdam: Elsevier.

Knowler, D., E. Barbier, and I. Strand (1997), 'The effects of pollution on open access fisheries: a case study of the Black Sea', Paper presented at the 8th European Association of Environmental and Resource Economists (EAERE) Annual Conference, Tilburg, 26–28 June.

Lassiter, R.R. (1986), '*A theoretical basis for modelling element cycling*', in Hallam and Levin (1986), pp. 341–80.

Ludwig, D., B. Walker, and C.S. Holling (1997), 'Sustainability, stability, and resilience', *Conservation Ecology* [online], **1** (1), URL: http:I/www.consecol.org.

Norgaard, R.B. (1984), 'Coevolutionary development potential', *Land Economics*, **60**, 160–73.

O'Neill, R.V., A.R. Johnson and A.W. King (1989), 'A hierarchical framework for the analysis of scale', *Landscape Ecology*, **3**, 193–205.

Pearce, D.W. and J.J. Warford (1993), *World without End*, New York: Oxford University Press.

Perrings, C. (1987), *Economy and Environment*, Cambridge: Cambridge University Press.

Perrings, C. (ed.) (1995), *The Economic Value of Biodiversity*, Chapter 12 of the *Global Biodiversity Assessment*, Cambridge: Cambridge University Press for United Nations Environment Programme.

Perrings, C. and B. Walker (1997), 'Biodiversity, resilience and the control of eco-logical–economic systems: the case of fire-driven rangelands', *Ecological Economics*, **22**, 73–83.

Pethig, R. (1994a), 'Ecological dynamics and the valuation of environmental change', in Pethig (1994b), pp. 3–22.

Pethig, R. (ed.) (1994b), *Valuing the Environment*, Dordrecht: Kluwer Academic Publishers.

Pielou, E.C. (1993), *Ecological Diversity*, New York: John Wiley.

Pimm, S.L. (1984), 'The complexity and stability of ecosystems,' *Nature*, **307**, 321–26.

Pimm, S.L. (1991), *The Balance of Nature?*, Chicago: University of Chicago Press.

Shaeffer, D.L., E. Herricks and H. Herster (1988), 'Ecosystem health: I. Measuring ecosystem health', *Environmental Management*, **12**, 445–55.

Stone, L., A. Gabric, and T. Berman (1996), 'Ecosystem resilience, stability and productivity: seeking a relationship.' *American Naturalist*, **148**, 892–903.

12. Stripping resources and investing abroad: a path to sustainable development?

John C.V. Pezzey*

INTRODUCTION

Behind this provocative title lies a fairly simple idea. Developing a dynamic economy optimally requires every sector of the economy to be used optimally. But developing an economy sustainably does not generally need every sector to be used sustainably, unless each and every sector is vital for survival. So in most cases it is very difficult, perhaps impossible, to derive logical, watertight rules for sustainable development which can be applied operationally at a purely sectoral level. Trying to find, as many have done in recent years, coherent rules for sustainable cities, sustainable transport, sustainable water, sustainable agriculture, sustainable forests and so on, will therefore usually give disappointing and often inconsistent results. Such rules may even provide a new disguise behind which special interests can argue for protecting a sector merely for its own sake, rather than for the sake of sustaining the whole economy.

This problem, that sustaining all the parts may not be needed in order to sustain the whole, was raised informally by Pezzey (1989, pp. 55–9 and 1992, pp. 347–9) and also by Little and Mirrlees (1990, p. 365) and Beckerman (1994, p. 193), among others. I suspect that one could develop a general theorem, which states the precise conditions under which sectoral sustainability is not necessary for sustaining the whole economy. However, what follows here is just one, formal illustration of such a theorem. It is a result for an economy with three main features, which are quite realistic for many countries. First, it is a 'capital-resource economy'. That is, it possesses both human-made capital, and depletable natural

* I am grateful for comments on earlier versions from Mick Common, James McTernan, Fanny Missfeldt, Cees Withagen, participants at the 8th European Association of Environmental and Resource Economists (EAERE) Annual Meetings in Tilburg, Netherlands in June 1997, and especially Pam Mason.

resources which could be renewable or non-renewable. (In this chapter 'capital' is always human-made, and a 'resource' is always natural.) Second, it is 'open' to the rest of the world, so that it exports and imports produced goods and resources. Third, it is 'small' in comparison to the rest of the world, so that nothing it does can affect the world prices of natural resources, or the world interest rate. Given further, maybe unrealistic features, such an economy can then develop sustainably by stripping (depleting) some or even all of its resources, investing enough of the proceeds abroad, and ultimately living on the interest on these investments.

In fact, the formal result found here is even stronger. It is that such an economy's plan for its future – its 'intertemporal welfare goal' – typically has no effect *at all* on how it manages its natural resources. Suppose it was originally planning to deplete some of its natural resources down to zero, in pursuit of a conventional goal of 'optimal development' which discounts the wellbeing of future generations. Then suppose it has some kind of ethical revolution, and all its citizens change their goal to sustainable development.[1] The result is that the economy still manages its resource sectors in exactly the same way. All that changes is that it saves and invests more abroad, so that it can sustain its future welfare once its resources are gone.

Such a result obviously conflicts with some of the strongest traditions in the 'environmental sustainability' literature. These propose three key rules for sectoral sustainability: to sustain renewable resources, to sustain the environment's assimilative capacity, and to deplete non-renewables only as fast as they can be substituted for (see, for example, Pearce 1988, p. 58 and Daly 1990, pp. 2 and 4). This conflict will be discussed in the conclusions, but first the 'strip resources and invest abroad' result for a small open economy must be explained. This is done next in words, with the formal underlying mathematics in an appendix. Then we see what happens if the economy is closed, or large and open. Then we discuss the fallacy of composition that would occur in the result if all economies tried to strip resources and invest abroad at once. Finally, we consider the implications of all this for the broader sustainability debate.

THE RESULT FOR A SMALL, OPEN ECONOMY

Three basic assumptions about the economy have already been mentioned. It has one non-depreciating, human-made capital stock and a number of depletable, natural resources, with initial stocks of both being given.[2] It is open to trade and is small in relation to both resource and capital markets in the rest of the world. The following further assumptions, some highly restrictive, are then needed to derive the result (see the appendix for mathematical details):

(1). The natural resources, which could be non-human species, do not have intrinsic rights to be sustained or preserved for their own sake. So we are ignoring any 'deep green' philosophy that resources do have rights.

(2). The resources are renewable. However, the result is in fact unaffected by the natural growth rate of the resource, and also applies to non-renewable resources, where the growth rate is zero.

(3). The economy lasts just two time periods, and then ceases to exist.

(4). The economy has a production process which transforms inputs of a capital stock and resource flows into a flow of a composite good. The good can be consumed in either time period; invested at home in the first period to increase the second-period capital stock; or invested abroad in the first period to yield a fixed, world rate of interest.

(5). There is no limit beyond which capital cannot substitute for resources in the production process, but some resource input to production remains essential.

(6). The economy has a 'representative agent'. This means that everyone in the economy is assumed to be identical, so that issues of within-generation equity are ignored.

(7). The representative agent's intertemporal welfare depends solely on his or her first- and second-period consumption of the composite good. Neither resource stocks nor resource flows directly affect intertemporal welfare. That is, the resources have no environmental (non-market) value.

(8). The economy is said to be sustainable if consumption is not lower in the second period than in the first. 'Sustainable' is thus distinct from 'environmentally sound' in that environmental quality is irrelevant. This differs from the majority of modern sustainability literature, such as Røpke (1994) and other papers in the same special issue.[3] I discuss sustainability definitions at length in Pezzey (1997), and there distinguish 'sustainedness' from 'sustainability', but for an efficient, two-period economy these two concepts both amount to consumption not falling from the first to the second period.[4]

(9). There is no uncertainty in the economy.

A more general theory of the sectoral sustainability problem would obviously use fewer assumptions. The result here depends crucially on assumptions (5) (substitutability), (7) (materialism) and (9) (certainty), and these would be challenged by most environmentalists. They would argue that many resources are ultimately non-substitutable, a direct source of environmental value, and subject to huge uncertainty. The degree to which these assumptions are right or wrong is a matter for important empirical or even ethical debates, to which I make no contribution here.

In the first period, the economy (or its representative agent) has four types of decision to make. First, how much of the resource to import, or to extract from its initial stock and export. Second, how much of its resource to extract and combine (together with any imported resource) at home with the given initial capital, to produce a certain amount of the good. These decisions determine the amount of production, and the resources available for the second period (after adding in natural growth between periods). The third decision is how much production to invest at home, which determines the second-period capital stock. The last is how much production to invest abroad. First-period consumption is then whatever production has not been invested.

In the second period, the only decision is how much of the resource to use for domestic production, which then determines how much to export (or import). Consumption is then the sum of domestic production, the return on the first-period foreign investment plus interest paid at the world rate, and the value of second-period resource exports.

The technical result of this model is that any change in the economy's intertemporal welfare goal – whether to achieving sustainability, to achieving maximum constant consumption as in Solow (1974), or to just giving more weight to the future – changes only the levels of its consumption and foreign investment. It does *not* change either resource 'management' (that is, resource trade, and resource use for domestic production) or domestic investment in the economy. So, *a sustainable economy does not necessarily require sustainable resource management*. There is no need in this model for further, sector-specific constraints on resource management such as the 'compensating investments' suggested by Daly (1990) or Barbier et al.(1990). The only investment needed to compensate future generations is the build-up of foreign investment while domestic resources are depleted, along the lines of the investment that Kuwait has built up against the day that its oil runs out. Nor is there any need to use especially low discount rates for 'environmental projects', thus avoiding the problem of how to define such projects in practice. Only if resources are non-substitutable in an uncertain and/or unowned way will any sectoral or project-level policy for sustainability make sense. If the non-substitutability was certain below some critical threshold of a fully-owned resource (thus breaking assumption (5) but not assumption (9)), prices would become infinite at that threshold, and resources would be sustained automatically by their owners' profitability calculations.

The result is formally proved in the appendix, but an intuitive explanation is as follows. Suppose the welfare goal is changed to a more 'conservationist' goal, which gives more weight to the future (that is, to period 2). This requires more saving and investment now. Because the economy is small and open, the world interest rate prevails in it, and is unchanged by any increase in the economy's foreign investment. But resource management is determined solely by the interest rate (which producers use to compute and maximize the discounted present value of their profits), and so also remains unchanged. And if the economy tried to increase investment domestically, the interest rate earned would fall below the world interest rate, so the economy would be better off making all its extra investment abroad.

This separation of decisions about production and resource management from decisions about consumption, saving and foreign investment happens because the world interest rate is unaffected by the small open economy. It is an international version of the 'separation' theorem of Fisher (1930, p. 271; see also Hirshleifer 1980, p. 497). I refer to the result as 'strip resources and invest abroad', because managing natural resources to maximize discounted profits can easily lead to resource stripping (that is, exhausting the stock towards zero, either in finite or infinite time). This is inevitable for non-renewable resources (for example, see Dasgupta and Heal 1974), but discounted profit maximization can also result in 'optimal extinction' of renewable resources if the discount rate (that is, the interest rate) is high enough (Clark 1990).[5] As already noted, investing abroad is then a better way of sustaining the economy's consumption than investing at home.

THE RESULT FOR A CLOSED, OR LARGE AND OPEN ECONOMY

What would be the effect of introducing a more conservationist welfare goal into an economy which has the same properties as before, except that it is closed (as ultimately only the global economy is), or large in relation to the rest of the world? The answer is as brief as the previous section was long. The increase in desired saving in period 1 is now large relative to the capital market, and so would lower the interest rate. This then automatically changes the economy's resource management policy to that which is necessary to achieve the new welfare goal (for example, sustainability), although the result is still not necessarily sustainable resource management. There is still no need for sectoral sustainability policies, be they compensating investments, or special discount rates for environmental projects.

A POSSIBLE FALLACY OF COMPOSITION IF MANY ECONOMIES ACT AT THE SAME TIME

The model described assumes that the small open economy changes its welfare goal on its own, while all the economies in the rest of the world make no change. What if, either by pure coincidence, or because of an international call such as the one issued by the 1992 Rio Earth Summit, a good proportion of the world's small, open economies change their welfare goal at the same time, say to sustainable development? Together they would amount to a large open economy. By the logic of the preceding paragraph, the equilibrium world interest rate would then change, as also would resource management and domestic investment in each economy. But if each economy assumes that all other economies have not changed their welfare goal, it will make plans which cannot in fact be realized.

To take an extreme example, suppose a two-period world consists of dozens of small, identical economies like the one formally modelled above. Suppose at first they all aim to maximize a conventional, discounted present value (PV) welfare function.[6] By symmetry, this would result in no resource trade, and each economy would act as if closed. Suppose also that the parameters of each economy mean that consumption in period 1 would be unsustainable. Now suppose that just one of these economies adds a sustainability constraint to its welfare goal before any plans are enacted. By the theory of the previous section, the resource management and domestic investment of this one sustainable economy would be the same as all the other, unsustainable economies. It would achieve sustainability first, by saving and investing abroad in period 1; and second, by reclaiming its investment in period 2, with interest added at the unchanged world rate, as consumption goods (made from capital and resources) imported from unsustainable economies.[7]

However, not every economy in this world can achieve sustainability in this way. If every economy tried to invest abroad at the same time, there would be no 'abroad' left to receive the investment! If every economy planned to do this in period 1, *ex post* there would be a significant world-wide increase in planned foreign investment. This would lower the world rate of interest, making domestic investment and resource conservation more attractive. But *ex ante*, if each economy does not realize the other economies' plans, it will expect too high a rate of interest. It will then save too little and deplete too much resource in period 1 to achieve its own sustainability, in a world where every other economy plans for sustainability, too. A global fallacy of composition would thus have occurred. What works as a sustainability strategy for one economy in isolation may not work for all economies together. It is thus important to investigate, possibly using the tools of game theory, whether and how such failures to make consistent sustainability plans can be avoided by world agencies and/or world futures markets. Unfortunately, this is beyond the scope of this chapter.

CONCLUDING DISCUSSION

This chapter has mainly studied a simple, two-period model of development in a small, open economy with human-made capital, depletable natural resources, no uncertainty, and many other restrictive assumptions. We saw that in this economy, adopting a new intertemporal welfare goal, such as sustainable development, typically requires no change at all in resource management or domestic investment. The economy can strip its natural resources down to nothing and still be developing sustainably, as long as it saves enough of the output from resource use and invests it abroad. This result does not hold when we change just one assumption and make the economy closed, or large and open. A new welfare goal will then require a change in resource management and domestic investment. However, this change will occur via market forces: the changed welfare goal changes saving; this changes the economy's interest rate; and a changed interest rate brings about the required change in resource management and domestic investment. So in all three types of economy (small open, closed, and large open), there is no need for sustainability policies (such as a programme of 'compensating investments', or especially low discount rates) to be targeted at specific resource sectors.

These results conflict directly with some of the 'strongest traditions in the environmental sustainability literature' mentioned in the introduction, which are worth giving in full here:

> In simple terms [sustainable development] argues for (a) development subject to a set of constraints which set resource harvest rates at levels no higher than managed or natural regeneration rates; and (b) use of the environment as a 'waste sink' on the basis that waste disposal rates should not exceed rates of (natural or managed) assimilation by the counterpart ecosystems. ... There are self-evident problems in advocating sustainable rates for exhaustible resources, so that 'sustainabilists' tend to think in terms of a resource set encompassing substitution between renewables and exhaustibles. (Pearce 1988, p. 58)

> For the management of renewable resources there are two obvious principles of sustainable development. First that harvest rates should equal regeneration rates (sustained yield). Second that waste emission rates should equal the natural assimilative capacities of the ecosystems into which the wastes are emitted. ... The quasi-sustainable use of nonrenewables requires that any investment in the exploitation of a nonrenewable resource must be paired with a compensating investment in a renewable substitute. (Daly 1990, pp. 2 and 4)

What are we to make of this conflict of views about sectoral sustainability? As a preliminary, recall that the word 'sustainable' has a purely intertemporal meaning here, and is quite distinct from 'environmentally desirable'. There will still be a general need for sectoral environmental policies to internalize external (non-market) costs, but that is not the issue here. Even ignoring all environmental externalities, which we have done throughout the chapter, the above conflict would remain.

The main conclusion is the trite, disappointing but important one that the truth is very complex. Justifying rules for sectoral sustainability is not as simple or obvious as Pearce or Daly claim. So much depends on the realism of the necessary assumptions, and Pearce and Daly's implicit assumptions do seem rather extreme. For example, their rules ignore trade, so they could only apply to a closed economy, and the only closed economy now is effectively the whole world economy. Current levels of consumption of renewable resources such as food and water are substantially in excess of minimum, non-substitutable needs in industrialized countries, and do not have to be sustained in order to achieve sustainable development as a whole.

However, the assumptions needed for my own result are just as extreme, in the opposite direction. I am certainly not claiming that they are all realistic. Indeed, by highlighting some simple, but unrealistic conditions required for the result to be true, this chapter is intended as a warning rather than a recommendation to policy makers in small open economies. To be sure that a 'strip resources and invest abroad' policy is wise, they must know with certainty that the resources have only private productive value and no intrinsic philosophical, popular amenity or publicly productive value; that capital will always be substitutable for resources in domestic production; and that few other countries are planning to adopt the same policy. If all countries followed the policy, there would be no abroad left to conserve natural resources and accept incoming investments.

So the result does not mean that such principles of 'environmental sustainability' should just be discarded. At its root, sustainability thinking is not a purely abstract, ethical concern for future generations, but a profound, practical concern that they are under threat from the way in which environmental resources are being treated by modern economies. If a country adopts a new welfare goal which gives more weight to the future, in practice it should probably make its resource management more conservative. However, this need not amount to sustaining each and every resource sector. Attention should also be given both to macroeconomic sustainability policies, such as the encouragement of higher saving and investment, and to the even trickier question of whether different countries' sustainability goals can be coordinated to avoid fallacies of composition.

To be able to reach any firmer conclusions, appropriate extensions of the simple model presented here, and tests of their empirical validity, will be required. The most obvious extensions to consider would be a formal separation between consumers and producers; corner as well as interior solutions; the inclusion of various national, transboundary and global resources which do have environmental value, such as the ozone layer or biodiversity; and last but by no means least, uncertainty.

NOTES

1. It is the study of a *change* in welfare goal which distinguishes this chapter from the literature on how to maintain constant consumption in open economies with natural resources (for example, Kemp and Long 1982; Asheim 1986; El Serafy 1989; Hartwick 1994; Vincent et al.1997; and Mason 1997). The assumption that the new welfare goal is adopted by everyone in the economy avoids the need that occurs in Pezzey (1989, Section 7) for government policies to persuade individuals to follow the goal.
2. The formal mathematics of the appendix assumes only one resource, but as noted there, the results can readily be extended to the case of many resources.
3. However, sustainability goals can affect environmental policies which control cumulative pollutants such as greenhouse gases (Howarth and Norgaard 1992).
4. In a multi-period model, I now define sustainedness as consumption not falling over time; while sustainability is consumption being no higher than the maximum sustainable level of consumption.
5. See Section 2.8 of Clark (1990) which ends 'If whaling companies expect to earn 10% on their investments and if the blue-whale population only increases by 5% per annum, the whalers could quite rationally plan to liquidate the blue-whale stocks (i.e. rationally from their point of view)'.
6. An example could be $W(C_1, C_2) = C_1{}^\eta + C_2{}^\eta/(1 + \delta)$, using the notation of the appendix, where $0 < \eta < 1$ and $\delta > 0$ is the discount rate for second-period instantaneous utility.
7. The whole arrangement could perhaps be seen as an example of 'exporting unsustainability' (Pearce et al. 1989, pp. 45–7). However, the cause of other countries' unsustainability that those authors envisaged was more their lack of knowledge and control of their natural resources, rather than their simple lack of desire for sustainability, which is the cause here.
8. If the resource is non-renewable ($G' \equiv 0$), (12A.15) is an identity and (12A.16)–(12A.18) are three equations in three variables, I_p, R_1, and $X_1 + X_2$. The split of total resource exports between periods 1 and 2 is then indeterminate.

REFERENCES

Asheim, Geir B. (1986), 'Hartwick's rule in open economies', *Canadian Journal of Economics*, **19** (3), 395–402.

Barbier, Edward B., Anil Markandya and David W. Pearce (1990), 'Environmental sustainability and cost–benefit analysis', *Environment and Planning A*, **22**, 1259–66.

Beckerman, Wilfred (1994), '"Sustainable development": is it a useful concept?', *Environmental Values* 3 (3), 191–209.

Clark, Colin W. (1990), *Mathematical Bioeconomics: The Optimal Management of Renewable Resources*, 2nd edn, New York: Wiley.

Daly, Herman E. (1990), 'Toward some operational principles of sustainable development', *Ecological Economics*, **2**, 1–6.

Dasgupta, Partha S. and Geoffrey M. Heal (1974) 'The optimal depletion of exhaustible resources', *Review of Economic Studies*, Symposium on the Economics of Exhaustible Resources, 3–28.

El Serafy, Salah (1989), 'The proper calculation of income from depletable natural resources', in Yusuf J. Ahmad, Salah El Serafy and Ernst Lutz (eds), *Environmental Accounting for Sustainable Development*, Washington, DC: World Bank, pp. 10–18.

Fisher, Irving (1930, 1954), *The Theory of Interest*, New York: Kelly & Millman.

Hartwick, John M. (1995), 'Sustainability and constant consumption paths in open economies with exhaustible resources', Review of International Economics, **3** (3), 275–83.

Hirshleifer, Jack (1980), *Price Theory and Applications*, 2nd edn, London: Prentice-Hall.

Howarth, Richard B. and Richard B. Norgaard (1992), 'Environmental valuation under sustainable development', *American Economic Review*, **82** (2), 473–7.

Kemp, Murray C. and Ngo Van Long (1982), 'Conditions for the survival of a small resource-importing economy', *Journal of International Economics* **13**, 135–42.

Little, I.M.D. and J.A. Mirrlees (1990), 'Project appraisal and planning twenty years on', in *Proceedings of the World Bank Annual Conference on Development Economics, 1990*, Washington, DC: World Bank.

Mason, Pamela (1997), 'An optimisation of El Serafy's rule and an extension to renewable resources', Mimeo, Department of Environmental Economics and Environmental Management, University of York.

Pearce, David W. (1998), 'Optimal prices for sustainable development', in D. Collard, D. Pearce and D. Ulph (eds), *Economics, Growth and Sustainable Environments*, New York: St Martin's Press.

Pearce, David, Anil Markandaya and Edward B. Barbier (1989), *Blueprint for a Green Economy*, London: Earthscan.

Pezzey, John (1989), 'Economic analysis of sustainable growth and sustainable development', Environment Department Working Paper No.15, World Bank, Washington, DC. Reprinted as *Sustainable Development Concepts: an Economic Analysis*, World Bank Environment Paper No. 2 (1992).

Pezzey, John (1992), 'Sustainability: an interdisciplinary guide', *Environmental Values*, **1**, 321–62.

Pezzey, John C.V. (1997), Sustainability constraints versus "optimality" versus intertemporal concern, and axioms versus data,' *Land Economics*, **73** (4), 448–66.

Røpke, Inge (1994), 'Trade, development and sustainability – a critical assessment of the "free trade dogma"', *Ecological Economics*, **9**, 13–22 (Special Issue on Trade and the Environment).

Solow, Robert M. (1974), 'Intergenerational equity and exhaustible resources', *Review of Economic Studies*, Symposium on the Economics of Exhaustible Resources, pp. 29–46.

Tietenberg, Thomas H. (1992), *Environmental and Natural Resource Economics*, 3rd edn, New York: Harper Collins.

Vincent, Jeffrey R., Theodore Panayotou and John M. Hartwick (1997), 'Resource depletion and sustainability in small open economies', *Journal of Environmental Economics and Management*, **33**, 274–86.

APPENDIX 12A PROOF THAT A CHANGED INTERTEMPORAL GOAL MAY NOT CHANGE RESOURCE MANAGEMENT IN A TWO-PERIOD MODEL

The model is of a two-period, small, open, representative-agent economy with one human-made capital stock and one depletable (renewable or non-renewable) resource flow as inputs to production. It could readily be extended, although at the expense of tedious notation, to include many resources, provided that the natural growth of each resource depends only on its own stock (that is, ecosystem interactions are ignored). Let:

K_i = non-depreciating capital stock in period i; $i = 1$ or 2, with K_1 = given initial capital

I_D = domestic investment in period 1; hence $K_2 = K_1 + 1_D$ (12A.1)

R_i = renewable, freely extractable and storable, resource flow that is essential input to domestic production

$Q(K_i, R_i)$ = output of composite consumption/investment good; twice continuously differentiable, with Q_{Ki}, $Q_{Ri} > 0$; Q_{KiKi}, $Q_{RiRi} < 0$; $Q_{KiRi} > 0$; $Q(Ki, 0) = Q(0, Ri) = 0$ (12A.2)

I_F = foreign investment by domestic economy in period 1

r = world interest rate, denominated in terms of the composite good, and independent of I_F because domestic economy is small

X_i = export of resource (if negative, denotes import)

p_i = world price of resource in terms of composite good; independent of X_i since domestic economy is small

C_i = consumption of composite good; hence

C_1 = $Q(K_1, R_1) - I_D - I_F + p_1 X_1$ (12A.3)

C_2 = $Q(K_2, R_2) + (1 + r)I_F + p_2 X_2$ (12A.4)

S_1 = given initial domestic resource stock; $G[S]$ = natural growth of stock; all the stock is exhausted at the end of period 2; hence

$R_2 + X_2 = S_1 - R_1 - X_1 + G[S_1 - R_1 - X_1]$ (12A.5)

$W(C_1, C_2)$ = intertemporal welfare function; twice continuously differentiable, with $\partial W / \partial C_i > 0$ and $\partial^2 W / \partial C_i^2 < 0$. Note that neither R_i nor S_i appear in $W(.)$, that is, the resource has no direct environmental value. (12A.6)

This whole model is an extension of Tietenberg's (1992, pp. 30–37) textbook model of sustainability. He did not include resource trade or capital, and focused on a pure, non-renewable resource-mining economy with $Q(R_i) = (a - c) R_1 - b R_i^2$, and effectively $W(C_1, C_2) = C_1 + C_2/(1 + r)$. He still had saving at a fixed interest rate (also r). However, he did not mention that such saving must be invested in the large world outside the economy (for otherwise there must be capital in the economy). Nor did he mention the coincidence that his time preference rate in $W(C_1,C_2)$ is also the world interest rate r, which makes the optimal amount of saving indeterminate in his model.

In the model defined by (12A.1)–(12A.6), the result to be proved is that changing the welfare function $W(.)$ makes no difference to the values of the variables R_i and X_i (domestic resource use, and resource trade) and I_D (domestic investment) which solve the open-economy problem:

$$\underset{R_1, I_D, I_F, X_1, X_2}{\text{Max}} \qquad W(C_1, C_2). \qquad (12A.7)$$

Using (12A.1), (12A.4) and (12A.5), we have

$$C_2 = Q(K_1 + I_D, S_1 - R_1 - X_1 + G[S_1 - R_1 - X_1] - X_2) + (1 + r) I_F + p_2 X_2, \qquad (12A.8)$$

so denoting partial derivatives by subscripts, the first-order conditions for an interior solution are:

$$\partial W/\partial R_1 = 0 \Rightarrow W_{C1}Q_{R1} = (1 + G')W_{C2}Q_{R2} \qquad (12A.9)$$
$$\partial W/\partial I_D = 0 \Rightarrow W_{C1} = W_{C2}Q_{K2} \qquad (12A.10)$$
$$\partial W/\partial I_F = 0 \Rightarrow W_{C1} = W_{C2}(1 + r) \qquad (12A.11)$$
$$\partial W/\partial X_1 = 0 \Rightarrow W_{C1}p_1 = (1 + G')W_{C2}Q_{R2} \qquad (12A.12)$$
$$\partial W/\partial X_2 = 0 \Rightarrow Q_{R2} = p_2. \qquad (12A.13)$$

Substituting (12A.11) and (12A.13) into (12A.9), (12A.10) and (12A.12) gives

$$W_{C1}/W_{C2} = 1 + r = (1 + G')Q_{R2}/Q_{R1} = (1 + G')p_2/p_1 = Q_{K2}. \qquad (12A.14)$$

This shows that a Hotelling rule appropriate to renewable resources,

$$p_2 = (1 + r)p_1/(1 + G'[S_1 - R_1 - X_1]), \qquad (12A.15)$$

must hold in the rest of the world if resources are to be traded in both time periods, as required for an interior solution. Obviously, if the change in welfare function is big enough, we shall move beyond an interior solution and one or more of the first-order conditions (12A.9)–(12A.13) will no longer be true.

Substituting (12A.14) into (12A.9)–(12A.13) gives the three equations

$$Q_{R1}(K_1,R_1) = p_1, \qquad (12A.16)$$
$$Q_{K2}(K_1 + I_D, S_1 - R_1 - X_1 + G[S_1 - R_1 - X_1] - X_2) = 1 + r, \qquad (12A.17)$$
$$Q_{R2}(K_1 + I_D, S_1 - R_1 - X_1 + G[S_1 - R_1 - X_1] - X_2) = (1 + r)p_1/(1 + G'). \qquad (12A.18)$$

Because of the strict concavity conditions in (12A.2), in principle the four equations (12A.15)–(12A.18) are sufficient to determine uniquely the values of the four variables I_D, R_1, X_1 and X_2. Together R_1, X_1 and X_2 determine R_2, and hence all aspects of resource management over time (R_1, R_2, X_1 and X_2).[8] But none of (12A.15)–(12A.18) contain the welfare function $W(.)$, so we conclude that

provided the solution remains interior, a change in intertemporal welfare goal has no effect on the economy's management of its resources or its domestic capital investment.

All that will change is foreign investment I_F, which is determined by (12A.11); hence total saving $I_D + I_F$, and consumption levels C_1 and C_2, will also change.

Since sustainable development (SD) is typically defined as an inequality constraint, it cannot be incorporated into a differentiable welfare function. So let us test whether imposing the SD constraint, which is here $C_1 \leq C_2$, also yields the above conclusion. Consider a case where $C_1 > C_2$ and $R_1 > R_2$ in the solution to the above equation set, that is, optimal consumption and resource use are both unsustainable. Maximizing $W(C_1,C_2)$ subject to the SD constraint $C_1 \leq C_2$ is then equivalent to maximizing C_1 subject to $C_1 = C_2$, which from (12A.8) means

$$I_F = \{Q(K_1,R_1) - I_D + p_1X_1 - p_2X_2 - Q(K_1 + I_D, S_1 - R_1 - X_1 + G[S_1 - R_1 - X_1] - X_2)\}/(2 + r), \qquad (12A.19)$$

hence

$$(2 + r)C_1 = \{(1 + r)[Q(K_1,R_1) - I_D + p_1X_1] + p_2X_2 + Q(K_1 + I_D, S_1 - R_1, -X_1 + G[S_1 - R_1 - X_1] - X_2)\}. \qquad (12A.20)$$

The first-order conditions for maximizing this C_1 with respect to R_1, I_D, X_1 and X_2 are

$$(1 + r)Q_{R1} = (1 + G')Q_{R2}, \quad 1 + r = Q_{K2},$$
$$(1 + r)p_1 = (1 + G')Q_{R2}, \text{ and } p_2 = Q_{R2}. \qquad (12A.21)$$

These are exactly equivalent to (12A.15)–(12A.18), which as already noted have at most one solution. So the SD constraint indeed does require an increase in foreign investment I_F (and hence an increase in total saving also) from the level determined by (12A.13) to the level determined in (12A.19); but *no* change in domestic resource use R_1, (which will still be unsustainable), investment I_D or resource exports X_1 and X_2.

However, if an economy is *closed*, or *large and open*, then the change in saving and investment caused by changing the welfare goal generally changes the interest rate path available to the economy. This then changes the path of resource management, although not necessarily to a sustainable path if the new goal is SD. In the above two-period example, if the economy is closed, then foreign investment I_F and resource trade X_1 and X_2 are all zero. The economy then chooses R_1 and I_D to maximize welfare

$$W \{Q[K_1,R_1] - I_D, \; Q[K_1 + I_D, \; S_1 - R_1]\}.$$

A change in $W\{.\}$ then generally changes R_1 and I_D. In particular, if maximizing the old $W\{.\}$ results in $C_1 > C_2$, an SD constraint will shift the economy to $C_1 = C_2$. Doing this in a Pareto-efficient way requires a shift to lower C_1 and higher C_2. It will also, given the strict concavity assumptions in (12A.2) and (12A.6), entail an increase in investment I_D and reductions in the interest rate r and first-period resource extraction R_1. But we cannot say in general if resource management is sustainable ($R_1 \leq R_2$) after the shift.

Index